THE COMPLETE ILLUSTRATED STEP BY STEP COOKBOOK

Compiled by Judith Ferguson
Photographed by Peter Barry
Designed by Philip Clucas and Sara Cooper
Recipes Prepared for Photography by
Jacqueline Bellefontaine

CLB 2208
This edition published 1989 by CLB Publishing Inc.
Airport Business Center, 29 Kripes Road, East Granby, CT 06026.
© 1988 Colour Library Books Ltd.
Text filmsetting by Words and Spaces, Hampshire, England.
Color separation by Hong Kong Graphic Arts Ltd., Hong Kong.
Printed and bound in Cordoba, Spain by Graficromo, S.A.
ISBN 0 86283 629 8

THE COMPLETE ILLUSTRATED
STEP BY STEP
COOKBOOK

CLB
PUBLISHING

CONTENTS

ACKNOWLEDGMENT

The publishers wish to thank the following suppliers for their kind assistance: Corning Ltd for providing Pyrex and other cookware; Habasco International Ltd for the loan of basketware, and Stent (Pottery) Ltd for the loan of glazed pottery oven-to-table ware. Thanks also to Old El Paso for permission to feature their recipes for Leg of Lamb with Chili Sauce, Spare Ribs in Chili and Cream Sauce, Mexican Kebabs, Mexican Beef Patties and Minute Steaks with Taco Sauce.

INTRODUCTION

Outside our kitchen windows is a wide world full of culinary delights that are there for the tasting. If we were to travel to eight different countries, what would we discover?

In France we find delicate crêpes with a multitude of interesting and delicious fillings. We can taste celebrated dishes like onion soup with a bubbling cheese topping, or rich beef stew aromatic with herbs and red wine.

A visit to Italy finds us developing a taste for fresh pasta, tender veal, an amazing selection of antipasti and vegetable dishes exciting enough to be a separate course.

Greek food offers a taste of the Mediterranean, of delicious eggplant, zucchini, artichokes, olives, and succulent lamb, all flavored with the characteristic combination of herbs and spices.

Spanish food is an unexpected delight, and dishes like Paella, with its golden saffron rice and mixture of chicken, seafood, and spicy sausage, are favorites far beyond the Spanish border, while combinations of fruit and meat in the same recipe challenge our usual ideas about main dishes.

Germany brings to mind rich cakes and pastries filled to overflowing with whipped cream. These high calorie treats are much loved, but Germans are health conscious, too. Quark, the low fat soft cheese so popular lately, originated here.

The last three countries on our lightning tour are places most of us may never visit – Poland, Mexico and China. Polish cuisine is very traditional, quite filling and perfect for cold weather. Christmas and Easter are special times in Poland's calendar, and the cuisine offers abundant ideas for these holidays.

Mexican food is sunny and vibrant. As in most countries that enjoy a warm climate, the taste of the food is spicy hot, but that can easily be adjusted to suit individual palates. Its festive colors make food perfect for parties.

Chinese food is known mainly through restaurants, and Cantonese dishes are the most popular. There is more to Chinese food, though: Peking cuisine, using pancakes and noodles instead or rice; Shanghai cuisine, offering many fish and seafood dishes, and Szechuan cuisine, with its rich, fiery sauces, are worth discovering.

Foreign travel has introduced us to hundreds of new ideas about what other people of the world eat. But though travel may broaden our taste experience, we are frequently more adventurous on foreign soil than we are in our own kitchens. The thought of faithfully trying to reproduce some sauce or pastry we have only tasted once is daunting, to say the least. We wonder, too, if those special ingredients will be available, and if not, whether they can successfully be substituted. Then there are the recipes; are we capable of tackling them without personal guidance. All these considerations can dampen creative and adventurous spirits, and send us back to those tired old recipes we are so familiar with.

This book can't offer you a world trip, but it can bring the cuisines of eight different countries into your kitchen; it can't offer you private lessons with famous chefs, but it can help you perfect your own skills. The recipes are broken down into numbered steps which will prove invaluable, however experienced the cook and complex or simple the recipe. Each recipe includes step by step photographs of some of the techniques and methods that make the preparation easier, while Cook's Notes offer information on cooking and preparation times, helpful hints on how to vary recipes to suit available ingredients, and how to prevent problems, or solve them. And to show you how your masterpiece will turn out, we have included a full page color photograph of each and every dish.

Bon Voyage!

FRENCH COOKING

INTRODUCTION

The bureaucrats of France have divided the country, for offical purposes, into 95 départements, rather like counties. The cooks of France have a better way. They still rely on the old names of the regions, each with its own contribution to the country's legendary cuisine.

Brittany is the home of crêpes, thin French pancakes. Normandy is famous for its rich cream and apples. Cider comes from those apples and Calvados, an incendiary brandy, comes from the cider. And the seas around the coasts provide an abundance of seafood.

Champagne's main contribution is obvious, but there are also rich dishes of Flemish influence coming from this region on the Belgian border.

Touraine and the Loire are known as the garden of France, with the finest fruits and vegetables and some of the loveliest wines.

Ile de France has Paris at its center, where hâute cuisine was born.

Alsace and Lorraine have been dominated by Germany more than once in their history and this is evident in many of their favorite dishes.

Burgundy and Bordeaux use their famous red and white wines to enhance their recipes, along with Dijon mustard from the former and truffles from the latter.

Franche Comté is a mountainous region that abounds with game and which produces robust dishes, many using its famous cheese.

Languedoc is on the Spanish border and its food shares many similarities with that of its neighbors, especially in the use of tomatoes, pepper and spicy sausage.

Provence is southern France, with all its color and warmth reflected in food such as Salade Niçoise and Ratatouille.

With the whole history of French cuisine before us and with only limited space, we didn't know where to begin, or end! Then we thought of the many well-loved classics, the ones that conjure up the essence of the French gastronomic experience. With those, we felt, we couldn't go wrong.

SERVES 6

QUICHE LORRAINE

The history of this egg and bacon flan goes back
to the 16th century in the Lorraine region. Traditionally
it doesn't contain cheese, but it's a tasty addition.

Pâte Brisée

½ cup butter
1½ cups all-purpose flour, sifted
Pinch salt
1 egg
2 tsps ice water

Filling

6 strips bacon, cut into large dice
1 tsp butter or margarine
2 shallots, finely chopped
2 eggs plus 2 egg yolks
1 cup heavy cream
Salt, pepper and grated nutmeg
¾ cup grated Gruyère cheese (optional)

1. Preheat the oven to 375°F. To prepare the pastry, sift the flour and salt into a large bowl. Rub in the butter until the mixture looks like fine breadcrumbs - this may also be done in a food processor. Beat the egg lightly and mix into the flour by hand or with the machine. If the dough seems crumbly, add some of the water. Chill well before using.

2. Roll the pastry out to a circle about ¼ inch thick on a well-floured surface. Roll the pastry over a rolling pin and unroll it onto a 8-9 inch flan dish. Gently press the pastry into the bottom and up the sides of the dish, being careful not to stretch it. Trim off the excess pastry by running the rolling pin over the rim of the dish or using a sharp knife. Prick the bottom of the pastry lightly With a fork.

Step 2 Use rolling pin to lift pastry into dish.

3. Place a circle of wax paper on top of the pastry and fill with dry beans, or rice. Bake for about 10 minutes, remove the paper and filling. Prick base again lightly and return to the oven for another 3 minutes or until just beginning to brown. Allow the pastry to cool while preparing the filling.

4. Place the bacon in a small frying pan and fry over gentle heat until the fat begins to run. Raise the heat and cook until lightly browned and crisp. Place the bacon on paper towels to drain and add the butter to the pan if insufficient fat left. Add the chopped shallots and cook until just beginning to color. Remove to the paper towel to drain with the bacon.

5. Beat the eggs and extra yolks, cream and seasonings together in a large bowl. Scatter the bacon and shallots over the bottom of the pastry case and ladle the custard filling on top of it. If using cheese, add with the custard.

6. Bake in the top half of the oven for about 25 minutes, or until the custard has puffed and browned and a knife inserted into the center comes out clean. Allow to cool slightly and then remove from the dish, or serve directly from the dish.

Cook's Notes

Time
Preparation takes about 25 minutes, plus time for chilling the pastry. Cooking takes about 40 minutes.

Preparation
Baking a pastry case without a filling is called baking blind.
By pricking the bottom of the pastry, lining it with paper and filling with rice or beans you help the pastry hold its shape.

Variation
Use basic pastry and custard recipes, but substitute other ingredients such as ham, shellfish or vegetables for the bacon.

MAKES 1 OMELET

OMELETTE ROUSSILLON

Roussillon is on France's border with Spain.
The Spanish influence is evident in the use of
tomatoes and peppers combined with eggs.

3 eggs
Salt and pepper
1 tbsp butter or margarine
¼ green pepper, cut into small dice
2 tomatoes, peeled, seeded and roughly chopped
2oz ham, cut into small dice

1. Break the eggs into a bowl, season with salt and pepper and beat to mix thoroughly. Heat an omelet pan and drop in the butter, swirling it so that it coats the bottom and sides. When the butter stops foaming, add pepper and ham. Cook for 1-2 minutes to soften slightly, and add the tomatoes.

2. Pour in the eggs and, as they begin to cook, push the cooked portion with the flat of the fork to allow the uncooked portion underneath. Continue to lift the eggs and shake the pan to prevent them from sticking.

3. When the egg on top is still slightly creamy, fold ⅓ of the omelet to the center and tip it out of the pan onto a warm serving dish, folded side down. Serve immediately.

Step 2 Push eggs with fork to let uncooked portion fall to the bottom of the pan.

Step 3 Fold ⅓ of the omelet to the middle.

Cook's Notes

Time
15 minutes preparation, 4-5 minutes cooking.

Preparation
To peel tomatoes, drop into boiling water for the count of 5 and remove to cold water. This loosens the peel.

Variations
Prepare the omelet in the same way, but use other ingredients such as mushrooms, chopped fresh herbs or spinach. If filling with cheese, sprinkle on before folding the omelet.

Serving Ideas
Accompany with French bread and a salad for a light lunch. May also be served as a first course.

SERVES 4-6
POTAGE À L'OIGNON GRATINÉ

Originally a Parisian specialty, every region in
France now has a recipe for onion soup.

¼ cup butter or margarine
2lbs onions, peeled and thinly sliced
2 tsps sugar
Pinch salt and pepper
1½ tbsps flour
1 tsp dried thyme
7 cups brown stock
½ cup dry white wine

Croûtes

12 1 inch slices French bread
1 tbsp olive oil
2 cups grated Gruyère cheese

Step 1 Brown the onions in a large saucepan with butter and sugar.

Step 3 Brush both sides of bread with olive oil and bake until lightly browned.

Step 4 Place the croûtes on soup and sprinkle with cheese.

1. Melt the butter in a large saucepan over a moderate heat. Stir in the onions and add the sugar. Cook, uncovered, over low heat, stirring occasionally, for 20-30 minutes or until the onions are golden brown.

2. Sprinkle the flour over the onions and cook for 2-3 minutes. Pour on the stock and stir to blend the flour. Add salt, pepper and thyme and return the soup to low heat. Simmer, partially covered, for another 30-40 minutes. Allow the soup to stand while preparing the croûtes.

3. Brush each side of the slices of bread lightly with olive oil and place them on a baking sheet. Bake in a preheated oven, 325°F, for about 15 minutes. Turn the slices over and bake for a further 15 minutes, or until the bread is dry and lightly browned.

4. To serve, skim fat from the soup and ladle soup into a tureen or individual soup bowls. Place the croûtes on top of the soup and sprinkle over the grated cheese. Place the soup in a hot oven and bake for 10-20 minutes, or until the cheese has melted. Brown under a preheated broiler, if desired, before serving.

Cook's Notes

Time
Preparation takes about 20 minutes. Cooking takes about 50-60 minutes - 40 minutes for the soup, 30 minutes for the croûtes and 10-20 minutes to melt the cheese.

Cook's Tip
The addition of sugar helps the onions to brown.

SERVES 10

PÂTÉ DE CAMPAGNE

This is the pâté of French restaurants
known also as pâté maison or terrine
de chef. It should be coarse textured.

¾lb pork liver, skinned and ducts removed
¾lb pork, coarsely ground
4oz veal, coarsely ground
8oz pork fat, coarsely ground
1 clove garlic, crushed
2 shallots, finely chopped
8oz bacon strips, rind and bones removed
3 tbsps cognac
½ tsp ground allspice
Salt and freshly ground black pepper
1 tsp chopped fresh thyme or sage
4oz smoked tongue or ham, cut into ¼ inch cubes
2 tbsps heavy cream
1 large bay leaf

1. Preheat the oven to 350°F.

2. Place the liver in a food processor and process once or twice to chop roughly. Add the ground meats and fat, shallots, garlic, cognac, allspice, salt and pepper and thyme and process once or twice to mix. Do not over-work the mixture; it should be coarse.

3. Stretch the strips of bacon with the back of a knife and line a terrine, metal baking pan or ovenproof glass dish. Stir the cream and the cubed tongue or ham into the meat mixture by hand and press it into the dish on top of the bacon.
Place the bay leaf on top and fold over any overlapping edges of bacon.

4. Cover the dish with a tight-fitting lid or two layers of foil

Step 3 Stretch the strips of bacon to line the terrine.

Step 5 Weight down the pâté with cans or scale weights.

and place the dish in a bain marie (dish of hand hot water) to come halfway up the sides of the terrine. Bake the pâté for 2 hours, or until the juices are clear. When it is done, remove it from the oven and remove the foil or lid.

5. Cover with fresh foil and weight down the pâté with cans of food or balance scale weights. Allow to cool at room temperature and then refrigerate the pâté, still weighted, until completely chilled and firm.

6. To serve, remove the weights and foil. Turn the pâté out and scrape off the fat. Slice through the bacon into thin slices.

Cook's Notes

Time
Preparation takes 25 minutes, plus refrigerating until firm.
Cooking takes about 2 hours.

Serving Ideas
The French often serve pâté with small pickled onions, and cornichons (small pickled gherkins). Serve as a first course with French bread or buttered toast, or with bread and salad for a light lunch.

Freezing
Cool and freeze in the dish. Pack well, label and store for up to 3 months. Allow to defrost in the refrigerator.

SERVES 4-6

GOUGÈRE AU JAMBON

This savory pastry dish originated in Burgundy, but is also popular in the Champagne district and indeed in many other districts as well. Serve it as an appetizer or main course.

Choux Pastry

½ cup water
4 tbsps butter or margarine
½ cup all-purpose flour, sifted
2 eggs, beaten
½ cup cheese, finely diced
Pinch salt, pepper and dry mustard

Ham Salpicon

1 tbsp butter or margarine
1 tbsp flour
½ cup stock
2oz mushrooms, sliced
2 tsps chopped fresh herbs
Salt and pepper
4oz cooked ham, cut into julienne strips
2 tbsps grated cheese and dry breadcrumbs mixed

Step 4 Beat in the egg gradually, but thoroughly.

Step 5 Spoon up the sides of the dish and fill the center with the salpicon.

1. Preheat oven to 400°F. Place the water for the pastry in a small saucepan. Cut the butter into small pieces and add to the water. Bring slowly to boil, making sure that the butter is completely melted before the water comes to a rapid boil. Turn up the heat and allow to boil rapidly for 30 seconds.

2. Sift the flour with a pinch of salt onto a sheet of paper. Take the pan off the heat and tip all the flour in at once. Stir quickly and vigorously until the mixture comes away from the sides of the pan. Spread onto a plate to cool.

3. Melt the butter in a small saucepan for the salpicon and add the flour. Cook for 1-2 minutes until pale straw colored. Gradually whisk in the stock until smooth. Add a pinch of salt and pepper and the chopped herbs. Stir in the sliced mushrooms and ham and set aside.

4. To continue with the pastry, add salt, pepper and dry mustard to the paste and return it to the saucepan. Gradually add the egg to the paste mixture, beating well between each addition–this may be done by hand, with an electric mixer or in a food processor. It may not be necessary to add all the egg. The mixture should be smooth and shiny and hold its shape when ready. If it is still too thick, beat in the remaining egg. Stir in the diced cheese by hand.

5. Spoon the mixture into a large ovenproof dish or 4 individual dishes, pushing the mixture slightly up the sides of the dish and leaving a well in the center. Fill the center with the ham salpicon and scatter over 2 tbsps grated cheese and dry breadcrumbs, mixed. Bake until the pastry is puffed and browned. Serve immediately.

Cook's Notes

Serving Ideas
Cooked in individual dishes, this makes a nice first course for 6. Cooked in a large dish this makes a main course for 4 with a salad or vegetables.

Time
Preparation takes about 30 minutes, cooking takes approximately 30-45 minutes if cooked in one large dish, 15-20 minutes for small individual dishes.

Variations
Vegetables, chicken, game or shellfish can be substituted for the ham.

SERVES 4

ARTICHAUTS AIOLI

Home-made mayonnaise is in a class by itself.
With the addition of garlic, it makes a perfect sauce
for artichokes – a typically Provençal appetizer.

4 medium-sized globe artichokes
1 slice lemon
1 bay leaf
Pinch salt

Sauce Aioli

2 egg yolks
1 cup olive oil
2 cloves garlic, peeled and crushed
Salt, pepper and lemon juice to taste
Chervil leaves to garnish

1. To prepare the artichokes, break off the stems and twist to remove any tough fibers. Trim the base so that the artichokes will stand upright. Trim the points from all the leaves and wash the artichokes well. Bring a large saucepan or stock pot full of water to the boil with the slice of lemon and bay leaf. Add a pinch of salt and, when the water is boiling, add the artichokes. Allow to cook for 25 minutes over a moderate heat. While the artichokes are cooking, prepare the sauce.

2. Whisk the egg yolks and garlic with a pinch of salt and pepper in a deep bowl or in a liquidizer or food processor. Add the olive oil a few drops at a time while whisking by hand, or in a thin steady stream with the machine running. If preparing the sauce by hand, once half the oil is added, the remainder may be added in a thin, steady stream. Add lemon juice once the sauce becomes very thick. When all the oil has been added, adjust the seasoning and add more lemon juice to taste.

Step 1 Trim the pointed ends from all the leaves of the artichoke.

Step 2 Add the oil to the egg yolks in a thin, steady stream to prevent curdling.

Step 3 Pull away one of the bottom leaves to see if the artichoke is cooked.

3. When the artichokes are cooked, the bottom leaves will pull away easily. Remove them from the water with a draining spoon and drain upside-down on paper towels or in a colander. Allow to cool and serve with the sauce aioli. Garnish with chervil.

Cook's Notes

Time
Preparation will take approximately 30 minutes and cooking approximately 25 minutes.

Cook's Tip
If this sauce or other mayonnaise needs to be thinned for coating, mix with a little hot water. A damp cloth under the mixing bowl will stop it spinning when making mayonnaise by hand.

Watchpoint
Sauce will curdle if oil is added too quickly. If it does, whisk another egg yolk and gradually beat curdled mixture into it. Sauce should come together again.

Serving Ideas
To eat, peel the leaves off one at a time and dip the fleshy part of the leaf into the sauce. Work down to the thistle or choke and remove with a teaspoon. Break artichoke bottom into pieces and dip into sauce.

SERVES 6-8

RATATOUILLE

This is probably one of the most familiar dishes from southern France. Either hot or cold, it's full of the warm sun of Provence.

2 eggplants, sliced and scored on both sides
4-6 zucchini, depending on size
3-6 tbsps olive oil
2 onions, peeled and thinly sliced
2 green peppers, seeded and cut into 1 inch pieces
2 tsps chopped fresh basil or 1 tsp dried basil
1 large clove garlic, crushed
2lbs ripe tomatoes, peeled and quartered
Salt and pepper
½ cup dry white wine

1. Lightly salt the eggplant slices and place on paper towels to drain for about 30 minutes. Rinse and pat dry. Slice the zucchini thickly and set them aside.

2. Pour 3 tbsps of the olive oil into a large frying pan and when hot, lightly brown the onions, green peppers and zucchini slices. Remove the vegetables to a casserole and add the eggplant slices to the frying pan or saucepan. Cook to brown both sides lightly and place in the casserole with the other vegetables. Add extra oil while frying the vegetables as needed.

3. Add the garlic and tomatoes to the oil and cook for 1 minute. Add the garlic and tomatoes to the rest of the vegetables along with any remaining olive oil in the frying pan. Add basil, salt, pepper and wine and bring to the boil over moderate heat. Cover and reduce to simmering. If the vegetables need moisture during cooking, add a little white wine.

Step 1 Score and salt the eggplants and leave to drain.

Step 2 Brown all the vegetables lightly.

Step 3 Combine all the ingredients and simmer gently.

4. When the vegetables are tender, remove them from the casserole to a serving dish and boil any remaining liquid in the pan rapidly to reduce to about 2 tbsps. Pour over the ratatouille to serve.

Cook's Notes

Time
Leave eggplants to stand 30 minutes while preparing remaining vegetables. Cook combined ingredients for approximately 35 minutes.

Cook's Tip
Vegetables in this stew are traditionally served quite soft. If crisper vegetables are desired, shorten the cooking time but make sure the eggplant is thoroughly cooked.

SERVES 6

FÈVES AU JAMBON

Touraine, where this dish comes from, is often called the "Garden of France." Some of the finest vegetables in the country are grown there.

2lbs lima beans
½ cup heavy cream
2oz ham, cut into thin strips
1 tbsps chopped parsley or chervil

1. If using fresh beans, remove them from their pods. Cook the beans in boiling salted water until tender, drain and keep warm.

2. Combine the cream and ham in a small saucepan. Add a pinch of salt and pepper and bring to the boil. Boil rapidly for 5 minutes to thicken the cream.

Step 2 Reduce the cream to thicken by boiling.

Step 3 Peel off outer skins of beans before adding to cream and ham.

Step 1 Remove fresh lima beans from their pods.

3. If desired, peel the outer skins from the beans before tossing with the cream and ham. Add parsley or chervil, adjust the seasoning and reheat if necessary. Serve immediately.

Cook's Notes

Time
Preparation takes 20-30 minutes, beans take approximately 15 minutes to cook.

Variation
Fresh peas may be used instead of beans, and cooked for 20-25 minutes.

Cook's Tip
The finished dish has better color if the beans are peeled.

SERVES 4

TOMATES À LA LANGUEDOCIENNE

This dish from the Languedoc region of southern France is similar to Provençal tomatoes, but is not as strong in flavor.

4 large ripe tomatoes
2 slices white bread, crusts removed
1 clove garlic, crushed
2 tbsps olive oil
1 tbsp chopped parsley
2 tsp chopped thyme or marjoram
Salt and pepper

1. Cut the tomatoes in half and score the cut surface. Sprinkle with salt and leave upside-down in a colander to drain. Allow the tomatoes to drain for 1-2 hours. Rinse the tomatoes and scoop out most of the juice and pulp.

2. Mix the olive oil and garlic together and brush both sides of the bread with the mixture, leaving it to soften. Chop the herbs and the bread together until well mixed.

Step 1 Scoop out seeds and juice to create space for the stuffing.

Step 2 Chop stuffing finely.

Step 3 Press in as much stuffing as possible.

3. Press the filling into the tomatoes and sprinkle with any remaining garlic and olive oil mixture.

4. Cook the tomatoes in an ovenproof dish under a preheated broiler under low heat for the first 5 minutes. Then raise the dish or the heat to brown the tomatoes on top. Serve immediately.

Cook's Notes

Time
Preparation takes about 15 minutes, tomatoes need 1-2 hours to drain. Cooking takes approximately 5-8 minutes.

Preparation
Can be prepared up to broiling and finished off just before serving.

Serving Ideas
Serve as a first course or a side dish. Especially nice with lamb or beef.

SERVES 4-6

HARICOTS VERTS À L'OIGNON

These slender green beans are the classic French vegetable. Quickly blanched, then refreshed under cold water, they can be reheated and still stay beautifully green.

1lb green beans
1oz butter
1 medium onion
Salt and pepper

Step 1 Top and tail the beans, but leave them whole.

Step 2 Finely chop the onion.

Step 3 Fry the onion in moderate heat until lightly browned.

1. Top and tail the beans.

2. Cook the beans whole in boiling salted water for about 8-10 minutes. Meanwhile, finely chop the onion.

3. Melt the butter and fry the finely chopped onion until lightly brown. Drain the beans and toss them over heat to dry. Pour the butter and onions over the beans and season with salt and pepper. Serve immediately.

Cook's Notes

 Watchpoint
Do not brown the onions too much as this will make them taste bitter.

 Time
Preparation takes about 15 minutes, cooking takes 8-10 minutes.

 Preparation
Trim the beans with a sharp knife or kitchen scissors in large handfuls.

SERVES 6

POMMES DAUPHINÉ

The food from the mountainous province of Dauphiné is robust fare. Comté is the finest cheese of the area and like Gruyère it is creamy rather than stringy when melted.

1 clove garlic, peeled and crushed with the flat of a knife
2 tbsps butter
2¼lbs potatoes, peeled and thinly sliced
½ cup light cream
Salt and pepper
1½ cups grated Comté or Gruyère cheese
⅓ cup butter cut into very small dice

1. Preheat the oven to 400°F. Rub the bottom and sides of a heavy baking dish with the crushed clove of garlic. Grease the bottom and sides liberally with the butter. Use a dish that can also be employed as a serving dish.

2. Spread half of the potato slices in the bottom of the dish, sprinkle with cheese, salt and pepper and dot with the butter dice. Top with the remaining slices of potato, neatly

Step 1 Rub the dish with garlic and butter well.

Step 2 Layer the potatoes with cheese and seasonings.

Step 3 Pour cream into the side of the dish.

arranged. Sprinkle with the remaining cheese, salt, pepper and butter.

3. Pour the cream into the side of the dish around the potatoes.

4. Cook in the top part of the oven for 30-40 minutes, or until the potatoes are tender and the top is nicely browned. Serve immediately.

Cook's Notes

Serving Ideas
A delicious side dish with poultry or roast meats, especially gammon.

Cook's Tip
Rubbing the dish with garlic gives just a hint of flavor.

Time
Preparation takes 25 minutes, cooking takes 30-40 minutes.

SERVES 4

POULET GRILLÉ AU LIMON

Crisp chicken with a tang of limes makes an elegant
yet quickly-made entrée. From the warm regions of
southern France, it is perfect for a summer meal.

2 2lb chickens
4 limes
1 tsp basil
⅓ cup olive oil
Salt, pepper and sugar

1. Remove the leg ends, neck and wing tips from the chicken and discard them.

2. Split the chicken in half, cutting away the backbone completely and discarding it.

3. Loosen the ball and socket joint in the leg and flatten each half of the chicken by hitting it with the flat side of a cleaver.

4. Season the chicken on both sides with salt and pepper and sprinkle over the basil. Place the chicken in a shallow dish and pour over 2 tbsps of olive oil. Squeeze the juice from 2 of the limes over the chicken. Cover and leave to marinate in the refrigerator for 4 hours.

5. Heat the broiler to its highest setting and preheat the oven to 375°F. Remove the chicken from the marinade and place in the broiler pan. Cook one side until golden brown and turn the pieces over. Sprinkle with 1 tbsp olive oil and brown the other side.

6. Place the chicken in a roasting dish, sprinkle with the

Step 2 Split the chicken in half and cut out the backbone.

Step 3 Bend chicken leg back to loosen ball and socket joint.

remaining oil and roast in the oven for about 25 minutes. Peel the remaining limes and slice them thinly. When the chicken is cooked, place the lime slices on top and sprinkle lightly with sugar. Place under the broiler for a few minutes to caramelize the sugar and cook the limes. Place in a serving dish and spoon over any remaining marinade and the cooking juices. Serve immediately.

Cook's Notes

 Time
Preparation takes about 25 minutes, plus 4 hours marinating, cooking takes about 35 minutes.

 Watchpoint
Sugar will burn and turn bitter quickly, so watch carefully while broiling.

 Variation
If limes are too expensive, use lemons instead. Vary the choice of herb.

 Serving Ideas
Tomato salad makes a good accompaniment.

Preparation
Chicken can be prepared and marinated overnight in the refrigerator.

 Cook's Tip
Marinating the chicken adds moisture as well as flavor.

SERVES 4

POULET SAUTÉ VALLÉE D'AUGE

This dish contains all the ingredients that Normandy
is famous for - butter, cream, apples and Calvados.

¼ cup butter or margarine
2 tbsps oil
3lbs chicken, cut into eight pieces
4 tbsps Calvados
⅓ cup chicken stock
2 apples, peeled, cored and coarsely chopped
2 sticks celery, finely chopped
1 shallot, finely chopped
½ tsp dried thyme, crumbled
⅓ cup heavy cream
2 egg yolks, lightly beaten
Salt and white pepper

Garnish

1 bunch watercress or small parsley sprigs
2 apples, quartered, cored and cut into cubes
2 tbsps butter
Sugar

Step 1 Brown the chicken a few pieces at a time, skin side down first.

Step 4 Cook diced apple until it begins to caramelize.

1. Melt half the butter and all of the oil in a large sauté pan over moderate heat. When the foam begins to subside, brown the chicken, a few pieces at a time, skin side down first. When all the chicken is browned, pour off most of the fat from the pan and return the chicken to the pan.

2. Pour the Calvados into a ladle or small saucepan and warm over gentle heat. Ignite with a match and pour, while still flaming, over the chicken. Shake the sauté pan gently until the flames subside. If the Calvados should flare up, cover the pan immediately with the lid.

3. Pour over the stock and scrape any browned chicken juices from the bottom of the pan. Set the chicken aside. Melt the remaining butter in a small saucepan or frying pan. Cook the chopped apples, shallot and celery and the thyme for about 10 minutes or until soft but not brown.

Spoon over the chicken and return the pan to the high heat. Bring to the boil, then reduce heat, cover the pan and simmer 50 minutes. When the chicken is cooked, beat the eggs and cream. With a whisk, gradually beat in some of the hot sauce. Pour the mixture back into a saucepan and cook over a low heat for 2-3 minutes, stirring constantly until the sauce thickens and coats the back of a spoon. Season the sauce with salt and white pepper and set aside while preparing the garnish.

4. Put the remaining butter in a small frying pan and when foaming, add the apple. Toss over a high heat until beginning to soften. Sprinkle with sugar and cook until the apple begins to caramelize. To serve, coat the chicken with the sauce and decorate with watercress or parsley. Spoon the caramelized apples over the chicken.

Cook's Notes

 Time
Preparation takes 25-30 minutes, cooking takes 55-60 minutes.

Watchpoint
Do not allow the sauce to boil once the egg and cream is added or it will curdle.

 Serving Ideas
Serve with sauté potatoes and fresh young peas.

SERVES 4

Coq au Vin

Originating from the Burgundy region, this dish is
probably the most famous chicken recipe in all of France.
It is very rich, definitely a cold weather meal.

8oz thick cut bacon strips
1½ cups water
2 tbsps butter or margarine
12-16 button onions or shallots
8oz mushrooms, left whole if small, quartered if large
1½ cups dry red wine
3lb chicken, cut into eight pieces
3 tbsps brandy
1 bouquet garni
1 clove garlic, crushed
3 tbsps flour
1½ cups chicken stock
2 tbsps chopped parsley
4 slices bread, crusts removed
Oil for frying
Salt and pepper

Step 1 Cut the
bacon into small
strips and blanch
to remove excess
salt.

1. Preheat oven to 350°F. Cut the bacon into strips about
¼ inch thick. Bring water the boil and blanch the bacon by
simmering for 5 minutes. Remove the bacon with a draining
spoon and dry on paper towels. Re-boil the water and drop
in the onions. Allow them to boil rapidly for 2-3 minutes and
then plunge into cold water and peel. Set the onions aside
with the bacon.

2. Melt half the butter in a large frying pan over moderate
heat and add the bacon and onions. Fry over high heat,
stirring frequently and shaking the pan, until the bacon and
onions are golden brown. Remove them with a draining
spoon and leave on paper towels. Add the remaining butter
to the saucepan and cook the mushrooms for 1-2 minutes.
Remove them and set them aside with the onions and
bacon.

3. Reheat the frying pan and brown the chicken, a few
pieces at a time. When all the chicken is browned, transfer
it to a large ovenproof casserole.

4. Pour the wine into a small saucepan and boil it to reduce
to about 1 cup. Pour the brandy into a small saucepan or
ladle and warm over low heat. Ignite with a match and pour
the brandy (while still flaming) over the chicken. Shake the
casserole carefully until the flames die down. If the brandy
should flare up, cover quickly with the casserole lid. Add the
bouquet garni and garlic to the casserole.

5. Pour off all but 1 tbsp of fat from the frying pan and stir in
the flour. Cook over gentle heat, scraping any of the
browned chicken juices from the bottom of the pan. Pour in
the reduced wine and add the stock. Bring the sauce to the
boil over high heat, stirring constantly until thickened. Strain
over the chicken in the casserole and cover tightly.

6. Place in the oven and cook for 20 minutes. After that
time, add the bacon, onions and mushrooms and continue
cooking for a further 15-20 minutes, or until the chicken is
tender. Remove the bouquet garni and season with salt
and pepper.

7. Cut each of the bread slices into 4 triangles. Heat
enough oil in a large frying pan to cover the triangles of
bread. When the oil is very hot, add the bread triangles two
at a time and fry until golden brown and crisp. Drain on
paper towels. To serve, arrange the chicken in a deep dish,
pour over the sauce and vegetables and arrange the fried
bread croûtes around the outside of the dish. Sprinkle with
chopped parsley.

Cook's Notes

Watchpoint
Make sure the oil for frying the
croûtes is hot enough when
the bread is added, otherwise croûtes
can be very oily.

Cook's Tip
Blanching the bacon in
boiling water removes excess
saltiness. Boiling the onions makes
them easier to peel.

Time
Preparation takes 30-40
minutes, cooking takes about
50 minutes.

SERVES 4

POULET FRICASSÉE

This is a white stew, enriched and thickened with an egg and cream mixture which is called a liaison in French cooking.

3lb chicken, quartered and skinned
¼ cup butter or margarine
2 tbsps flour
2 cups chicken stock
1 bouquet garni
12-16 small onions, peeled
12oz button mushrooms, whole if small, quartered if large
Juice and grated rind of ½ lemon
2 egg yolks
⅓ cup heavy cream
2 tbsps chopped parsley and thyme
Salt and pepper
3 tbsps milk (optional)
Garnish with lemon slices

1. Melt 3 tbsps of the butter in a large sauté pan or frying pan. Place in the chicken in 1 layer and cook over gentle heat for about 5 minutes, or until the chicken is no longer pink. Do not allow the chicken to brown. If necessary, cook the chicken in two batches. When the chicken is sufficiently cooked, remove it from the pan and set aside.

2. Stir the flour into the butter remaining in the pan and cook over very low heat, stirring continuously for about 1 minute, or until a pale straw color. Remove the pan from the heat and gradually beat in the chicken stock. When blended smoothly, add lemon juice and rind, return the pan to the heat and bring to the boil, whisking constantly. Reduce the heat and allow the sauce to simmer for 1 minute.

3. Return the chicken to the pan with any juices that have

Step 3 Tie a bay leaf, sprig of thyme and parsley stalks together to make a bouquet garni.

accumulated and add the bouquet garni. The sauce should almost cover the chicken. If it does not, add more stock or water. Bring to the boil, cover the pan and reduce the heat. Allow the chicken to simmer gently for 30 minutes.

4. Meanwhile, melt the remaining butter in a small frying pan, add the onions, cover and cook very gently for 10 minutes. Do not allow the onions to brown. Remove the onions from the pan with a draining spoon and add to the chicken. Cook the mushrooms in the remaining butter for 2 minutes. Set the mushrooms aside and add them to the chicken 10 minutes before the end of cooking.

5. Test the chicken by piercing a thigh portion with a sharp knife. If the juices run clear, the chicken is cooked. Transfer chicken and vegetables to a serving plate and discard the bouquet garni. Skim the sauce of any fat and boil it rapidly to reduce by almost half.

6. Blend the egg yolks and cream together and whisk in several spoonfuls of the hot sauce. Return the egg yolk and cream mixture to the remaining sauce and cook gently for 2-3 minutes. Stir the sauce constantly and do not allow it to boil. If very thick, add milk. Adjust the seasoning, stir in the parsley and spoon over the chicken in a serving dish. Garnish with lemon slices.

Cook's Notes

Time
Preparation takes about 30 minutes, cooking takes about 30-40 minutes.

Serving Idea
Serve with boiled potatoes or rice.

Cook's Tip
Pour boiling water over the onions and leave to soak 10 minutes to make them easier to peel. Alternatively, prepare as for Coq au Vin.

Watchpoint
A fricassée is a white stew. Cook gently to avoid browning the ingredients.

SERVES 4-6

SALADE NIÇOISE

Almost everyone knows what Salade Niçoise is, but there are so many variations that it need never be ordinary.

1 head Romaine lettuce
2 hard-boiled eggs, quartered
2 large tomatoes, quartered
6 anchovy fillets
10 pitted black olives
1 tbsp capers
¼ cucumber, diced but not peeled
1 can tuna fish, drained
4 large artichoke hearts, quartered

Dressing

⅓ cup olive oil
2 tbsps white or red wine vinegar
½ clove garlic, crushed
1 tsp mustard
Salt, pepper and lemon juice

Step 2 If anchovy fillets are thick, cut in half. Eggs, tomatoes, and artichoke hearts may be cut into smaller pieces if desired.

Step 2 Whisk the dressing ingredients well to blend thoroughly.

1. Wash the lettuce well, pat dry and break into bite-size pieces.

2. Prepare the remaining ingredients and toss with the lettuce in a large bowl, taking care not to break up the eggs. Mix the dressing ingredients together and whisk until well emulsified. Pour the dressing over the salad just before serving.

Step 1 Break well washed lettuce into bite-sized pieces.

Cook's Notes

Serving Ideas
Makes a light lunch with French bread or a first course.

Time
Preparation takes about 20 minutes, cooking approximately 9-10 minutes to hard-boil the eggs.

Variations
Add cubed new potatoes or lightly cooked green beans or lima beans. Substitute shrimp for tuna, if desired.

Preparation
If cooking eggs in advance, leave them in cold water to prevent a gray ring forming around the yolks.

SERVES 4

MOULES MARINIÈRE

Brittany and Normandy are famous for mussels and for cream
and so cooks combined the two in one perfect seafood dish.

3lbs mussels
1½ cups dry cider or white wine
4 shallots, finely chopped
1 clove garlic, crushed
1 bouquet garni
½ cup heavy cream
3 tbsps butter, cut into small pieces
2 tbsps finely chopped parsley

1. Scrub the mussels well and remove the beards and any barnacles from the shells. Discard any mussels that have cracked shells and do not open when lightly tapped. Put the mussels into a large bowl and soak in cold water for at least 1 hour. Meanwhile, chop the parsley very finely.

2. Bring the cider or wine to the boil in a large stock pot and add the shallots, garlic and bouquet garni. Add the mussels, cover the pan and cook for 5 minutes. Shake the pan or stir the mussels around frequently until the shells open. Lift out the mussels into a large soup tureen or individual serving bowls. Discard any mussels that have not opened.

3. Reduce the cooking liquid by about half and strain into another saucepan. Add the cream and bring to the boil to thicken slightly. Beat in the butter, a few pieces at a time. Adjust the seasoning, add the parsley and pour the sauce over the mussels to serve.

Step 1 Break off thick stems from parsley and chop leaves very finely.

Step 2 Whilst cooking the mussels, stir or shake them frequently until the shells open.

Step 3 Beat the butter into the thickened cream and cooking liquid, a few pieces at a time.

Cook's Notes
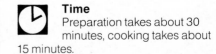

Preparation
Soak mussels with a handful of flour or cornmeal in the water. They will then expel sand and take up the flour or cornmeal, which plumps them up.

Serving Ideas
Serve as a first course with French bread, or double the quantity of mussels to serve for a light main course.

Time
Preparation takes about 30 minutes, cooking takes about 15 minutes.

RAIE AU BEURRE NOIR

It is amazing how the addition of simple ingredients
like browned butter, vinegar, capers and parsley can
turn an ordinary fish into a French masterpiece.

4 wings of skate
1 slice onion
2 parsley stalks
Pinch salt
6 black peppercorns

Beurre Noir

4 tbsps butter
2 tbsps white wine vinegar
1 tbsp capers
1 tbsp chopped parsley (optional)

Step 1 Place the skate in a pan with the poaching liquid and flavouring ingredients.

1. Place the skate in one layer in a large, deep pan. Completely cover with water and add the onion, parsley stalks, salt and peppercorns. Bring gently to the boil with pan uncovered. Allow to simmer 15-20 minutes, or until the skate is done.

2. Lift the fish out onto a serving dish and remove the skin and any large pieces of bone. Take care not to break up the fish.

Step 2 Carefully remove any skin or large bones from the cooked fish, with a small knife.

3. Place the butter in a small pan and cook over high heat until it begins to brown. Add the capers and immediately remove the butter from the heat. Add the vinegar, which will cause the butter to bubble. Add parsley, if using, and pour immediately over the fish to serve.

Step 3 Pour sizzling butter over the fish to serve.

Cook's Notes

Variations
Chopped black olives, shallots or mushrooms may be used instead of or in addition to the capers. Add lemon juice instead of vinegar, if desired.

Cook's Tip
When the skate is done, it will pull away from the bones in long strips.

Time
Preparation takes about 20 minutes, cooking takes 15-20 minutes for the fish and about 5 minutes to brown the butter.

SERVES 4

ROUGETS À LA PROVENÇALE

Red Mullet is a very attractive fish, with a flavor quite
like shrimp. It is also known as "woodcock of the sea"
because it is often served with the liver left inside.

2 tbsps olive oil
1 clove garlic, crushed
2 shallots, finely chopped
1lb ripe tomatoes, peeled, seeded and sliced
2 tsps chopped marjoram and parsley mixed
⅓ cup dry white wine
Salt, pepper and pinch saffron
Oil for frying
2 small bulbs fennel, quartered and cored
4 red mullet, about 6oz each
Flour mixed with salt and pepper

Step 3 To scale fish, run the blunt end of a knife from the tail to the head.

1. Heat 2 tbsps olive oil in a deep saucepan and add the garlic and shallots. Cook 1-2 minutes to soften slightly, then add tomatoes, herbs, wine, salt, pepper and saffron. Allow to simmer, uncovered, for 30 minutes and set aside while preparing the fennel and fish.

2. Pour about 4 tbsps oil into a large frying pan or sauté pan. Place over moderate heat and add the fennel. Cook quickly until the fennel is slightly browned. Lower the heat and cook a further 5-10 minutes to soften the fennel.

3. Scale the fish, remove the gills and clean, leaving in the liver if desired. Wash the fish and dry thoroughly. Trim the fins and roll the fish in seasoned flour, shaking off the excess.

4. When the fennel is tender, remove it from the pan and set it aside. Fry the fish until golden brown on both sides, about 2-3 minutes per side. Arrange the fish in a warm

Step 3 Remove the fins with kitchen scissors.

Step 3 Gut the fish, cut along the stomach and remove insides, leaving liver if desired.

serving dish and surround with the fennel. Reheat the sauce and spoon over the fish. Serve remaining sauce separately.

Cook's Notes

Time
Preparation takes about 30 minutes unless the fish are already cleaned. Cooking takes approximately 40 minutes.

Watchpoint
Red mullet spoils quickly, so use on day of purchase.

Cook's Tip
Saffron is expensive, so use a pinch of turmeric as a substitute for color.

SERVES 4

Truite Meunière aux Herbes

The miller (meunier) caught trout fresh from the mill stream and his wife used the flour which was on hand to dredge them with, or so the story goes.

4 even-sized trout, cleaned and trimmed
Flour
Salt and pepper
½ cup butter
Juice of 1 lemon
2 tbsps chopped fresh herbs such as parsley, chervil, tarragon, thyme or marjoram
Lemon wedges to garnish

1. Trim the trout tails to make them more pointed. Rinse the trout well.

2. Dredge the trout with flour and shake off the excess. Season with salt and pepper. Heat half the butter in a very large sauté pan and, when foaming, place in the trout. It may be necessary to cook the trout in two batches to avoid overcrowding the pan.

3. Cook over fairly high heat on both sides to brown evenly. Depending on size, the trout should take 5-8 minutes per side to cook. The dorsal fin will pull out easily when the trout are cooked. Remove the trout to a serving dish and keep them warm.

4. Wipe out the pan and add the remaining butter. Cook over moderate heat until beginning to brown, then add the lemon juice and herbs. When the lemon juice is added, the butter will bubble up and sizzle. Pour immediately over the fish and serve with lemon wedges.

Step 1 Trim the trout tails with scissors to make them neater.

Step 2 Coat trout in flour, shaking off excess.

Step 3 Brown the trout on both sides. Dorsal fin will pull out easily when done.

Cook's Notes

Time
Preparation takes 15-20 minutes, cooking takes 5-8 minutes per side for the fish and about 5 minutes to brown the butter.

Preparation
If trout is coated in flour too soon before cooking it will become soggy.

Serving Ideas
Serve with new potatoes and peeled, cubed cucumber quickly sautéed in butter and chopped dill.

SERVES 6

ROGNONS À LA DIJONNAISE

Veal kidneys are lighter in color and milder in flavor than lamb's kidneys. Since they must be quickly cooked, kidneys make an ideal sauté dish.

¼ cup unsalted butter
3-4 whole veal kidneys
1-2 shallots, finely chopped
1 cup dry white wine
⅓ cup butter, softened
3 tbsps Dijon mustard
Salt, pepper and lemon juice to taste
2 tbsps chopped parsley

1. Melt the unsalted butter in a large sauté pan. Cut the kidneys into 1 inch pieces and remove any fat or core. When the butter stops foaming, add the kidneys and sauté them, uncovered, until they are light brown on all sides, about 10 minutes. Remove the kidneys from the pan and keep them warm.

2. Add the shallots to the pan and cook for about 1 minute, stirring frequently. Add the wine and bring to the boil, stirring constantly and scraping the pan to remove any browned juices. Allow to boil rapidly for 3-4 minutes until the wine is reduced to about 3 tbsps. Remove the pan from the heat.

3. Mix the remaining butter with the mustard, add salt and pepper and whisk the mixture into the reduced sauce. Return the kidneys to the pan, add the lemon juice and parsley and cook over low heat for 1-2 minutes to heat through. Serve immediately.

Step 1 Slice the kidneys and remove any fat or core.

Step 2 Add wine to the pan and scrape to remove browned juices (deglaze).

Step 3 Whisk the butter and mustard mixture gradually into the reduced sauce.

Cook's Notes

Variations
If veal kidneys are not available, use lamb kidneys instead.

Time
Preparation takes about 25 minutes, cooking 15-17 minutes.

Cook's Tip
Use unsalted butter for sautéeing or shallow frying because it does not burn as quickly as salted butter.

Watchpoint
Kidneys and all offal need careful, quick cooking or they will toughen.

SERVES 6

CARBONNADE À LA FLAMANDE

This carbonnade is a rich stew cooked in the
Flemish style with dark beer.

2 tbsps oil
1½lbs chuck steak
1 large onion, thinly sliced
2 tbsps flour
1 clove garlic, crushed
1 cup brown ale
1 cup hot water
Bouquet garni, salt and pepper
Pinch sugar and nutmeg
Dash red wine vinegar
6 slices French bread cut about ½ inch thick
French or Dijon mustard

1. Preheat the oven to 325°F. Place the oil in a large, heavy-based frying pan. Cut the meat into 2 inch pieces and brown quickly on both sides in the oil. Brown the meat 5-6 pieces at a time to avoid crowding the pan.

2. Remove the meat when browned, lower the heat and add the onion. Cook until the onion is beginning to soften and color. Stir in the flour and add the garlic. Add the hot water and ale.

3. Add the bouquet garni, season with salt and pepper, add the sugar, nutmeg and vinegar. Bring to the boil on top of the stove. Transfer to an ovenproof casserole with the meat, cover and cook in the oven for 2-2½ hours.

4. Fifteen minutes before serving, skim off any fat from the surface and reserve it. Spread the mustard on the bread and spoon some of the fat over each slice.

Step 1 Cut the meat into 2 inch pieces and brown in the oil.

Step 4 Spread the bread with mustard and spoon reserved fat over each slice.

Step 5 Place bread on top of casserole and push down slightly.

5. Place the bread on top of the casserole, pushing it down slightly. Cook a further 15-20 minutes, uncovered, or until the bread is browned and crisp.

 Time
Preparation takes about 30 minutes, cooking takes 2-2¾ hours.

 Watchpoint
Add the ale gradually to the hot casserole as it may foam up and boil over.

 Preparation
The casserole may be prepared in advance and the bread added just before reheating to serve.

 Variations
Add carrots or mushrooms, if desired.

 Freezing
Prepare the casserole in advance without the bread topping. Cool it completely, pour into a freezer container, cover, label and freeze for up to 3 months.

SERVES 4-6

FILET DE PORC AUX PRUNEAUX

Tours, situated on the River Loire, is where this dish originated.
It is a rich dish with its creamy sauce and wine-soaked prunes.

2-3 small pork tenderloins
1lb pitted prunes
2 cups white wine
3 tbsps butter or margarine
1-2 tbsps flour
Salt and pepper
1 tbsp redcurrant jelly
1 cup heavy cream

1. Soak the prunes in the white wine for about 1 hour and then put them into a very low oven to soften further. If the prunes are the ready-softened variety, soak for 20 minutes and omit the oven cooking.

2. Slice the pork fillet on the diagonal into 1-inch-thick pieces. Flatten them slightly with the palm of the hand. Dredge them with the flour, and melt the butter in a heavy pan. When the butter is foaming, put in the pork and cook until lightly browned on both sides. It may be necessary to cook the pork fillet in several batches.

3. Add half the soaking liquid from the prunes, cover the pan and cook very gently on moderate heat for about 45 minutes. If necessary, add more wine from the prunes while the pork is cooking.

4. When the pork is tender, pour liquid into a small saucepan and bring to the boil. Reduce by about ¼ and add the redcurrant jelly. Stir until dissolved and then add the cream. Bring the sauce back to the boil and allow to boil rapidly, stirring frequently. When the sauce is reduced and

Step 1 Cook the prunes in wine until softened.

Step 2 Slice the pork fillet and flatten the slices with the palm of the hand.

Step 4 Whisk the redcurrant jelly into the boiling sauce.

thickened slightly, pour over the meat and reheat. Add the prunes and transfer to a serving dish. Sprinkle with chopped parsley if desired.

Cook's Notes

Variation
Substitute water or stock for half of the wine measurement.

Time
Preparation about 25 minutes, cooking about 45 minutes.

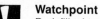

Watchpoint
Pork fillet is very lean meat and can easily dry out. Be careful not to over-cook and make sure to use enough liquid.

Cook's Tip
Pork fillet may be cooked in a moderate oven for the same length of time.

SERVES 6

RAGOÛT DE VEAU MARENGO

There is an Italian influence evident in this stew recipe.
Pie veal is relatively inexpensive, thus making this
recipe easier on the budget than most veal dishes.

3lbs lean pie veal
4 tbsps flour, mixed with salt and pepper
4 tbsps olive oil
2 shallots, finely chopped
½ clove garlic, crushed
⅓ cup dry white wine
1 cup brown stock
8oz canned tomatoes, drained and crushed
1 bouquet garni
2 strips lemon peel
4oz mushrooms, whole if small, quartered if large
3 tbsps butter or margarine
2 tbsps chopped parsley (optional)

1. Preheat oven to 325°F. Dredge the pieces of veal with the seasoned flour.

2. Pour the oil into a large sauté pan or heatproof casserole and place over a moderate heat. When the oil is hot, cook the veal 5-10 pieces at a time, depending upon the size of the pan. Brown the veal well on all sides, remove from the pan and set aside.

3. Add the shallots and garlic to the pan, lower the heat and cook until softened, but not colored. Return the veal to the pan, add the wine, stock, tomatoes, bouquet garni and lemon peel. Bring to the boil on top of the stove, cover and cook in the oven for 1¼ hours, or until the veal is tender.

4. Meanwhile, melt the remaining butter in a frying pan and add the mushrooms and toss over a moderate heat for 2-3 minutes, stirring occasionally. When the veal is cooked, skim the surface of the sauce to remove excess fat and add the mushrooms with their cooking liquid to the veal. Cook for a further 10-15 minutes then remove the bouquet garni and the lemon peel.

Step 2 Brown the veal well on all sides.

Step 3 Cook the shallots and garlic gently until softened but not colored.

Step 4 Tilt the pan to make it easier to skim off excess fat.

5. Transfer the veal and mushrooms to a serving dish and reduce the sauce to about 1½ cups by boiling rapidly. Adjust the seasoning and pour the sauce over the veal and mushrooms before serving. Reheat if necessary and garnish with chopped parsley, if desired.

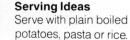

Cook's Notes

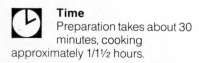

Time
Preparation takes about 30 minutes, cooking approximately 1/1½ hours.

Serving Ideas
Serve with plain boiled potatoes, pasta or rice.

! Watchpoint
Do not allow garlic to brown as it will turn bitter.

SERVES 6

NAVARIN PRINTANIER

This is a ragôut or brown stew traditionally made with
mutton chops. Substitute lamb for a milder taste.
Printanier means that a selection of vegetables is added.

⅓ cup vegetable oil
12 even-sized lamb cutlets
Flour mixed with salt, pepper and a pinch dried thyme
2 shallots, finely chopped
1 clove garlic, crushed
2 cups brown stock
½ cup dry white wine
5 tomatoes, peeled, seeded and coarsely chopped
1 bouquet garni

Spring Vegetables

12 new potatoes, scrubbed but not peeled
8 baby carrots, scraped (if green tops are in good
    condition, leave on)
6 small turnips, peeled and left whole
12oz frozen petits pois
8oz green beans cut into 1 inch lengths on the diagonal
12 green onions, roots ends trimmed and green tops
    trimmed about 3 inches from the ends
1 tbsps chopped parsley (optional)

Remove the cores
from the
tomatoes.

Plunge into
boiling water for a
few seconds.

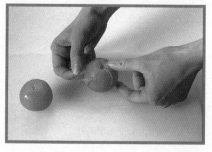

Refresh in cold
water then peel
off skins.

1. Preheat the oven to 350°F. Heat about half the oil in a large, heavy-based frying pan. Dredge the lamb cutlets with the flour mixture, shaking off the excess. Brown the lamb cutlets 4 at a time, adding more oil if necessary. When the cutlets are brown on all sides, remove them to a heavy casserole.

2. Remove most of the oil from the pan and cook the shallots and garlic over moderate heat, stirring constantly. Add the stock and bring to the boil, scraping the bottom of the pan to remove the browned meat juices. Allow to boil rapidly to reduce slightly, then add the tomatoes.

3. Pour the sauce over the lamb, turning the cutlets to coat all of them with the sauce. Add the bouquet garni, cover tightly and cook in the oven for about 30 minutes, or until the lamb is tender.

4. After about 10 minutes, add the potatoes and carrots to the lamb.

5. Add the turnips, green beans, peas and green onions 15 minutes before the end of cooking time.

6. After 30 minutes, remove the lamb and any vegetables that are tender. Boil the sauce rapidly to reduce it and cook any vegetables that need extra time. Pour the sauce over the lamb and vegetables to serve and sprinkle with chopped parsley, if desired.

Cook's Notes

Variations
Substitute other vegetables as
desired, but always cook root
vegetables first. Canned tomatoes may
be substitued for fresh ones.

Time
Preparation takes 30-40
minutes, cooking about 30-35
minutes.

SERVES 6

Poires au Vin Rouge

A marvellous recipe for using firm cooking pears to their best advantage. They look beautiful served in a glass bowl.

2 cups dry red wine
Juice of half lemon
1 strip lemon peel
1 cup sugar
1 small piece stick cinnamon
6 small ripe but firm pears, peeled, but with the
   stalks left on

1. Bring the wine, lemon juice and peel, sugar and cinnamon to the boil in a deep saucepan or ovenproof casserole that will accommodate 6 pears snugly. Stir until the sugar dissolves and then allow to boil rapidly for 1 minute.

2. Peel the pears lengthwise and remove the small eye from the bottom of each pear. Place the pears upright in the simmering wine. Allow to cook slowly for 20 minutes, or until they are soft but not mushy. If the syrup does not completely cover the pears, allow the pears to cook on their sides and turn and baste them frequently. Cool the pears in the syrup until lukewarm and then remove them. Remove the cinnamon stick and the lemon peel and discard.

3. If the syrup is still very thin, remove pears, boil to reduce slightly or mix 1 tbsp arrowroot with a little cold water, add some of the warm syrup and return the arrowroot to the rest of the syrup. Bring to the boil, stirring constantly until thickened and cleared. Spoon the syrup over the pears and refrigerate or serve warm. Pears may be decorated with slivered toasted almonds and served with lightly whipped cream if desired.

Step 2 Peel the pears lengthwise and remove the eye from the bottom.

Step 2 Place the pears in the simmering wine, upright or on their sides.

Step 3 Spoon the syrup over the pears and decorate with almonds.

Cook's Notes

Variations
Pears may be cooked au Vin Blanc with a dry white wine or in fruit juice.

Cook's Tip
Add a few drops of red food coloring to the syrup if the pears appear too pale when cooked.

Time
Preparation takes about 25 minutes, cooking 20 minutes.

SERVES 6

MOUSSE AU CHOCOLAT BASQUE

This mousse is a dark chocolate mixture which
sets to a rich cream in the refrigerator.

6oz semi-sweet chocolate
Scant ⅓ cup water
1 tbsp butter
3 eggs, separated
2 tbsps rum

1. Chop the chocolate into small pieces and combine with
the water in a heavy-based saucepan. Cook over very
gentle heat so that the chocolate and water form a thick
cream. Remove from the heat, allow to cool slightly and
then beat in the butter.

2. Add the rum and beat in the egg yolks one at a time.

Step 1 Melt
chopped
chocolate in water
over gentle heat.

Step 2 Beat in
egg yolks one at
a time.

Step 3 Fold
lightly whipped
egg whites into
the chocolate
mixture.

3. Whip the egg whites until stiff but not dry and fold
thoroughly into the chocolate mixture. Pour into small pots
or custard cups and chill overnight. Finish with whipped
cream and chocolate curls to serve, if desired.

Cook's Notes

! Watchpoint
Never melt chocolate over
direct heat without using
some liquid. Do not over-whip egg
whites; this will make the mousse
grainy in texture.

Variations
Add strong coffee in place of
water, or flavor with grated
orange rind. Use juice instead of the
water and add Grand Marnier instead
of rum.

Time
Preparation takes 20 minutes,
cooking takes approximately
10 minutes to melt the chocolate.

SERVES 6

SOUFFLÉ AU CITRON FROID

A cold soufflé is really a mousse in disguise. It doesn't "rise" in the refrigerator, but is set above the rim of its dish with the help of a paper collar and gelatine.

3 eggs, separated
¾ cup sugar
Grated rind and juice of 2 small lemons
1 tbsp gelatine dissolved in 3-4 tbsps water
¾ cup cream, lightly whipped

Decoration

½ cup cream, whipped
Thin strips lemon rind or lemon twists
Finely chopped almonds or pistachios

Step 2 When thick enough, mixture will leave a ribbon trail.

1. Tie a double thickness of wax paper around a soufflé dish to stand about 3 inches above the rim of the dish.

2. Beat the egg yolks in a large bowl until thick and lemon colored. Add the sugar gradually and then the lemon rind and juice. Set the bowl over a pan of hot water and whisk until the mixture is thick and leaves a ribbon-trail. Remove the bowl from the heat and whisk a few minutes longer.

3. Melt the gelatine and the water until clear, pour into the lemon mixture and stir thoroughly. Set the bowl over ice and stir until beginning to thicken.

4. Whip the egg whites until stiff but not dry and fold into the lemon mixture along with the lightly whipped cream. Pour into the prepared soufflé dish and chill in the refrigerator until the gelatine sets completely. To serve, peel off the paper carefully and spread some of the cream on the sides of the mixture. Press finely chopped nuts into the cream. Pipe the remaining cream into rosettes on top of the soufflé and decorate with strips of rind or lemon twists.

Step 4 Fold the egg whites and cream into the mixture and pour into the prepared dish.

Step 4 Peel off the paper carefully.

Cook's Notes

Time
Preparation takes about 25-30 minutes.

Watchpoint
Do not allow gelatine to boil; it will lose its setting qualities.

Cook's Tip
If gelatine sets before cream and egg whites are added, gently reheat the lemon mixture, stirring constantly until soft again.

Preparation
Do not fill the dish more than 1½ inches above the rim of the dish or, once decorated, the mixture will collapse.

SERVES 6

CRÊPES AU CHOCOLAT ET FRAMBOISES

Crêpes Suzette may be more famous, but these.
filled with chocolate and raspberry, are incredibly delicious.

Crêpe Batter

1½ cups milk and water mixed
4 eggs
Pinch salt
2 cups all-purpose flour, sifted
1 tbsp sugar
4 tbsps melted butter or oil

Filling

8oz semi-sweet dessert chocolate, grated
4oz seedless raspberry jam
Whipped cream and chopped, browned hazelnuts

Step 1 Cook until edges are brown then turn over.

Step 1 When underside is lightly speckled with brown, slide onto a plate.

1. Put all the ingredients for the crêpes into a food processor or blender and process for about 1 minute, pushing down the sides occasionally. Process a few seconds more to blend thoroughly. Leave, covered, in a cool place for 30 minutes to 1 hour. The consistency of the batter should be that of thin cream. Add more milk if necessary. Brush a crêpe pan or small frying pan lightly with oil and place over high heat. When a slight haze forms, pour a large spoonful of the batter into the pan and swirl the pan to cover the base. Pour out any excess into a separate bowl. Cook on one side until just beginning to brown around the edges. Turn over and cook on the other side until lightly speckled with brown. Slide each crêpe onto a plate and repeat using the remaining batter. Reheat the pan occasionally in between cooking each crêpe. The amount of batter should make 12 crêpes.

2. As the crêpes are cooked, sprinkle them evenly with grated chocolate and divide the raspberry jam among all the crêpes. Roll them up so that the jam shows at the ends, or fold into triangles.

3. Reheat in a moderate oven for about 10 minutes before serving. Top with whipped cream and a sprinkling of browned nuts.

Cook's Notes

 Time
Preparation takes about 30 minutes, cooking takes about 30 minutes.

 Variation
To make savory crêpes, leave out the sugar but prepare them in the same way.

 Watchpoint
Batter works best when only one quarter water to three quarters milk used in the mixture. The batter must stand for at least 30 minutes before use to allow it too thicken properly.

 Freezing
Allow crêpes to cool completely and stack between sheets of nonstick or wax paper. Place in a plastic bag and freeze for up to 3 months. Defrost completely but separate and reheat as needed.

MAKES 12

ECLAIRS

Think of French pastry and eclairs immediately spring
to mind. French patisseries - pastry shops - sell
them filled and iced in many different flavors.

Choux Pastry

⅞ cup water
⅓ cup butter or margarine
¾ cup all-purpose flour, sifted
3 eggs

Crème Patissière

1 whole egg
1 egg yolk
¼ cup sugar
1 tbsp cornstarch
1½ tbsps flour
1 cup milk
Few drops vanilla extract

Glacé Icing

1lb confectioners' sugar
Hot water
Few drops vanilla extract

1. Preheat the oven to 350°F.

2. Combine the water and butter for the pastry in a deep
saucepan and bring to the boil. Once boiling rapidly, take
the pan off the heat. Stir in the flour all at once and beat just
until the mixture leaves the sides of the pan. Spread out
onto a plate to cool. When cool, return to the saucepan and
gradually add the beaten egg. Beat in well in between each
addition of egg until the paste is smooth and shiny –
should be of soft dropping consistency, but holding its
shape well. It may not be necessary to add all the egg. Pipe
or spoon into strips of about 3 inches long, spaced well
apart on lightly-greased baking sheets.

3. Sprinkle the sheets lightly with water and place in the
oven. Immediately increase oven temperature to 375°F.

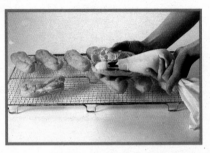

Step 6 Cut the
eclairs almost in
half. Pipe or
spoon in the
crème patissière.

Make sure the pastry is very crisp before removing it from
the oven, this will take about 20-30 minutes cooking time. If
the pastry is not crisp, return to the oven for a further
5 minutes.

4. To prepare the Crème Patissière, separate the whole
egg and reserve the white. Mix the egg yolks and sugar
together, sift in the flours and add about half the milk, stirring
well. Bring the remainder of the milk to the boil and pour
onto the yolk mixture, stirring constantly. Return the mixture
to the pan and stir over heat until boiling point is reached.
Take off the heat and whip the egg white until stiff but not
dry. Fold the egg white into the mixture and return to the
heat. Cook gently for about 1 minute, stirring occasionally.
Add the vanilla extract at this point. Pour the mixture into a
bowl and press a sheet of wax paper directly onto the
surface of the crème and leave it to cool.

5. Sift the confectioners' sugar into a bowl and add hot
water, stirring constantly until the mixture is of thick coating
consistency. The icing should cover the back of a wooden
spoon but run off slowly. Add the vanilla extract.

6. To assemble the eclairs, cut the choux pastry almost in
half lengthwise and either pipe or spoon in the Crème
Patissière. Using a large spoon, coat the top of each eclair
with a smooth layer of glacé icing. Allow the icing to set
before serving.

Cook's Notes

 Time
Preparation takes about 40
minutes, cooking takes about
30-40 minutes.

 Cook's Tip
Water sprinkled on the baking
sheet creates steam to help
pastry rise.

 Preparation
1-2 tsps oil added to the icing
will keep it shiny when set.

ITALIAN COOKING

INTRODUCTION

The food of Italy is among the best-loved in the world. The ingredients reflect all the warmth, color and variety that the country has to offer. There are beautiful lemons, limes and oranges in the orchards up and down the peninsula. Miles and miles of coastline mean a plentiful supply of fish and seafood. Tomatoes, peppers and most other vegetables flourish in the sun throughout spring and summer. Herbs, garlic and the fragrant bouquet of olive oil all provide taste interest. Cheeses and cured meats are superb in quality and selection.

When putting together a traditional Italian meal, begin with an antipasto, which means "before the pasta." Follow with a pasta dish or soup, but not both. Then choose a main course of fish, meat or poultry accompanied by polenta, risotto or potatoes and a salad. A sweet is served next, and this can be as rich as Zuppa Inglese or as simple as fresh fruit. Cheese is considered an antipasto and not the final course.

Vegetables are highly prized in Italy and often appear as a separate course before the main dish. Sicilian Caponata is a perfect choice, hot or cold.

If all that food seems too much, turn to Italy's best-known contributions, pizza and pasta. Once you make your own pizza dough, you won't go back to frozen pizzas again! Home-made pasta is also a wonderful thing and easy to make, too, but if you can't find time, try to buy fresh pasta, which is readily available these days.

There is room for endless creativity with sauces for pastas and toppings for pizzas so boredom need never set in. Just add a salad and perhaps a glorious pudding like cassata for an authentic taste of Italy that is as close as your kitchen.

SERVES 6-8

BRUSCHETTA WITH TOMATOES

Cooked over a wood fire in the traditional way, or more
conveniently in the oven, tomatoes, basil and crisp bread
make an unusual and informal appetizer.

18 slices of crusty Italian bread, cut 1 inch thick
2 cloves garlic, crushed
½ cup olive oil
Salt and pepper
18 large fresh basil leaves
4-5 ripe tomatoes, depending on size

Step 3 Warm the oil in a small saucepan and pour over the bread.

Step 1 Toast the bread in the oven until golden brown on both sides and spread each side with some of the garlic.

Step 4 Slice the tomatoes with a serrated knife and arrange on top of the bread with the basil leaves.

1. Place the bread slices on a baking sheet and toast for about 10 minutes on each side at 375°F.

2. Spread some of the garlic on both sides of each slice.

3. Heat the oil gently in a small saucepan. Arrange the bread on a serving plate and immediately pour over the warm oil. Sprinkle with salt and pepper.

4. Slice the tomatoes in ½ inch rounds. Place one basil leaf and one slice of tomato on each slice of bread and serve immediately.

Cook's Notes

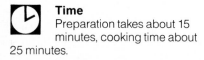

Time
Preparation takes about 15 minutes, cooking time about 25 minutes.

Variations
French bread may be used if Italian bread is not available, but the taste will be different. White or brown bread may be used.

Serving Ideas
May be served as a first course or as cocktail savories.

SERVES 4

MELON AND PROSCIUTTO

This is one of the best-loved Italian appetizers. It deserves
to be, because the flavor of a ripe melon and the richness
of Italian ham complement one another perfectly.

1 large ripe melon
16 thin slices prosciutto ham

Step 1 Cut the melon in half and scoop out the seeds.

Step 2 Cut the melon in quarters and carefully remove the rind. Cut into thin slices.

Step 3 Roll up the melon in the prosciutto to serve.

1. Cut the melon in half lengthwise, scoop out the seeds and discard them.

2. Cut the melon into quarters and carefully pare off the rind. Cut each quarter into four slices.

3. Wrap each slice of melon in a slice of prosciutto and place on a serving dish. Alternatively, place the melon slices on the dish and cover with the slices of prosciutto, leaving the ends of the melon showing. Serve immediately.

Cook's Notes

Time
Preparation takes about 20 minutes.

Variations
Place the slices of prosciutto flat on serving plates or roll them up into cigar shapes. Serve with quartered fresh figs instead of melon.

SERVES 6-8

SEAFOOD TORTA

A very stylish version of a fish flan, this makes
a perfect accompaniment to an Italian aperitif or
serves as a light supper dish with salad.

Pastry

2 cups all-purpose flour, sifted
½ cup unsalted butter
Pinch salt
4 tbsps cold milk

Filling

4oz whitefish fillets (plaice, sole or cod)
8oz cooked shrimp
4oz flaked crab meat
½ cup white wine
½ cup water
Large pinch hot pepper flakes
Salt and pepper
2 tbsps butter
2 tbsps flour
1 clove garlic, crushed
2 egg yolks
½ cup heavy cream
Chopped fresh parsley

Step 5 Press a sheet of wax paper on the pastry and fill with beans, rice or baking beans to weight down.

1. To prepare the pastry, sift the flour into a bowl or onto a work surface. Cut the butter into small pieces and begin mixing them into the flour. Mix until the mixture resembles fine breadcrumbs – this may also be done in a food processor. Make a well in the flour, pour in the milk and add the pinch of salt. Mix with a fork, gradually incorporating the butter and flour mixture from the sides until all the ingredients are mixed. This may also be done in a food processor.

2. Form the dough into a ball and knead for about 1 minute. Leave the dough in the refrigerator for about 1 hour.

3. To prepare the filling, cook whitefish fillets in the water and wine with the red pepper flakes for about 10 minutes or until just firm to the touch. When the fish is cooked, remove it from the liquid and flake it into a bowl with the shrimp and the crab meat. Reserve the cooking liquid.

4. Melt the butter in a small saucepan and stir in the flour. Gradually strain on the cooking liquid from the fish, stirring constantly until smooth. Add garlic, place over high heat and bring to the boil. Lower the heat and allow to cook for 1 minute. Add to the fish in the bowl and set aside to cool.

5. On a well-floured surface, roll out the pastry and transfer it with a rolling pin to a tart pan with a removable base. Press the dough into the pan and cut off any excess. Prick the pastry base lightly with a fork and place a sheet of wax paper inside. Fill with rice, dried beans or baking beans and chill for 30 minutes. Bake the pastry shell blind for 15 minutes in a 375°F oven.

6. While the pastry is baking, combine the egg yolks, cream and parsley and stir into the fish filling. Adjust the seasoning with salt and pepper. When the pastry is ready, remove the paper and beans and pour in the filling.

7. Return the tart to the oven and bake for a further 25 minutes. Allow to cool slightly and then remove from the pan. Transfer to a serving dish and slice before serving.

Cook's Notes

Time
Filling takes about 15-20 minutes to prepare. Pastry takes about 20 minutes to prepare plus 1 hour refrigeration. Tart takes about 40 minutes to cook.

Variation
Substitute lobster for the whitefish for a special occasion or dinner party first course.

Freezing
Make the pastry in advance and wrap it very well. Label and freeze for up to 3 months. Defrost at room temperature before using. Also freeze uncooked in the flan dish.

SERVES 8-10

MINESTRONE

Everyone's favorite Italian soup doesn't always have to contain pasta. Our's substitutes potatoes and is hearty enough to serve as a meal.

8oz dried white cannellini beans
2 tbsps olive oil
1 large ham bone, preferably prosciutto
1 onion, chopped
2 cloves garlic, crushed
4 sticks celery, sliced
2 carrots, diced
1 small head Savoy cabbage or 1lb fresh spinach, well washed
4oz green beans, cut into 1 inch lengths
8oz tomatoes, peeled, seeded and diced
1 dried red chili pepper
10 cups water (or half beef stock)
Salt and pepper
1 sprig fresh rosemary
1 bay leaf
3 potatoes, peeled and cut into small dice
3 zucchini, trimmed and cut into small dice
1 tbsp chopped fresh basil
1 tbsp chopped fresh parsley
Grated Parmesan cheese
Salt and pepper

1. Place the beans in a large bowl, cover with cold water and leave to soak overnight.

2. Heat the oil in a large stock pot and add ham bone, onion and garlic. Cook until onion has softened but not colored. Add the celery, carrots, cabbage and green beans. If using spinach, reserve until later.

3. Drain the beans and add them to the pot with the tomatoes and the chili pepper. Add the water and bring to the boil, skimming the surface as necessary. Add the rosemary and bay leaf and simmer, uncovered, until the beans are tender, about 1¼ hours.

4. Add the potatoes and cook for the further 20 minutes.

5. Add the zucchini and spinach and cook, skimming the surface, about 20 minutes longer. Remove the ham bone, rosemary and bay leaf and add basil and parsley. Serve with Parmesan cheese.

Step 1 Soak beans overnight in enough water to cover. They will swell in size.

Step 3 Using a metal spoon, skim any fat from the surface of the soup as it cooks.

Cook's Notes

Time
Preparation takes about 20 minutes plus overnight soaking for the beans. Cooking takes about 2 hours.

Watchpoint
The beans must be thoroughly cooked - it can be dangerous to eat them insufficiently cooked.

Serving Ideas
If desired, cooked pasta may be substituted for the potatoes and added at the end of cooking time.

Variation
Other varieties of white beans may be used and canned beans may also be used. If using canned beans, add them with zucchini and spinach. Other vegetables such as broccoli, turnips, leeks or quartered Brussels sprouts, may be substituted.

SERVES 4-6

SPINACH GNOCCHI

Gnocchi are dumplings that are served like pasta. A dish of gnocchi can be served as a first course or as a light main course, sprinkled with cheese or accompanied by a sauce.

4oz chopped, frozen spinach
8oz ricotta cheese
3oz Parmesan cheese
Salt and pepper
Freshly grated nutmeg
1 egg, slightly beaten
3 tbsps butter

Step 3 Shape the gnocchi mixture with well-floured hands into ovals or balls.

Step 1 Press the spinach between two plates to remove excess moisture.

Step 5 Gnocchi will float to the surface of the water when cooked. Remove with a draining spoon.

1. Defrost the spinach and press it between two plates to extract all the moisture.

2. Mix the spinach with the ricotta cheese, half the Parmesan cheese, salt, pepper and nutmeg. Gradually add the egg, beating well until the mixture holds together when shaped.

3. With floured hands, form the mixture into oval shapes. Use about 1 tbsp mixture for each gnocchi.

4. Lower into simmering water, 3 or 4 at a time, and allow to

cook gently until the gnocchi float to the surface, about 1-2 minutes.

5. Remove with a draining spoon and place in a well buttered ovenproof dish.

6. When all the gnocchi are cooked, sprinkle on the remaining Parmesan cheese and dot with the remaining butter.

7. Reheat 10 minutes in a hot oven and brown under a preheated broiler before serving.

Cook's Notes

Time
Preparation takes about 15 minutes, cooking takes about 20 minutes.

Serving Ideas
Accompany with a tomato or cheese sauce for a light meal with a salad and hot bread.

Cook's Tip
Gnocchi are best served soon after they are cooked. If allowed to stand overnight they become very heavy.

SERVES 4

TOMATO SALAD RUSTICA

An informal salad with a country flavor, this is
perfect with barbecued meat, poultry or fish.

1lb tomatoes
1 onion
4-6 anchovies
Milk
2 tbsps capers
1 tsp chopped fresh oregano or basil
6 tbsps olive oil
1 tbsp lemon juice

Step 1 Remove the cores from the quartered tomatoes and slice again if large.

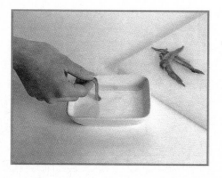

Step 1 Soak the anchovies in milk, rinse well and dry before using.

Step 2 Hold the onion with a fork to steady it while slicing into rings.

1. Soak the anchovies in a little milk before using, rinse, pat dry and chop. Cut the tomatoes into quarters and remove the cores. Slice each quarter in half again and place them in a serving bowl.

2. Slice the onion into rounds and then separate into rings. Scatter over the tomatoes. Cut the anchovies into small pieces and add to the tomatoes and onions along with the capers.

3. Mix the herbs, salt, pepper, oil and lemon juice together until well emulsified and pour over the salad. Mix all the ingredients gently and leave to stand for about 30 minutes before serving.

Cook's Notes

Cook's Tip
Soaking the anchovies in milk removes some of the strong taste and saltiness of the fish.

Time
Preparation takes about 20 minutes. Salad must stand for 30 minutes before serving.

Serving Ideas
Serve as a side dish with broiled meat, poultry or fish, or with a combination of other salads in an antipasti selection.

Variations
Use red onions or green onions for a change. Add sliced black olives if desired.

SERVES 4-6

PEPPER SALAD WITH CAPERS

Capers, the flower buds of a plant that flourishes in the warm
Italian climate, are a favorite ingredient in Italian cooking.

3 large peppers, red, green and yellow
6 tbsps olive oil
1 clove garlic, peeled and finely chopped
Basil leaves, roughly chopped
Fresh marjoram roughly chopped
2 tbsps capers
1 tbsp white wine vinegar

1. Cut the peppers in half and remove the core and seeds. Press with the palm of the hand or the back of a knife to flatten. Brush the skin side with oil and place the peppers under a preheated broiler.

2. Broil the peppers until the skins are well charred. Wrap in a towel and leave for 15 minutes. Unwrap and peel off the charred skin.

3. Cut the peppers into thick strips and arrange on a serving dish. Scatter over the chopped garlic, basil leaves, marjoram and capers.

4. Mix together the remaining olive oil with the vinegar and salt and pepper and pour over the salad. Refrigerate for 1 hour before serving.

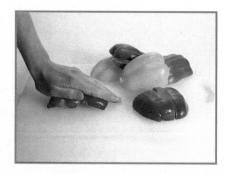

Step 1 Flatten the pepper halves with the palm of the hand or a large knife.

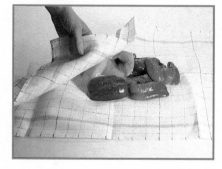

Step 2 Brush lightly with oil and broil until the skins are charred. Wrap in towels and leave for 15 minutes.

Cook's Notes

Time
Preparation takes about 30 minutes plus 1 hour refrigeration.

Preparation
The peppers may also be roasted in a hot oven for about 30 minutes. Alternatively, pierce whole peppers with a fork and hold them over a gas flame to char the skin.

Watchpoint
The peppers must become very charred on the outside before the skin will peel well.

Cook's Tip
Instead of chopping them, the basil leaves may be rolled up and cut into strips with kitchen scissors.

Variation
The salad may be prepared with all red or all yellow peppers instead of the combination of the three colors. If using only red peppers, substitute red wine vinegar.

SERVES 6

SICILIAN CAPONATA

Vegetables, so important in Italian cuisine, are
often served separately. This combination makes an
excellent appetizer, vegetable course or accompaniment.

1 eggplant
Salt
½ cup olive oil
1 onion, sliced
2 sweet red peppers, cored, seeded and cut into
   1 inch pieces
2 sticks celery, sliced thickly
1lb canned plum tomatoes
2 tbsps red wine vinegar
1 tbsp sugar
1 clove garlic, crushed
12 black olives, pitted
1 tbsp capers
Salt and pepper

1. Cut the eggplant in half and score the cut surface.
Sprinkle with salt and leave to drain in a colander or on
paper towels for 30 minutes. Rinse, pat dry and cut into 1
inch cubes.

2. Heat the oil in a large sauté pan and add the onion,
peppers and celery. Lower the heat and cook for about 5
minutes, stirring occasionally. Add the eggplant and cook a
further 5 minutes.

3. Sieve the tomatoes to remove the seeds and add the
pulp and liquid to the vegetables in the sauté pan. Add the
remaining ingredients except the olives and capers and
cook for a further 2 minutes.

4. To remove the stones from the olives, roll them on a flat
surface to loosen the stones and then remove them with a
swivel vegetable peeler. Alternatively, use a cherry pitter.
Slice the olives in quarters and add to the vegetables with
the capers.

5. Simmer, uncovered, over moderate heat for 15 minutes
to evaporate most of the liquid. Adjust the seasoning and
serve hot or cold.

Step 1 Halve
eggplant and
score cut surface.
Sprinkle with salt
and leave to
drain.

Step 4 Roll black
olives on a flat
surface to loosen
stones.

Cook's Notes

Preparation
Scoring and salting the
eggplant helps remove any
bitter taste. Be sure to rinse all the salt
off before cooking.

Cook's Tip
When serving cold, caponata
may be prepared two days
in advance.

Serving Ideas
Caponata may be served as a
first course or in an antipasti
selection. Also serve as a side dish.

SERVES 6-8

FLAGEOLET, TUNA AND TOMATO SALAD

Tuna and tomatoes are two popular ingredients in Italian antipasto dishes.
Add beans, with their pale green color, for an attractive and easy first course or salad.

1lb canned flageolet beans (substitute white haricot beans or butter beans)
6oz canned tuna in oil
Juice of 1 lemon
Chopped fresh herbs (parsley, oregano, basil or marjoram)
8 tbsps olive oil
Salt and pepper
6-8 tomatoes, sliced

1. Drain the beans, rinse and leave in a colander to dry. Drain the tuna and flake it into a bowl.

2. Chop the herbs finely and mix with lemon juice, oil, salt and pepper. Add the beans to the tuna fish in the bowl and pour over the dressing, tossing carefully. Do not allow the tuna to break up too much.

3. Adjust the seasoning and pile the salad into a mound in a shallow serving dish. Cut the tomatoes into rounds about ¼ inch thick and place against the mound of salad. Serve immediately.

Step 2 Chop the herbs finely with a large knife using a mixture of different herbs, if desired.

Step 3 Mound the salad in the serving dish and place the tomatoes around it.

Cook's Notes

🕐 **Time**
Preparation takes about 15 minutes.

✿ **Serving Ideas**
If desired, serve the salad on individual plates lined with radicchio or curly endive.

 **Variations**
Add chopped green onions or red onions to the salad or add finely chopped garlic.

SERVES 4

SPIRALI WITH SPINACH AND BACON

Pasta doesn't have to have a sauce that cooks for hours.
This whole dish takes about 15 minutes. True Italian "fast food"!

12oz pasta spirals
8oz fresh spinach
3oz bacon
1 clove garlic, crushed
1 small red or green chili pepper
1 small red sweet pepper
1 small onion
3 tbsps olive oil
Salt and pepper

1. Cook the pasta in boiling salted water about 10-12 minutes or until just tender. Drain the pasta in a colander and rinse it under hot water. Keep the pasta in a bowl of water until ready to use.

2. Tear the stalks off the spinach and wash the leaves well, changing the water several times. Set aside to drain.

3. Remove the rind and bones from the bacon, if necessary, and dice the bacon finely. Cut the chili and the red pepper in half, remove the stems, core and seed, and slice finely. Slice the onion thinly.

4. Roll up several of the spinach leaves into a cigar shape and then shred them finely. Repeat until all the spinach is shredded.

5. Heat the oil in a sauté pan and add garlic, onion, peppers and bacon. Fry for 2 minutes, add the spinach and fry for a further 2 minutes, stirring continuously. Season with salt and pepper.

6. Drain the pasta spirals and toss them in a colander to remove excess water. Mix with the spinach sauce and serve immediately.

Step 2 Tear stalks off the spinach and wash the leaves well.

Step 3 Slice red pepper and chili pepper in half, remove seeds and core and shred finely with a large, sharp knife.

Step 4 Roll up the leaves in several layers to shred them faster.

Cook's Notes

Time
Pasta takes about 10-12 minutes to cook. Sauce takes about 4 minutes to cook. Preparation takes about 20 minutes.

Preparation
Wash spinach leaves in cold water to keep them crisp, and change the water about three times to make sure all the grit is washed away.

Watchpoint
Handle chilis with care and wash hands well after chopping chilis as the juice tends to stick to the skin.

SERVES 6

LASAGNE NAPOLETANA

This is lasagne as it is cooked and eaten in Naples.
With its layers of red, green and white it looks as delicious
as it tastes and is very easy to prepare and assemble.

9 sheets spinach lasagne pasta

Tomato Sauce

3 tbsps olive oil
2 cloves garlic, crushed
2lbs fresh tomatoes, peeled, or canned tomatoes, drained
2 tbsps chopped fresh basil, six whole leaves reserved
Salt and pepper
Pinch sugar

Cheese Filling

1lb ricotta cheese
4 tbsps unsalted butter
2 cups Mozzarella cheese, grated
Salt and pepper
Pinch nutmeg

1. Cook the pasta for 8 minutes in boiling salted water with 1 tbsp oil. Drain and rinse under hot water and place in a single layer on a damp cloth. Cover with another damp cloth and set aside.

2. To prepare the sauce, cook the garlic in remaining oil for about 1 minute in a large saucepan. When pale brown, add the tomatoes, basil, salt, pepper and sugar. If using fresh tomatoes, drop into boiling water for 6-8 seconds. Transfer to cold water and leave to cool completely. This will make the peels easier to remove.

3. Lower the heat under the saucepan and simmer the sauce for 35 minutes. Add more seasoning or sugar to taste.

4. Beat the ricotta cheese and butter together until creamy and stir into the remaining ingredients.

5. To assemble the lasagne, oil a rectangular baking dish and place 3 sheets of lasagne on the base. Cover with one third of the sauce and carefully spread on a layer of cheese. Place another 3 layers of pasta over the cheese and cover with another third of the sauce. Add the remaining cheese filling and cover with the remaining pasta. Spoon the remaining sauce on top.

6. Cover with foil and bake for 20 minutes at 375°F. Uncover and cook for 10 minutes longer. Garnish with the reserved leaves and leave to stand 10-15 minutes before serving.

Step 5 Place pasta on the base of an oiled baking dish. Spread tomato sauce over.

Step 5 Carefully spread the softened cheese mixture on top of the tomato sauce.

Cook's Notes

Cook's Tip
Lasagne can be assembled the day before and refrigerated. Allow 5-10 minutes more cooking time in the oven if not at room temperature.

Time
Preparation takes about 25 minutes, cooking takes about 1-1¼ hours.

Variations
Use plain pasta instead, if desired. If using pre-cooked lasagne pasta, follow the baking times in the package directions.

SERVES 4

PENNE WITH
HAM AND ASPARAGUS

The Italian word penne means quills,
due to the diagonal cut on both ends.

8oz penne
12oz fresh asparagus
4oz cooked ham
2 tbsps butter or margarine
1 cup heavy cream

Step 1 Peel the asparagus stalks with a swivel vegetable peeler.

1. Using a swivel vegetable peeler, scrape the sides of the asparagus spears starting about 2 inches from the top. Cut off the ends of the spears about 1 inch from the bottom.

2. Cut the ham into strips about ½ inch thick.

3. Bring a sauté pan of water to the boil, adding a pinch of salt. Move the pan so it is half on and half off direct heat. Place in the asparagus spears so that the tips are off the heat. Cover the pan and bring back to the boil. Cook the asparagus spears for about 2 minutes. Drain and allow to cool.

4. Cut the asparagus into 1 inch lengths, leaving the tips whole.

5. Melt the butter in the sauté pan and add the asparagus and ham. Cook briefly to evaporate the liquid, and add the cream. Bring to the boil and cook for about 5 minutes to thicken the cream.

6. Meanwhile, cook the pasta in boiling salted water with 1 tbsp oil for about 10-12 minutes.

7. Drain the pasta and rinse under hot water. Toss in a colander to drain and mix with the sauce. Serve with grated Parmesan cheese, if desired.

Step 4 Cut ham and cooked asparagus into 1 inch lengths. Leave the asparagus tips whole.

Step 5 Boil the cream with the asparagus and ham for about 5 minutes to thicken.

Cook's Notes

Time
Pasta takes 10-12 minutes to cook. Sauce takes about 8 minutes to cook. Preparation takes about 20 minutes.

Variations
If using frozen instead of fresh asparagus, do not peel or pre-cook. Substitute broccoli spears for the asparagus and prepare in the same way. If using peas instead of asparagus, cook them in the butter with the ham, add the cream and cook 5 minutes.

Serving Ideas
May be served as a first course in smaller amounts.

SERVES 4

SPAGHETTI AMATRICIANA

This is another quickly cooked sauce with a rich, spicy taste.
Use less of the chili pepper for a less fiery flavor.

1 onion
6 strips Canadian bacon
1lb ripe tomatoes
1 red chili pepper
1½ tbsps oil
12oz spaghetti

1. Slice the onion thinly. Remove rind from the bacon and cut into thin strips.

2. Drop the tomatoes into boiling water for 6-8 seconds. Remove with a draining spoon and place in cold water, and leave to cool completely. This will make the peels easier to remove.

3. When the tomatoes are peeled, cut them in half and remove the seeds and pulp with a teaspoon. Rub the seeds and pulp through a strainer and retain juice to use in the sauce if desired. Chop the tomato flesh roughly and set it aside.

4. Cut the stem off the chili pepper and cut the pepper in half lengthwise. Remove the seeds and core and cut the pepper into thin strips. Cut the strips into small dice.

5. Heat the oil in a sauté pan and add the onion and bacon. Stir over medium heat for about 5 minutes, until.the onion is transparent. Drain off excess fat and add the tomatoes and chili and mix well. Simmer the sauce gently, uncovered, for about 5 minutes, stirring occasionally.

6. Meanwhile, cook the spaghetti in boiling salted water with 1 tbsp oil for about 10-12 minutes. Drain and rinse in hot water and toss in a colander to dry. To serve, spoon the sauce on top of the spaghetti and sprinkle with freshly grated Parmesan cheese, if desired.

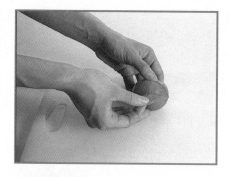

Step 2 Placing tomatoes in boiling water and then in cold water makes the skins easier to remove.

Step 3 Cut the peeled tomatoes in half and remove the seeds and pulp with a teaspoon. Cut the flesh roughly.

Step 4 Remove the stems, seeds and cores from the chili pepper, cut into thin strips and then chop into fine dice.

Cook's Notes

Time
Spaghetti takes about 10-12 minutes to cook, sauce takes about 8 minutes to cook, preparation takes about 20-25 minutes.

Cook's Tip
It is not necessary to use the whole chili pepper; use as much as desired.

Watchpoint
Wash hands very well after handling chili peppers or use rubber gloves while chopping them.

SERVES 4

HOME-MADE TAGLIATELLE WITH SUMMER SAUCE

Pasta making is not as difficult as you might think.
It is well worth it, too, because home-made pasta is in a class by itself.

Pasta Dough

1 cup all-purpose flour
1 cup bread flour
2 large eggs
2 tsps olive oil
Pinch salt

Sauce

1lb unpeeled tomatoes, seeded and cut into small dice
1 large green pepper, cored, seeded and cut in small dice
1 onion, cut in small dice
1 tbsps chopped fresh basil
1 tbsp chopped fresh parsley
2 cloves garlic, crushed
½ cup olive oil and vegetable oil mixed

1. Place the flours in a mound on a work surface and make a well in the center. Place the eggs, oil and salt in the center of the well.

2. Using a fork, beat the ingredients in the center to blend them and gradually incorporate the flour from the outside edge. The dough may also be mixed in a food processor.

3. When half the flour is incorporated, start kneading using the palms of the hands and not the fingers. This may also be done in a food processor. Cover the dough and leave it to rest for 15 minutes.

4. Divide the dough in quarters and roll out thinly with a rolling pin on a floured surface or use a pasta machine, dusting dough lightly with flour before rolling. If using a machine, follow the manufacturer's directions. Allow the sheets of pasta to dry for about 10 minutes on a floured surface or on tea towels. Cut the sheets into strips about ¼ inch wide by hand or machine, dusting lightly with flour while cutting. Leave the cut pasta to dry while preparing the sauce.

5. Combine all the sauce ingredients, mixing well. Cover and refrigerate overnight.

6. Cook the pasta for 5-6 minutes in boiling salted water with a spoonful of oil. Drain the pasta and rinse under very hot water. Toss in a colander to drain excess water. Place the hot pasta in serving dish. Pour the cold sauce over and toss.

Step 3 Knead with palms of hands to bring dough together until smooth.

Step 4 Roll the dough out thinly and cut into thin strips.

 Cook's Notes

 Time
Preparation takes about 30 minutes, cooking takes about 5-6 minutes.

 Watchpoint
Pasta must remain very hot to balance the cold sauce.

Serving Ideas
This basic pasta recipe can be used with other shapes of pasta such as lasagne, cannelloni, ravioli, farfalle (butterflies or bows), or cut into very fine noodles.

SERVES 4

PIZZA WITH PEPPERS, OLIVES & ANCHOVIES

Pizza really needs no introduction. It originated in Naples and has been adopted everywhere. Change the toppings to suit your taste.

Pizza Dough

½oz fresh yeast
½ tsp sugar
¾ cup lukewarm water
2 cups all-purpose flour
Pinch salt
2 tbsps oil

Topping

2 tsps olive oil
1 onion, finely chopped
1 clove garlic, crushed
1lb canned tomatoes
1 tbsp tomato paste
½ tsp each oregano and basil
1 tsp sugar
Salt and pepper
½ red pepper
½ green pepper
½ cup black olives, pitted
2oz canned anchovies, drained
1 cup Mozzarella cheese, grated
2 tbsp grated Parmesan cheese

1. Cream the yeast with the sugar in a small bowl, add the lukewarm water and leave to stand for 10 minutes to prove. Bubbles will appear on the surface when ready.

2. Sift flour and salt into a bowl, make a well in the center and add the oil and the yeast mixture. Using a wooden spoon, beat the liquid in the center of the well, gradually incorporating the flour from the outside until it forms a firm dough.

3. Turn the dough out onto a floured surface and knead for 10 minutes, or until the dough is smooth and elastic. Place in a lightly oiled bowl or in a large plastic bag, cover or tie the bag and leave to stand in a warm place for 30 minutes, or until the dough has doubled in bulk.

4. Knock the dough back and knead it into a smooth ball. Flatten the dough and roll out into a circle on a floured surface. The circle should be about 10 inches in diameter.

5. To prepare the topping, heat the oil in a heavy-based saucepan and add the onion and the garlic. Cook until the onion and garlic have softened but not colored. Add the tomatoes and their juice, tomato paste, herbs, sugar, salt and pepper. Bring the sauce to the boil and then allow to simmer, uncovered, to reduce. Stir the sauce occasionally to prevent sticking. When the sauce is thick and smooth, leave it to cool. Spread the cooled sauce over the pizza dough. Sprinkle half the cheese on top of the tomato sauce and then arrange the topping ingredients. Sprinkle with remaining cheese and bake in a 400°F oven for 15-20 minutes or until the cheese is melted and bubbling and the crust is brown.

Step 4 When the dough has doubled in bulk, knock back before kneading again lightly.

Cook's Notes

Time
Dough takes about 40 minutes to make, including the rising. The tomato sauce needs to cook for 10-15 minutes. Pizza takes 15-20 minutes to bake.

Variations
Other ingredients, such as Italian hams and sausages, fish and shellfish, capers, green olives, or zucchini, may be used as toppings.

SERVES 4-6
PIZZA RUSTICA

This farmhouse pie is really a cross between quiche
and pizza. Whichever you think it resembles most,
there is no question that it is delicious.

Pizza Dough
(see recipe for Pizza with Peppers, Olives and Anchovies)

Filling
Grated Parmesan cheese
4oz prosciutto or Parma ham, sliced
2 tomatoes, peeled, seeded and roughly chopped
2oz Mozzarella cheese, diced
1 tbsp chopped fresh parsley
1 tbsp chopped fresh basil
2 eggs, lightly beaten
5 tbsps heavy cream
2oz Fontina cheese, finely grated
Pinch nutmeg
Salt and pepper

Step 2 Roll out the dough, place in a dish and press up the sides to form an edge.

1. Prepare the dough as for the Pizza with Peppers, Olives and Anchovies. When the dough has doubled in bulk, knock it back and knead lightly. Flatten the dough into a circle or rectangle and roll out. Roll to a circle about 10 inches in diameter or a rectangle about 11x7 inches.

2. Lightly oil the baking dish, place in the dough and press out with floured fingertips to form a raised edge on the sides of the dish.

3. Sprinkle the base of the dough with some of the Parmesan cheese and place on a layer of ham. Cover the ham with the chopped tomato. Mix the remaining ingredients together and pour over the tomato and ham.

4. Bake on the lowest shelf of the oven for about 35 minutes at 375°F. The top of the pizza should be nicely browned and the edge of the dough should be golden when the pizza is ready. Serve hot.

Step 3 Fill with Parmesan, ham and tomatoes.

Step 3 Mix cream, cheese and eggs together and pour onto the pizza.

Cook's Notes

Time
Pizza dough takes 40 minutes to make, including rising time. Bake pizza for 35 minutes.

Freezing
Pizzas can be prepared and frozen in their unbaked form. When cooking from frozen, allow an extra 10 minutes. Pizza dough bases may also be frozen unfilled. Allow to defrost before topping.

Variations
If Fontina cheese is not available, substitute Gruyère or Emmental. Vary the filling ingredients using different vegetables and meats as desired.

SERVES 4-6

LIVER VENEZIANA

As the name indicates, this recipe originated
in Venice. The lemon juice offsets the rich
taste of liver in this very famous Italian dish.

Risotto

9oz Italian rice
3 tbsps butter or margarine
1 large onion, chopped
4 tbsps dry white wine
2 cups chicken stock
¼ tsp saffron
2 tbsps grated fresh Parmesan cheese
Salt and pepper

Liver

1lb calves' or lambs' liver
Flour for dredging
3 onions, thinly sliced
2 tbsps butter or margarine
3 tbsps oil
Salt and pepper
Juice of ½ a lemon
1 tbsp chopped parsley

1. Melt the butter for the risotto in a large sauté pan, add the onion and cook until soft but not colored, over gentle heat.

2. Add the rice and cook for about a minute until the rice looks clear.

3. Add the wine, stock, saffron and seasoning. Stir well and bring to the boil. Lower the heat and cook gently, stirring frequently until the liquid has evaporated. This will take about 20 minutes.

4. Meanwhile, skin the liver and cut out any large tubes.

5. Cut the liver into strips and toss in a sieve with the flour to coat.

6. Heat the butter or margarine and 1 tbsp oil in a large sauté or frying pan. Cook the onions until golden. Remove the onions from the pan to a plate. Add more oil if necessary, raise the heat under the pan and add the liver. Cook, stirring constantly, for about 2 minutes. Return the onions and add the lemon juice and parsley. Cook a further 2 minutes or until the liver is done. Season with salt and pepper and serve with the risotto.

7. To finish the risotto, add the cheese and salt and pepper to taste when the liquid has evaporated, and toss to melt the cheese.

Step 3 Lower the heat and cook gently, stirring frequently until the liquid has evaporated.

Step 5 Cut the liver into strips and toss with flour in a sieve to coat each piece evenly.

 *Cook's Notes*

 Time
Risotto takes about 30 minutes to prepare and cook. Liver takes about 4 minutes to cook.

! **Watchpoint**
Liver and all organ meats need quick cooking or they will toughen.

 Preparation
Tossing the liver and flour together in a sieve coats each piece of meat more evenly than can be done by hand.

 Cook's Tip
If desired, add 4 tbsps stock to the recipe for a little more sauce.

SERVES 4

VEAL SCALOPPINE WITH PROSCIUTTO AND CHEESE

Veal is the meat used most often in Italian cooking. Good veal is tender and quick cooking, but expensive. Save this recipe for your next dinner party!

8 veal escalopes
2 tbsps butter or margarine
1 clove garlic, crushed
1 sprig rosemary
8 slices prosciutto ham
8 slices Mozzarella cheese
3 tbsps sherry
½ cup beef stock
Salt and pepper

Step 3 Place a slice of ham on top of each slice of veal and pour over the sherry and stock and add the rosemary.

Step 2 Cook the veal on both sides until lightly browned.

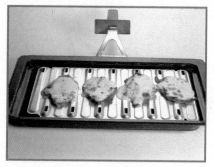

Step 6 Place the meat under a preheated broiler and cook to melt the cheese and lightly brown the top.

1. Pound the veal escalopes out thinly between two pieces of wax paper with a meat mallet or a rolling pin.

2. Melt the butter or margarine in a sauté pan and add the veal and garlic. Cook until the veal is lightly browned on both sides.

3. Place a piece of prosciutto on top of each piece of veal and add the sherry, stock and sprig of rosemary to the pan. Cover the pan and cook the veal for about 10 minutes over

gentle heat, or until done.

4. Remove the meat to a heatproof serving dish and top each piece of veal with a slice of cheese.

5. Bring the cooking liquid from the veal to the boil and allow to boil rapidly to reduce slightly.

6. Meanwhile, broil the veal to melt and brown the cheese. Remove the sprig of rosemary from the sauce and pour the sauce around the meat to serve.

Cook's Notes

 Time
Preparation takes about 15 minutes, cooking takes 15-20 minutes.

Variations
White wine may be substituted for the sherry, if desired. 1 tsp of tomato paste may be added to the sauce. Use chicken, turkey or pork instead of the veal.

SERVES 4-8

PORK ROULADES WITH POLENTA

Polenta, either boiled or fried, is a staple dish in
Italy as potatoes are elsewhere in the world.

8oz coarse yellow cornmeal
6 cups chicken stock
Salt and white pepper

Roulades

8 pork escalopes or steaks
8 slices Parma ham
4 large cup mushrooms
4 tbsps grated Parmesan cheese
1 tbsp chopped fresh sage
Seasoned flour for dredging
4 tbsps olive oil
1 small onion, finely chopped
2 sticks celery, finely chopped
1 clove garlic, crushed
6 tbsps brown stock
½ cup dry white wine
4oz canned plum tomatoes, drained and juice reserved
1 tsp tomato paste
Salt and pepper
6 tbsps dry Marsala
Fresh sage leaves for garnish

1. Bring the chicken stock for the polenta to the boil in a large stock pot and start adding the cornmeal in a very slow, steady stream, stirring continuously. Add salt and pepper and continue cooking over very low heat, stirring frequently, for about 55 minutes.

2. Flatten the pork escalopes or steaks and place a slice of Parma ham on top of each. Chop the mushrooms and divide among the pork escalopes, spooning on top of the ham slices. Sprinkle over the Parmesan cheese and the fresh sage.

3. Fold the sides of the pork escalopes into the center to seal them, and roll up the pork jelly roll fashion. Secure each roll with a wooden pick stick. Dredge each roulade in flour, shaking off the excess.

4. Heat the olive oil in a large sauté pan or frying pan and add the pork roulades, seam side down first. Cook on all sides until nicely browned. Remove the roulades and keep them warm.

5. Add the onion and celery to the oil in the pan and cook until lightly browned. Add the garlic and all the remaining ingredients except the Marsala. Reserve the juice from the tomatoes for later use if necessary. Bring the sauce to the boil, breaking up the tomatoes. Return the roulades to the pan, cover and cook over moderate heat for about 15-20 minutes or until the pork is completely cooked. Add reserved tomato juice, as necessary, if liquid is drying out.

6. When the pork is cooked, remove to a dish and keep it warm. Add the Marsala to the sauce and bring to the boil. Allow to boil 5-10 minutes. The sauce may be puréed in a food processor and also sieved if desired.

7. To assemble the dish, spoon the polenta on a serving plate. Remove the wooden picks from the roulades and place on top of the polenta. Spoon the sauce over the meat and garnish the dish with fresh sage leaves.

Step 2 Place all the filling ingredients on top of the pork scallops, fold in the sides and roll up. Secure with wooden picks.

Cook's Notes

Time
Polenta takes almost 1 hour to cook. Roulades will take about 20 minutes to prepare and 20 minutes to cook.

Watchpoint
Be sure to stir the polenta often and add more liquid if it begins to dry out as it can easily stick to the pan.

Variations
Double the quantity of cornmeal and cut the cooking time down to 30-35 minutes. Spoon into a lightly oiled pan and allow to cool. This version of polenta can be cut into squares and fried in hot oil. Serve as an accompaniment to any meat.

SERVES 6-8

CRESPELLE ALLA BOLOGNESE

Almost all countries in the world have a kind of
pancake, and crespelle are the Italian version. Use
other fillings and sauces for lots of variety.

Bolognese Filling

2 tbsps butter or margarine
1 tbsp olive oil
2 onions, finely chopped
8oz ground beef
1 small green pepper, seeded, cored and finely chopped
4oz canned plum tomatoes
1 tbsp tomato paste
½ cup beef stock
1 bay leaf
2 tsps chopped basil
1 tsp chopped oregano
2 tbsps sherry
Salt and pepper

Crespelle Batter

3 eggs
1 cup all-purpose flour
Pinch salt
1 cup water
2 tsps olive oil
Melted butter

Tomato sauce

1 tbsp butter or margarine
1 clove garlic, crushed
1 onion, finely chopped
1lb canned plum tomatoes
Salt, pepper and a pinch of sugar
Fresh basil leaves

1. Heat the butter and oil in a deep saucepan for the Bolognese filling. Put in the onion and cook slowly until soft but not colored. Increase the heat and add the beef. Stir the beef while cooking, until all the meat is brown. Add chopped pepper, tomatoes and their juice, tomato paste, stock, herbs, salt and pepper to taste and simmer gently for about 45 minutes or until the mixture thickens, stirring occasionally. Add the sherry and cook for a further 5 minutes and set aside.

2. Sift the flour for the crespelle with a pinch of salt. Break the eggs into a bowl and beat to mix thoroughly. Mix the flour into the eggs gradually, beating all the time until the mixture is smooth. Add water and the oil and stir in well. Cover the bowl with a damp cloth and leave in a cool place for 30 minutes.

3. Heat the crêpe pan or a 7 inch frying pan. Lightly grease with the melted butter and pour a large spoonful of the batter into the center of the pan. Swirl the pan to coat the base evenly. Fry until the crespelle is brown on the underside, loosen the edge with a pallete knife, and turn over and brown the other side. Stack and wrap in a clean towel until needed.

4. To make the tomato sauce, melt the butter in a small saucepan and cook garlic and onion slowly for about 5 minutes, or until softened but not colored. Reserve whole basil leaves for garnish and chop 2 tsps. Add the tomatoes to the onions and garlic along with the basil, salt, pepper and a pinch of sugar. Cook for about 10-15 minutes or until the onions are completely soft. Drain to remove the seeds, pressing the pulp against the strainer to extract as much liquid as possible.

5. To assemble, lay the crespelle out on a large, clean work surface and put 2 heaped spoonfuls of Bolognese filling into each. Roll up and place in an ovenproof dish. Repeat until all the crespelle have been filled.

6. Put into a 400°F oven and heat for about 8 minutes. Heat the tomato sauce and spoon over the crespelle before serving. Garnish with basil leaves and serve immediately.

Cook's Notes

Time
Preparation takes about 45 minutes, cooking takes about 1 hour 15 minutes.

Preparation
The crespelle batter must stand for 30 minutes to allow the starch to swell for the batter to thicken properly.

Variations
Crespelle can be used with a variety of fillings and toppings, both sweet and savory.

SERVES 4-6

CHICKEN CACCIATORE

The name means Chicken the Hunter's Way, and that
means the addition of mushrooms. Though not
traditional, pasta is a good accompaniment.

3 tbsps oil
4oz mushrooms, quartered, if large
3lb chicken, skinned if desired and cut into pieces
1 onion
2 cloves garlic
½ cup vermouth
1 tbsp white wine vinegar
½ cup chicken stock
1 tsp oregano
1 sprig fresh rosemary
1lb canned tomatoes
2oz black olives, pitted
2 tbsps chopped parsley
Salt and pepper

1. Heat the oil in a heavy-based frying pan and cook the
mushrooms for about 1-2 minutes. Remove them and set
aside. Brown the chicken in the oil and transfer the browned
pieces to an ovenproof casserole.

2. Chop the onion and garlic finely. Pour off all but 1 tbsp
of the oil in the frying pan and reheat the pan. Cook the
onion and garlic until softened but not colored. Add the
vermouth and vinegar, and boil to reduce by half. Add the
chicken stock, tomatoes, oregano, rosemary, salt and
pepper. Break up the tomatoes and bring the sauce to the
boil. Allow to cook for 2 minutes.

3. Pour the sauce over the chicken in the casserole, cover
and cook at 350°F for about 1 hour.

4. To remove the stones from the olives, roll them on a flat
surface to loosen the stones and then use a swivel
vegetable peeler to extract them. Alternatively, use a cherry
pitter.

5. Add mushrooms and olives during the last 5 minutes of
cooking.

Step 2 Cut onion
in half lengthwise
leaving the root
end intact.
Holding the knife
parallel to the
chopping board,
cut the onion in
thin horizontal
slices, but not
through to the
root end.

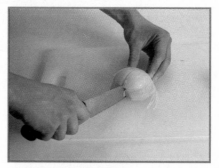

Step 2 Cut the
onion lengthwise
in thin strips,
leaving the onion
attached at the
root end.

Step 2 Cut cross-
wise through the
onion; the onion
will fall apart into
small dice.

6. Remove the rosemary before serving, and sprinkle with
chopped parsley.

Cook's Notes

Time
Cooking takes approximately
1 hour 15 minutes,
preparation takes about 25-30 minutes.

Cook's Tip
Pitted black olives are
available in some
delicatessens.

Serving Idea
Serve with spaghetti or pasta
shapes and sprinkle with
grated Parmesan cheese.

SERVES 4

TURKEY MARSALA

Marsala is a dessert wine from Sicily which complements chicken, veal or turkey surprisingly well. It is traditional, but sherry will serve as a substitute if Marsala is unavailable.

4 turkey breast fillets or escalopes
4 tbsps butter or margarine
1 clove garlic
4 anchovy fillets, soaked in milk
Capers
4 slices Mozzarella cheese
2 tsps chopped marjoram
1 tbsp chopped parsley
3 tbsps Marsala
½ cup heavy cream
Salt and pepper

1. Flatten the turkey breasts between two sheets of wax paper with a meat mallet or rolling pin if necessary.

2. Melt butter in a sauté pan and, when foaming, add the garlic and the turkey. Cook for a few minutes on each side until lightly browned. Remove them from the pan.

3. Drain the anchovy fillets and rinse them well. Dry on paper towels. Put a slice of cheese on top of each turkey fillet and arrange the anchovies and capers on top of each. Sprinkle with the chopped herbs and return the turkey to the pan.

4. Cook the turkey a further 5 minutes over moderate heat, until the turkey is done and the cheese has melted. Remove to a serving dish and keep warm. Return the pan to the heat and add the Marsala. Scrape the browned pan juices off the bottom and reduce the heat. Add the cream and whisk in well. Lower the heat and simmer gently, uncovered, for a few minutes to thicken the sauce. Season the sauce with salt and pepper and spoon over the turkey fillets to serve.

Step 1 Flatten the turkey breasts between two sheets of wax paper with a rolling pin or meat mallet.

Step 3 Place a slice of cheese on top of each turkey breast and top with anchovies, capers and herbs.

Step 4 Cook until turkey is done and the cheese has melted.

Cook's Notes

Time
Preparation takes about 25 minutes and cooking about 15 minutes.

Watchpoint
Turkey breast fillets are very lean so can dry out easily if over-cooked.

Serving Suggestions
Accompany the Turkey Marsala with new potatoes and lightly cooked zucchini.

SERVES 6

TURKEY KEBABS

You don't have to buy a whole turkey for these! Small portions are now readily available at supermarkets and butchers.

3lbs turkey meat
2 tsps chopped sage
1 sprig rosemary
Juice of 1 lemon
2 tbsps olive oil
Salt and pepper
4oz bacon, rinds and bones removed
Whole sage leaves

Step 2 Stretch the bacon by scraping it with the blunt side of a knife.

Step 1 Remove the turkey bones and cut the meat into small, even-sized pieces.

Step 3 Cut the bacon into halves and wrap around a piece of turkey. Thread the ingredients onto skewers.

1. Remove any bones from the turkey and cut the meat into even-sized pieces. Combine the chopped sage, rosemary, lemon juice, oil, salt and pepper in a large bowl and add the turkey meat. Stir once or twice to coat evenly, cover and leave in the refrigerator overnight.

2. Cut the bacon in half and wrap around some of the pieces of turkey. Leave other pieces of turkey unwrapped.

3. Thread the bacon, wrapped turkey, plain turkey and whole sage leaves onto skewers, alternating the ingredients.

4. Cook in a preheated 400°F oven for about 40 minutes. Alternatively, cook for 30 minutes and place the kebabs under a preheated broiler for 10 minutes to crisp the bacon. Baste frequently with the marinade while cooking. Pour any remaining marinade and pan juices over the kebabs to serve.

Cook's Notes

 Time
Kebabs take about 20 minutes to assemble and need to marinate overnight. Cooking takes about 40 minutes.

 Serving Ideas
Serve with a green salad, fried polenta or risotto.

 Variation
Use chicken, if desired.

WHITE BEAN SOUP WITH SALAMI

Dried bean soups have been popular in Germany for hundreds of years.
The addition of salami is a contemporary touch.

12oz dried white beans
2 leeks
2 tbsps butter or margarine
1 tsp chopped fresh herbs
1 cup beef stock
11oz German salami
1 cup milk
4 tbsps chopped parsley
½ tsp ground nutmeg
Salt and pepper

1. Soak the beans overnight in enough water to cover. They will swell in size. Put into fresh water and bring to the boil. Allow to simmer for about 1 hour, or until the beans are tender. Remove all but 2 cups of the cooking liquid and reserve it.

2. Trim the tops of the leeks, leaving on some of the green. Trim the root ends and cut the leeks almost in half lengthwise. Rinse well under cold running water. Slice thinly into rounds. Heat the butter in a sauté pan and when foaming add the leeks. Sauté for about 1 minute, add the herbs and the stock and bring to the boil. Pour the mixture into the pot with the beans and stir well.

3. Skin the salami with a small sharp knife and cut into ½ inch cubes. Add the salami to the beans.

4. Bring the milk to the boil in a heavy-based pan and, when boiling, add to the beans, stirring well. Add salt and pepper and cook for a further 30 minutes, or until the beans are completely tender. Add reserved cooking liquid if beans dry out. Add nutmeg and garnish with chopped parsley to serve.

Step 1 Soak the beans overnight in a large stock pot or bowl with enough water to cover. They will swell considerably in size.

Step 2 Trim the leeks, cut them almost in half lengthwise, rinse well and cut into thin rounds.

Step 3 Peel the salami with a sharp knife and cut into cubes.

Cook's Notes

Time
Beans need overnight soaking and cooking for about 1 hour before other ingredients are added.

Preparation
Leeks have to be cut in half to be washed because sand and dirt get into the layers as the vegetables grow.

Cook's Tip
When using dried pulses, make sure they are thoroughly cooked before eating. It can be dangerous to eat undercooked or uncooked pulses.

SERVES 4

POTATO SOUP

North Germany, where potatoes are used most
frequently, is where this soup originated.
Different sausages are used in other areas.

3 tbsps butter or margarine
2 carrots, peeled and cut in ½ inch pieces
2 sticks celery, cut into ½ inch pieces
1lb potatoes, peeled and cut into 1 inch cubes
3-4 tbsps flour
6 cups water or light stock
Salt and white pepper
1 bay leaf
3 tbsps chopped fresh dill
6 Frankfurters

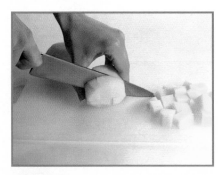

Cut the slices into
1 inch wide strips
and then into cubes.

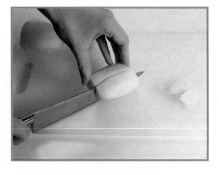

Cut the potato
into even-sized
cubes and square
off the ends
slightly. Cut into 1
inch thick slices.

Step 1 Cook the
vegetables in the
butter until they
begin to take on a
light brown color.

1. Melt the butter in a large stock pot or saucepan and when foaming add the vegetables. Cook, stirring frequently until all the vegetables take on a little color. Sprinkle over the flour and cook over low heat until it begins to brown. Pour on the water or stock, add salt, pepper and bay leaf and stir well.

2. Partially cover and cook for about 30 minutes, or until the potatoes are tender.

3. Pour the soup through a colander, but do not push the vegetables through. Return the liquid to the pan and add the dill.

4. Slice the Frankfurters thinly on the diagonal. Add to the soup and bring back to the boil. Simmer for about 5 minutes and return the vegetables to the pan. Cook to heat the vegetables through and remove the bay leaf. Transfer to a soup tureen, or spoon into individual soup bowls.

Cook's Notes

 Time
Preparation takes about 20 minutes, cooking takes about 35 minutes.

 Watchpoint
Do not allow the vegetables to brown too much; they will give an unattractive color to the soup.

 Preparation
If the potatoes are cut slightly larger than the other vegetables, they will cook in the same length of time without falling apart.

Cook's Tip
Soup may be prepared in advance and kept in the refrigerator overnight. Reheat the next day.

SERVES 4-6

MEAT SALAD

A salad made with a selection of cooked meats
is a favorite throughout Germany. Serve it as
a first course or as part of a cold buffet.

1lb diced cooked beef, veal, ham or tongue
2 dill pickles
1 medium onion
1 tbsp capers
1 tbsp chopped parsley
1 tsp German mustard
1 medium boiled potato, peeled and diced
Salt and pepper
1 hard-boiled egg

Dressing

2 tbsps olive oil
3 tbsps wine vinegar
3 tbsps cold beef stock

Step 1 To slice an
onion, peel and
cut in half through
the root end.
Place flat side
down on a cutting
board.

1. Cut the dill pickles into thin slices and combine with the
meat in a large bowl. Slice the onion thinly and add it to the
bowl. Add the remaining salad ingredients except the
eggs.

2. Combine the dressing ingredients and whisk well. Pour
over the salad and toss gently to coat all the ingredients
thoroughly. Chill for 2 hours before serving.

3. To slice the egg evenly, use an egg slicer. Peel the egg,
place it in the slicer and pull down the wire cutter. Carefully
remove the slices and use the best looking ones to garnish
the top of the salad. Further slices may be combined with
the rest of the ingredients.

Step 1 Using a
large, sharp knife,
cut crosswise into
thin slices. If
desired, the slices
may be cut in half
again so they are
not so long.

Step 3 Use a
wire egg slicer to
make uniform
slices of egg.
Once the egg is
sliced through,
turn the egg slicer
carefully over into
the palm of your
hand and gently
extract the egg
slices.

Cook's Notes

 Time
Preparation takes about 20
minutes with 2 hours to chill.

 Variation
Use a combination of 3 or 4
different meats. Cooked or
smoked sausage may also be used.

 Economy
Leftover cooked meat can be
used.

SERVES 6-8

HOT POTATO SALAD WITH BACON

If Germany has a national salad this must be it.
It is perfect with any of the country's many sausage varieties.

6-8 even-sized potatoes (waxy variety)
Pinch salt
4oz bacon, diced
1 onion
½ cup white wine vinegar
½ cup water or beef stock
3 tbsps sour cream (optional)
2 tbsps chopped parsley
Salt and pepper

Step 2 Follow the natural lines in the onion, and make a series of vertical cuts through the onion, but not completely through the root end.

Step 2 To chop the onion finely, place onion half, cut side down, on a chopping board and with a large sharp knife make a series of cuts parallel to the flat surface almost to the root end .

Step 2 Cut through the onion crosswise into large or small pieces, as desired.

1. Boil the potatoes in their jackets in lightly salted water to cover. When the potatoes are just tender, drain and peel while still hot. Cut into thin slices and place in a serving dish.

2. Fry the bacon in a large frying pan or sauté pan. While the bacon is frying, chop the onion very finely. Once the bacon is pale golden brown add the onions and continue to sauté slowly until they become transparent but not brown. Remove the pan from the heat and carefully pour in the

vinegar and the water or stock. Do this gradually so that the hot fat does not spatter.

3. Bring to the boil and remove from the heat. Stir in the sour cream, if using, and pour the mixture over the potatoes. Lift the potatoes so that the dressing runs over them evenly. Sprinkle with salt and pepper and parsley. Serve immediately.

Cook's Notes

Time
Preparation takes about 25 minutes, cooking takes about 20 minutes for the potatoes to cook and about 15 minutes to complete the recipe.

Watchpoint
Do not overcook the potatoes or they will fall apart in the salad.

Cook's Tip
To peel a potato while it is still hot, hold it in several thicknesses of paper towels.

SERVES 4-6

MUSHROOM SALAD

No doubt this salad was first made with wild mushrooms
gathered in Germany's forests. It is equally good with
mushrooms gathered from the greengrocer!

1lb mushrooms
1 medium onion
3 tbsps oil
1 tbsp chopped parsley
1 dill pickle, diced
3-4 tomatoes, peeled, seeded and diced
4 tbsps oil
1 tbsp wine vinegar
Salt and pepper
Pinch sugar

1. Slice the mushrooms thinly and chop the onion finely.
Heat 3 tbsps oil in a large sauté pan and add the mushrooms and onions. Cook for about 2-3 minutes to soften
slightly. Remove from the heat and allow to cool.

2. When the mushrooms and onions have completely
cooled, add the parsley, dill pickle and tomatoes. Mix
together the oil and vinegar, sugar and salt and pepper and
pour over the other ingredients. Stir gently to coat evenly
and allow to stand for 1-2 hours in the refrigerator before
serving.

To make tomatoes
easier to peel, first
drop them into
boiling water.

Use a small,
sharp knife to
remove the peel.

Cook's Notes

Serving Ideas
To serve as a first course,
spoon the mushroom salad
on top of curly endive or finely
shredded lettuce. Serve with melba
toast, brown bread and butter or rolls.

Variation
If German mushrooms such
as Steinpilz or Pfifferlinge are
available in cans, they may be used
instead of fresh mushrooms. Drain and
rinse before using. Cook the onions on
their own and add to the mushrooms.

Cook's Tip
The salad may be prepared a
day in advance. Add the
tomatoes 1 hour before serving.

SERVES 6

SPAETZLE

These little Bavarian dumplings are incredibly
easy to make, and are a delicious alternative
to potatoes, rice or pasta.

2¼ cups all-purpose flour
1 tsp salt
1 egg, well beaten
¼-⅔ cup water
3 tbsps butter or margarine
4 tbsps dry breadcrumbs or 2 tbsps poppy seeds

1. Sift the flour and salt into a bowl. Make a well in the center and pour in the beaten egg.

2. Using a wooden spoon, stir the egg, gradually incorporating the outside ingredients. At the same time, gradually begin adding the water until the batter is stiff but smooth. It may not be necessary to add all the water.

3. Spread the dough flat on a plate or on a floured board. With a sharp knife, scrape off small pieces of dough and drop into boiling salted water. Cook only one small batch of spaetzle at a time. The dough will sink and then rise to the surface as it cooks.

4. Once the spaetzle have risen, allow them to boil gently for about 5-8 minutes, or until the dough is completely cooked through to the center.

5. Remove them from the water with a slotted spoon and drain. Repeat until all the dough is used.

6. If desired, melt the butter in a large frying pan and add the dry breadcrumbs. Cook until golden brown and crisp and toss with the hot spaetzle. Alternatively, pour the melted butter over the spaetzle and toss with the poppy seeds.

Step 2 Gradually beat the egg and the water into the sifted flour and salt using a wooden spoon.

Step 3 When the dough is stiff but smooth, press it onto a plate or floured board. With a sharp knife, scrape off small pieces of dough to drop into boiling salted water.

Step 4 Cook for 5-8 minutes after spaetzle rise to surface. They will swell in size.

Cook's Notes

Time
Preparation takes about 10 minutes, cooking takes about 25-30 minutes to cook all the batches of spaetzle.

Preparation
The dough may also be prepared in a food processor. Add the egg to the flour and pour the water through the funnel with the machine running. Stop the machine occasionally to check the consistency of the dough.

Serving Ideas
Serve spaetzle with any meat, poultry or game dishes that have a sauce.

SERVES 4

STUFFED TOMATOES

Use summer's ripe tomatoes to their
best advantage as an appetizer or side
dish with a creamy cheese filling.

4 beefsteak tomatoes
4oz German Camembert or Bavarian Brie
2 green onions
4 anchovy fillets
1 tbsp capers
2 tsps caraway seeds
Salt and freshly ground black pepper

Step 1 Remove
the pulp and
seeds from the
tomatoes with a
teaspoon.

Step 1 Remove
the stalk from the
top of each
tomato. Slice off
the bottom of
each tomato.

Step 2 Soak the
anchovies in milk
for about 5
minutes to remove
the salt.

1. Remove the core from the bottom of each tomato. Cut a slice from the rounded end of each tomato and scoop out the pulp and seeds with a small teaspoon. Strain out the seeds and use the pulp and juice for the filling.

2. Place the anchovies in a little milk and leave to soak for about 5 minutes. Rinse, pat dry and chop. If the capers are large, chop them roughly. Chop the green onions finely and

mash with the cheese, capers, anchovies, caraway seeds, salt and pepper. Add the reserved tomato juice and pulp and mix the ingredients together thoroughly.

3. Spoon the filling into the tomatoes and place them on serving plates. Top with the reserved tomato slices and serve chilled.

Cook's Notes

Time
Preparation takes about 15 minutes. Tomatoes should be chilled for at least 30 minutes before serving.

Variation
If beefsteak tomatoes are not available, substitute 2 ripe tomatoes per person.

Serving Ideas
Tomatoes may be served in a vinaigrette dressing. Accompany with brown bread and butter or rolls.

SERVES 4

Imperial Asparagus

Green asparagus, such a common type in most
other countries, is imported into Germany
and is quite expensive and hard to find.

2lbs white asparagus
3 tbsps butter or margarine
3 tbsps flour
1 cup chicken stock or asparagus cooking liquid
½ cup German white wine
2 egg yolks
4 tbsps heavy cream
Salt and white pepper
Pinch sugar

Step 2 Cook the asparagus in a sauté pan of boiling salted water. Place all the asparagus tips in one direction and set that part of the pan off the heat.

Step 1 Hold the trimmed asparagus spears in the palm of your hand and take off the outer skin in thin strips using a swivel vegetable peeler.

Step 6 Whisk the eggs and cream together and beat in a little hot sauce to raise the temperature of the eggs before adding back to the hot sauce.

1. Trim the ends of the asparagus to remove the top parts and to make the spears the same length. Using a swivel vegetable peeler, pare the stalks up to the tips.

2. To cook the asparagus, tie the spears in a bundle and stand them upright in a deep saucepan of lightly salted boiling water. Alternatively, place the spears in a large sauté pan of boiling salted water. If using a sauté pan, place half on and half off the heat, with the tips of the asparagus off the heat.

3. Cook, uncovered, for about 12-15 minutes, or until the asparagus is tender. Drain and reserve the cooking liquid. Keep the asparagus warm in a covered serving dish.

4. To prepare the sauce, melt the butter in a heavy-based saucepan and stir in the flour off the heat. Gradually beat in the asparagus cooking liquid or chicken stock and add the wine. Stir until the sauce is smooth and then place over a low heat.

5. Bring the sauce to the boil, stirring constantly, and allow to boil for about 1-2 minutes, or until thickened.

6. Beat the egg yolks and cream together and add a few spoonfuls of the hot sauce. Return the egg and cream mixture to the pan, stirring constantly. Reheat if necessary, but do not allow the sauce to boil once the egg is added. Add salt and white pepper and a pinch of sugar if desired. Pour over the asparagus to serve.

Cook's Notes

Time
Preparation takes about 30 minutes, cooking takes about 12-15 minutes for the asparagus and about 10 minutes for the sauce.

Variation
White asparagus is often difficult to find outside Germany, so use green asparagus as an alternative.

Serving Ideas
Serve as a vegetable side dish with ham and new potatoes, or as a first course on its own.

SERVES 6

CRUMB FRIED CHICKEN

A southern speciality, this dish has
a slightly misleading name since most
of the "frying" is done in the oven!

3lb chicken
2 eggs, mixed with a pinch of salt
1 cup breadcrumbs
½ cup Parmesan cheese
¼ tsp powdered ginger
4 tbsps butter or margarine
3 tbsps oil
Lemons and parsley for garnish

1. Preheat the oven to 400°F. To joint the chicken, first cut off the legs, bending them backwards to break the ball and socket joint. Cut in between the ball and socket joint to completely remove the legs.

2. Cut down the breastbone with sharp poultry shears to separate the two halves. Use the poultry shears to cut through the rib cage. Use the notch in the shears to separate the wing joints from the back.

3. Cut the quarters into two pieces each. Use a sharp knife to separate the drumstick from the thigh. Cut the breasts in half, leaving some of the white meat attached to the wing joint. Cut through the bones with poultry shears.

4. Mix the breadcrumbs, Parmesan cheese and powdered ginger together. First dip the chicken into the egg and then coat with the crumbs.

5. Heat the oil in a large frying pan or sauté pan and add the butter. When hot, place in the chicken, skin side down first. Cook both sides until golden brown.

6. Transfer with a slotted spoon to a baking sheet and place in the oven for 20-30 minutes, or until the juices run clear when the chicken is tested with a knife or a fork. Serve garnished with small bunches of parsley and lemon wedges or slices.

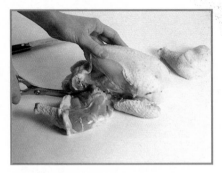

Step 1 First remove the legs from the chicken. Bend the leg backwards to break the ball and socket joint and cut in between.

Step 2 Use poultry shears to cut down the breastbone and through the rib cage. Use the notch to cut through the wing joint.

Step 3 Use poultry shears to cut through the bones, separating the breast joint into two. Use a sharp knife to separate the drumstick from the thigh.

Cook's Notes

Time
Preparation takes about 30 minutes. If using pre-jointed chicken, allow about 15-20 minutes for preparation. Chicken will take about 10-15 minutes to brown and 20-30 minutes to finish cooking in the oven.

Preparation
Mix the crumbs, cheese and ginger on a sheet of wax paper. Place the chicken on the crumbs and shake the paper from side to side to coat easily and completely.

Variation
If desired, leave out the Parmesan cheese and ginger and add extra breadcrumbs, paprika, salt, pepper and a pinch of thyme.

SERVES 6
CHICKEN FRICASSEE

Food in the Rhine Valley shows a considerable French influence while still retaining its own distinctive character, as shown in this fricassee with German cheese topping.

3lb chicken
1 stick celery, chopped
2 carrots, chopped
1 turnip, peeled and chopped
1 small onion, finely chopped
Water to cover
Pinch salt and pepper
2 tbsps butter
2 tbsps flour
1 egg yolk
1 cup cream
1 can artichoke hearts, drained and halved
Salt, pepper and a pinch nutmeg
1 tbsp chopped fresh parsley
1oz Tilsit cheese, thinly sliced

1. Place the chicken in a large stock pot with the vegetables and enough water to cover. Cook over medium heat for about 1 hour, or until the chicken is tender and juices run clear when the thigh is pierced with a fork.

2. Remove the chicken and allow to cool. Strain the stock and reserve it. Keep the vegetables to add to the sauce. When the chicken is cool, skin it and remove the meat from the bones. Discard the skin and bones and chop the meat roughly.

3. Melt the butter in a large pan and stir in the flour off the heat. Place the pan back over low heat and cook until the flour is a pale straw color. Pour in about 2 cups of the strained stock gradually. Whisk well and bring the sauce to the boil. Add the chicken, reserved vegetables and the artichoke hearts. Cook for about 10 minutes over low heat and then remove to a heated serving dish with a draining spoon.

4. Mix the egg and cream together and combine with a few spoonfuls of the hot sauce. Put the egg and cream back to the sauce and stir well. Heat gently, but do not allow to boil. Season with salt, pepper and a pinch of nutmeg.

5. Cut the cheese into strips or triangles and arrange attractively on top. Place under a preheated broiler to brown the cheese. Sprinkle with the chopped parsley and serve immediately.

Step 1 When the chicken is cooked, the leg joint will move easily and the juices will run clear when the thickest part of the thigh is pierced with a fork.

Step 3 Cook the flour and the butter together until the mixture is a pale straw color.

Step 3 Gradually add the stock, beating well after each addition.

Cook's Notes

Time
Preparation takes about 20 minutes, cooking takes about 1 hour 15 minutes.

Watchpoint
Do not allow the sauce to boil once the egg and cream have been added or the mixture will curdle.

Freezing
Any leftover stock may be frozen in small containers or in an ice cube tray for convenience.

GARNISHED PEPPER STEAK

This is an unusual German recipe
not only because of its garnish but
also because beef is so seldom used.

2 sirloin or rump steaks about 4oz each in weight
1 clove garlic, crushed
Salt and freshly ground black pepper
Oil

Sauce
1 shallot, finely chopped
2 tbsps small capers
2 oz sliced mushrooms
1 tbsp flour
½ cup beef stock
2 tsps German mustard
1 tsp Worcestershire sauce
4 tbsps German white wine
1 tsp lemon juice
Pinch each of thyme and rosemary

Garnish
4 baby ears of corn, cut in half
½ green pepper and ½ red pepper, seeded, cored and
  thinly sliced
2 peperonata, stem and seeds removed and cut in half
2 ripe tomatoes, peeled, seeded and cut into thin strips
2oz bone marrow (optional)

Step 1 Press the steaks firmly against the base of the pan using a spatula.

Step 2 Sprinkle the flour over the shallot, capers and mushrooms in the frying pan and cook to brown it lightly.

1. Rub the crushed garlic, salt and pepper into both sides of each steak. Heat a large frying pan and brush the surface lightly with oil. Place the steaks in the hot pan and press them down firmly with a spatula to seal. Turn over and repeat. Remove the steaks to a plate and add 1 tbsp of oil to the pan.

2. Add the shallot, capers and mushrooms and cook for about 1 minute. Sprinkle on the flour and cook to brown slightly. Pour on the stock and stir in well. Add the remaining sauce ingredients and bring to the boil.

3. Add the corn and peppers to the sauce and return the steaks to the pan. Cook 6-8 minutes until the steaks reach desired doneness. Add the remaining ingredients to the sauce, slpowdered the bone marrow, if using. Transfer the steaks to a heated serving plate, reheat the sauce and spoon over the steaks to serve.

Cook's Notes

Time
Preparation takes about 30 minutes, cooking takes about 20 minutes in total.

Preparation
Sealing the steaks on both sides helps to seal in the meat juices.

Serving Ideas
Serve with rice, pasta or spaetzle or sauté potatoes.

Variation
If desired, canned pimento may be substituted for the fresh red pepper. Sliced dill pickle may also be added as part of the garnish.

SERVES 6

SAUSAGE, APPLE & PEPPER KEBABS

Not a traditional dish, these kebabs nevertheless have a
sweet-sour flavor characteristic of northern cooking.

½ cup honey (set)
1 tsp chopped fresh dill
½ cup white wine vinegar
1lb schinkenwurst, cut in 2 inch pieces
2 large cooking apples, cored but not peeled
1 large red pepper, cored, seeded and cut into 2 inch
  pieces

Step 1 Mix the honey and herbs together and gradually beat in the vinegar.

Step 3 Quarter and core the apple, but do not peel. Cut lengthwise or crosswise into smaller pieces.

Step 4 Cut peppers in half and remove the core and seeds. Also cut out any white pith as this tends to be bitter.

1. Mix together the honey and the herbs. Gradually whisk in the vinegar to blend thoroughly.

2. Cut the sausage and place in the marinade, stirring to coat evenly. Allow to marinate for about 2 hours.

3. Cut the apple in quarters and remove the cores. Cut in half again crosswise or lengthwise as desired.

4. Cut the pepper in half and remove the core and seeds and any white pith inside. Rinse under cold running water to remove all the seeds. Cut the pepper into pieces about the same size as the sausage and apple. Thread the ingredients onto skewers, alternating the pepper, sausage and apple. Brush with the marinade and place under a pre-heated broiler. Cook for about 5-6 minutes, turning 2 or 3 times and brushing frequently with the marinade. Pour over any additional marinade to serve.

Cook's Notes

 Time
The sausage needs about 2 hours to marinate. Preparation will take about 15 minutes, cooking takes about 5-6 minutes.

 Preparation
The kebabs may be cooked over an outdoor barbecue grill, as well.

 Variation
Other types of sausage, such as bratwurst, bierwurst or knackwurst, may be used.

Serving Ideas
Serve on a bed of rice and accompany with a green salad.

 Cook's Tip
For extra flavor, the apples may also be mixed in with the marinade. The vinegar will keep them from going brown.

SERVES 4

BLACKBERRY VEAL STEAKS

Veal, with its mild taste, is the perfect background
for rich and flavorful sauces like this one
with its unusual combination of ingredients.

4 even-sized veal steaks
Seasoned flour
3 tbsps butter or margarine
2 shallots, finely chopped
⅓ cup blackberry liqueur
½ a green pepper, thinly sliced
2oz oyster mushrooms
3 tbsps heavy cream
2 tbsps butter, cut into small pieces
Salt and pepper
Fresh, frozen or canned blackberries for garnishing

Step 1 Place the veal in the butter and cook to brown on both sides.

Step 1 Once the steaks have been dredged with flour, shake off the excess to leave just a thin coating.

Step 3 Make sure the sauce is very hot and remove the pan from the heat. Whisk in the butter, a piece at a time.

1. Dredge the steaks with the seasoned flour and shake off the excess. Melt the butter or margarine in a large sauté pan and, when foaming, place in the steaks. Cook on both sides until browned and then lower the heat. Cover the pan and cook for about 15 minutes, or until just tender.

2. Remove the veal steaks to a serving dish and keep them warm. Add the chopped shallots to the pan and cook until

beginning to soften. Add the blackberry liqueur and bring to the boil. Lower the heat and add the pepper and mushrooms. Add enough stock to barely cover, reduce the heat and simmer for about 5 minutes. Pour in the cream and bring to the boil.

3. Remove the vegetables from the sauce with a draining spoon and place them over the veal steaks. Reheat the sauce and beat in the butter, a little at a time. Pour the sauce over the veal steaks and serve garnished with blackberries.

Cook's Notes

Time
Preparation takes about 30 minutes, cooking takes about 25-30 minutes.

Preparation
Beating the butter in at the end makes the sauce shiny and also helps to thicken it.

Variation
If blackberry liqueur is not available, substitute blackcurrant (Crème de Cassis). Substitute any other type of mushroom for oyster mushrooms.

SERVES 4

ROLLED VEAL ESCALOPES

Roulades – filled meat rolls – are extremely
popular in Germany, and a dish using veal is always
a favorite. Combine the two and you can't go wrong!

4 veal escalopes
8-16 slices German salami or cervalat
2 tbsps butter or margarine
2 tbsps oil
1 tsp chopped sage
6 tbsps white wine
⅓ cup quark or fromage frais
Salt and white pepper
Fresh sage leaves for garnish

Step 2 Top each piece of veal with salami and roll up. Tie or secure with wooden picks.

Step 1 Place escalopes between two sheets of wax paper or plastic wrap and flatten with a meat mallet or rolling pin. If using a rolling pin, hit with middle rather than the end.

Step 3 Place the veal rolls, seam side down first, in the butter and brown to a good, even color.

1. Bat out the escalopes between two sheets of damp wax paper or plastic wrap using a meat mallet or rolling pin. When flattened, cut each in half to make squarish pieces.

2. Top each piece with a slice of salami and roll up like a jelly roll. Secure with wooden picks. Alternatively, tie in three places with fine string.

3. Heat the butter and oil in a frying pan or a sauté pan and

fry the meat rolls until evenly browned all over. Sprinkle with the chopped sage and add the wine. Simmer without the lid for about 15 minutes.

4. Remove the rolls, discard the picks or string and transfer the rolls to a warm serving dish. Cover and keep warm.

5. Whisk the quark into the pan liquid over a low heat until smooth and heated through. Pour this over the rolls to serve, and garnish with fresh sage leaves.

Cook's Notes

 Time
Preparation takes about 25 minutes, cooking takes about 20 minutes.

 Variation
Turkey breasts may be used instead of the veal.

 Watchpoint
Quark will curdle if allowed to boil, so heat very gently.

 Serving Ideas
Serve with puréed spinach and sauté potatoes. Spinach pasta is also a good accompaniment.

SERVES 4

ZIGEUNERSCHNITZEL

A Hungarian influence is evident with the use of
paprika and peppers in this traditional veal escalope
dish. The name literally means gypsy cutlets.

8 veal escalopes
Seasoned flour
3 tbsps butter or margarine
1 onion
1 red and 1 green pepper, thinly sliced
2 tbsps flour
1 tbsp paprika
½ – 1 cup beef stock
½ cup plain yogurt

Step 3 Slice onion thinly and add to pan. Add the pepper slices and sauté for 3 minutes until soft but not browned.

1. Trim the escalopes to remove any fat. Bat them out if desired. Dredge in the seasoned flour and shake off the excess.

2. Melt the butter or margarine in a large frying pan or sauté pan and, when foaming, place in the escalopes. It may be necessary to cook them in two or four batches. Lower the heat and brown slowly on both sides for about 8 minutes in total. Remove and keep warm.

3. Slice the onion thinly and add to the pan. Add the pepper slices and sauté for about 3 minutes. Remove and set aside with the veal.

4. Add the flour to the pan and allow it to cook slowly until golden brown. Add the paprika and cook for 1 minute.

5. Whisk in the stock gradually to prevent lumps and bring to the boil. Replace the veal and vegetables, cover and cook for 10 minutes, or until the veal is tender.

6. Beat the yogurt until smooth and drizzle over the veal to serve.

Step 6 Beat the yogurt well to remove any lumps and to thin it slightly. If still too thick to run easily from the spoon, add water or milk.

Step 6 Drizzle yogurt onto the veal over the prongs of a fork or over a tea-spoon. If desired, use a knife and swirl the yogurt partially into the sauce.

Cook's Notes

Time
Preparation takes about 30 minutes, cooking takes about 15-20 minutes. Veal dries out very quickly, so brown slowly to avoid toughening.

Preparation
Always remove the white pith from inside the peppers as this tends to be bitter. This dish may be prepared in advance and reheated slowly before serving. Do not add the yogurt until ready to serve.

Cook's Tip
If the yogurt is too thick to drizzle properly, thin with a little water or milk. Cook paprika and most spices briefly before adding any liquid to the recipe. This will develop the flavor and eliminate any harsh taste.

SERVES 4

TROUT IN ASPIC

A dish using crystal-clear aspic is always
impressive, and home-made aspic has a flavor
that is well worth the effort to make.

---

6 cups water
Pinch salt and 6 black peppercorns
2 bay leaves and 2 parsley stalks
1 small onion, diced
1 cup dry white wine
4 even-sized rainbow trout, gutted and well washed
2 egg whites
2 level tbsps powdered gelatine
Lemon slices, capers and sprigs of fresh dill for garnish

---

1. Combine the water, vinegar, salt, peppercorns, bay leaves, parsley stalks, sliced onion and wine in a large saucepan or fish kettle. Bring to the boil and allow to simmer for about 30 minutes.

2. Cool slightly and add the fish. Cover and bring back to the simmering point. Allow the fish to cook gently for 5 minutes. Cool in the liquid, uncovered, until lukewarm.

3. Carefully remove the fish, drain and peel the skin off both sides while the fish is still slightly warm. Strain the liquid and reserve it.

4. Carefully lift the fillets from both sides of the trout, taking care not to break them up. Make sure they are completely free of skin and bones and place them on individual plates, or onto one large serving plate that has a slight well in the center.

5. Pour the reserved fish cooking liquid into a large, deep saucepan and add the egg whites. Place the pan over the heat and whisk by hand using a wire balloon whisk. Allow the mixture to come to the boil, whisking constantly. Egg whites should form a thick frothy crust on top.

6. Stop whisking and allow the liquid and egg whites to boil up the side of the pan. Take off the heat and allow to subside. Repeat the process twice more and then leave to settle.

7. Line a colander with several thicknesses of paper towels or a clean tea towel. Place in a bowl and pour the fish cooking liquid and the egg white into the colander. Leave to drain slowly. Do not allow the egg white to fall into the clarified liquid.

8. When all the liquid has drained through, remove about 1 cup and dissolve the gelatine in it. Heat again very gently if necessary to dissolve the gelatine thoroughly. Return the gelatine to the remaining stock, place the bowl in a bowl of ice water to help thicken the gelatine.

9. Decorate the trout and the base of the dish with lemon slices, capers and fresh dill. When the aspic has become syrupy and slightly thickened, spoon carefully over the decoration to set it. Place in the refrigerator until set.

10. The aspic may be reheated gently by placing the bowl in a pan of hot water. Do not stir the aspic too vigorously or bubbles will form. Chill again until almost set and cover the trout completely in a layer of aspic. Place in the refrigerator until completely set and serve cold.

Step 9 Decorate the top of the fish and set with a bit of aspic. When firm, cover the trout with the remaining aspic.

Cook's Notes

Time
Preparation takes about 40 minutes to 1 hour. Cooking time for the trout is about 35 minutes. The aspic takes about 15 minutes to clarify.

Preparation
Adding egg whites to a stock removes any sediment that makes the stock cloudy. The sediment remains in the egg whites, hence it is important not to let the crust fall back into the clarified stock.

Cook's Tip
If the aspic is still cloudy after straining, pour back through the colander and the egg white crust into a clean bowl. This usually produces a very clear aspic.

SERVES 6

STUFFED SOLE

Fish is traditionally more popular in Northern Germany than in other parts of the country. This dish is elegant enough for a formal dinner party.

4 tbsps butter or margarine
2 tbsps flour
1½ cups fish or vegetable stock
3oz button mushrooms, sliced
6oz peeled, cooked shrimp
4oz canned, frozen or fresh cooked crabmeat
4 tbsps heavy cream
2 tbsps brandy
1oz fresh breadcrumbs
Salt and pepper
6-12 sole fillets, depending upon size
4 tbsps melted butter

Step 3 Cut fillets in half along the natural line that divides them.

1. Preheat the oven to 350°F. Melt 4 tbsps butter and add the flour. Cook for about 3 minutes over gentle heat or until pale straw colored. Add the stock and bring to the boil. Add the mushrooms and allow to cook until the sauce thickens.

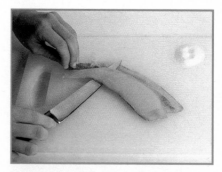

Step 3 Using a filleting knife, begin at the tail end and, using a sawing motion, slide the knife along the skin at a slight angle. Hold the end of the skin tightly with fingers dipped in salt.

Step 3 Spread stuffing on one side of each fillet, and roll up. Secure with wooden picks.

2. Add the cream and re-boil the sauce. Remove the sauce from the heat and add the brandy, shrimp, crab and breadcrumbs.

3. Skin the sole fillets and spread the filling on the side that was skinned. Roll up and arrange in a buttered baking dish. Spoon melted butter over the top and cook in the pre-heated oven for 20-30 minutes, until the fish is just firm.

Cook's Notes

 Time
Preparation takes about 30 minutes and cooking takes 20-30 minutes.

 Cook's Tip
When skinning fish, dip fingers into salt to get a better grip on slippery fish skin.

 Preparation
Filling may be prepared in advance and covered with a sheet of damp wax paper or plastic wrap to prevent a skin from forming on top. Filling is best used when completely cool.

 Serving Ideas
Serve with a green vegetable such as broccoli, asparagus or spinach. Accompany with new potatoes tossed in parsley butter.

 Variation
For special occasions, substitute lobster for the crabmeat for an elegant dinner party.

SERVES 4-6

SHRIMP MARINATED IN WHITE WINE

Dishes like this one from Schleswig-Holstein have a distinctly Scandinavian flavor, despite the use of an unmistakably German wine.

2lbs peeled uncooked shrimp

Marinade

1 cup Mosel wine
4 tbsps lemon juice
1 tbsp chopped fresh dill
Pinch salt and black pepper
1 clove garlic, crushed
1 bay leaf
Chopped parsley for garnishing
4 tbsps butter or margarine

Step 1 Peel the shrimp and remove any black veins along the rounded side.

1. Peel the shrimp and remove the black vein along the top. If desired, the tail ends of the shell may be left attached. Place the shrimp in a shallow dish.

2. Combine all the marinade ingredients except the chopped parsley and the butter. Pour the marinade over the shrimp and turn several times to coat well. Marinate for at least 2 hours in the refrigerator.

3. Melt the butter or margarine in a large frying pan. Remove the shrimp from the marinade with a slotted spoon and place them in the butter. Cook over moderate heat for 8-10 minutes, stirring frequently for even cooking.

4. Pour the marinade into a deep saucepan. Boil rapidly until it thickens and reduces by about ¾.

5. Place the cooked shrimp in a large serving dish or in individual dishes and pour over the reduced marinade. Sprinkle with chopped parsley and serve immediately.

Step 3 When the shrimp are cooked, they will curl up slightly, become opaque and turn pink. Do not overcook them or they will toughen.

Step 4 Place the marinade in a saucepan and boil rapidly to reduce to a syrupy consistency.

Cook's Notes

 Watchpoint
Do not cook the shrimp too long or over heat that is too high as they will toughen.

 Cook's Tip
If serving cold, the shrimp may be prepared a day in advance.

 Serving Ideas
Serve the shrimp with rolls or brown bread. If serving cold, chill well and serve on a bed of lettuce leaves.

SERVES 4-6

WEINSCHAUM

This is a light and luscious pudding that
can also be a sauce. Its name means "wine foam,"
which describes it perfectly.

2 cups Rhine or Mosel wine
½ cup water
4 eggs
½ cup sugar
Orange zest or crystallized rose or violet petals for
decoration

Step 1 Combine all the ingredients in the top of a heavy boiler and whisk until mixture thickens.

Step 2 Check the base of the bowl or heavy boiler. If very hot, place in a bowl of ice water and continue whisking.

Step 2 When thick enough, lift beaters or whisk and draw a trail of mixture across the bowl. It should stay and hold its shape on top. This is a ribbon trail.

1. Place the wine and water in the top of a double boiler over boiling water. Make sure the top of the double boiler does not actually touch the boiling water. Add the eggs and sugar and beat the ingredients vigorously with a wire whisk or an electric mixer.

2. When the custard thickens, it should hold a ribbon trail when the whisk or the beaters are lifted.

3. Spoon into serving dishes and decorate with strips or orange zest or crystallized flower petals. Serve hot or chill thoroughly before serving.

Cook's Notes

Time
Cooking will take approximately 10 minutes. If serving cold, chill for at least 1 hour.

Watchpoint
Do not allow the custard to boil. If the bottom of the bowl gets too hot, remove it and dip into ice water.

Variation
If serving cold, ⅓ cup lightly whipped cream may be folded into the chilled custard.

SERVES 6-8

RED FRUIT PUDDING

No pudding could be easier to prepare than this
light, tangy sweet, which is perfect after a rich
meal, and so popular it's Germany's national dessert.

2 cups German redcurrant fruit juice
2 cups German raspberry juice
1 strip lemon peel
½-1 cup sugar
½ cup Mosel wine
6 tbsps cornstarch
2 tbsps lemon juice or additional wine
Whipped cream
Fresh redcurrants and raspberries to garnish

Step 2 Return mixture to the saucepan gradually, whisking constantly.

Step 2 Dissolve cornstarch in wine and stir in a few spoonfuls of hot sauce.

Step 2 Bring to the boil, stirring constantly until the mixture begins to thicken and clear.

1. Combine the fruit juices in a large, heavy-based saucepan, add the lemon peel and heat gently.

2. Dissolve the cornstarch in the wine and stir a few spoonfuls of the hot juice into the mixture. Return the mixture to the saucepan, whisking continuously. Bring to the boil and stir until thickened. Add sugar to taste and simmer gently until the sugar dissolves completely.

3. When the mixture thickens and clears, remove it from the heat and add lemon juice or the additional white wine.

4. Pour into a large glass serving bowl or individual dessert glasses and chill until set.

5. To serve, pipe or spoon whipped cream on the top and decorate with fresh redcurrants and raspberries.

Cook's Notes

Time
Preparation takes about 10 minutes, cooking takes about 10-15 minutes.

Preparation
If bottled currant juice and raspberry juice are not available, use 1lb each fresh redcurrants and raspberries. Place fruit in a large saucepan with 2 cups water and bring slowly to the boil. Cook until the fruit is very soft. Strain the juice and make up to the required amount with water.

Variation
If desired, fold pieces of red fruit such as raspberries, strawberries or redcurrants into the pudding once it has thickened.

SERVES 6

QUARKSPEISE

A Westphalian specialty, this pudding is a delightfully different combination of pumpernickel bread, low fat soft cheese and tangy cranberries.

3oz pumpernickel bread made into crumbs
3 tbsps brandy
2½ cups quark
⅓-½ cup sugar
8oz whole cranberry sauce or fresh raspberries
3 slices pumpernickel, cut in small squares or triangles, for decoration

Step 2 Mix the quark, sugar and brandy-soaked crumbs together.

Step 1 Leave the pumpernickel to soak in the brandy until the crumbs soften and swell slightly.

Step 3 Layer up the mixture with cranberry sauce or fresh raspberries in glass dessert dishes.

1. Place the pumpernickel crumbs in a bowl and sprinkle over the brandy. Stir to coat evenly and leave to stand.

2. Combine the quark and sugar together and mix thoroughly. When the crumbs have softened, fold into the quark.

3. Spoon a layer of quark-pumpernickel mixture into the

bottom of each of 6 glass dessert dishes. Spoon over a layer of cranberry sauce or raspberries. Continue layering up the pumpernickel-quark mixture and cranberries or raspberries, ending with a layer of quark on top. Decorate the top with the squares or triangles of pumpernickel and a fresh raspberry or spoonful of sauce. Chill before serving.

Cook's Notes

 Time
Preparation takes about 15 minutes, plus chilling time.

 Buying Guide
Quark is a low fat, soft cheese now readily available in supermarkets and delicatessens.

 Variation
Other fruit or preserves may be used.

MAKES 1 CAKE

APPLE, PEAR OR PLUM CAKE

Cakes don't always have to be iced sponge
layers. Kuchen in Germany are often made like
flans, using a very versatile biscuit-like pastry.

Pastry

1½ cups all-purpose flour with 1½ tsps baking powder
Salt
3 tbsp sugar
Dash vanilla extract or 1 tsp grated lemon rind
½ cup plus 2 tbsps butter or margarine
2 egg yolks or 1 whole egg
1-2 tbsps milk or water

Filling

1lb dessert apples, pears or plums
Sugar for dredging

Step 1 Rub the butter into the dry ingredients by hand or with a food processor until the mixture resembles fine breadcrumbs.

1. Sift the flour with the salt and sugar into a large bowl. Add the baking powder, if using, with the flour. Rub in the butter or margarine until the mixture resembles fine breadcrumbs.

2. Make a well in the center and place in the egg yolks or the whole egg. Add the vanilla or lemon rind and 1 tbsp milk or water. Mix into the flour with a fork. If the pastry appears too dry, add the additional milk or water.

3. Knead together quickly with the hand to smooth out. If the mixture is too soft, wrap well and chill briefly.

4. Press the pastry on the base and up the sides of a flan dish, preferably one with a removable base. Chill 15 minutes.

5. Meanwhile, prepare the fruit. Peel, core and quarter the apples and slice thinly. Peel, core and quarter the pears and slice those thinly, lengthwise. Cut the plums in half and remove the stones. Slice thinly. Arrange the chosen fruit on the base of the flan in straight lines or circles with the slices slightly overlapping. Sprinkle on sugar and bake in a preheated oven at 400°F until the pastry is pale golden brown and the fruit is soft. Allow to cool and sprinkle with additional sugar before serving.

Step 2 Make a well in the center of the flour and place in the egg and milk or water. Mix together with a fork.

Step 3 Press the pastry into the flan dish, making sure the base and sides are of even thickness. Trim off any excess pastry around the edges.

Cook's Notes

Time
Preparation takes about 30 minutes, cooking takes about 35-40 minutes.

Cook's Tip
If the pastry begins to brown around the edges before the remaining pastry and fruit is cooked, cover the browned parts with foil, shiny side out.

Serving Ideas
Serve with whipped cream, ice cream or pouring cream. Custard sauce is also a nice accompaniment.

MAKES 1 CAKE

CHERRY CAKE

This cake has a pastry base and
custard filling so it is really more
flan than cake, and quite irresistible.

1 recipe pastry from Apple, Pear or Plum Cake

1¼ lbs fresh cherries
2 egg yolks
⅓ cup light cream
1 slice white or whole-wheat bread, made into crumbs
½ cup toasted hazelnuts, chopped
½ cup sugar
Cinnamon or nutmeg

Step 3 Sprinkle breadcrumbs over the base of the pastry to absorb the juice from the fruit as it cooks, and to keep the bottom from going soggy.

Step 2 Remove the stones from the cherries with a swivel peeler, cherry pitter or by cutting in half.

Step 4 Arrange the cherries evenly over the pastry, sprinkle with cinnamon and sugar, and pour the egg yolk and cream filling over the top.

1. Prepare the pastry as before and line a flan dish with a removable base.

2. Wash the cherries and remove the stems and stones. Use a swivel vegetable peeler or a cherry pitter to remove the stones. Alternatively, cut them in half to remove the stones easily.

3. Sprinkle the top of the pastry with the breadcrumbs and

then spread the cherries over evenly. Sprinkle with sugar and a pinch of cinnamon or nutmeg if desired. Scatter over the hazelnuts.

4. Beat the egg yolks and cream together and pour over the top. Bake in a preheated oven at 400°F until the pastry is pale brown and the filling has risen and set. Serve warm or cold cut into wedges.

Cook's Notes

Time
Preparation takes about 30 minutes, cooking takes about 20-30 minutes.

Variation
Other berries may be used instead of cherries. Apples, pears, plums or apricots can also be used. If using canned fruit, be sure to drain well.

Cook's Tip
This cake does not keep well, so serve on the day it is made.

SERVES 6

APPLE FILLED PANCAKES

These light, puffy pancakes make a delicious brunch dish as
well as a sweet, and are popular in Southern Germany.

Filling

3 tbsps butter or margarine
1½lbs cooking apples, peeled, cored and cut into
    ¼-inch-thick wedges
2 tbsps brown sugar
½ tsp ground allspice

Pancakes

4 eggs
1½ cups milk
½ cup all-purpose flour
½ tbsp sugar
Pinch salt
6 tbsps butter or margarine
Powdered sugar

1. Melt the butter for the filling in a large frying pan over
moderate heat. When just foaming, add the apples and
sprinkle with sugar and allspice. Cook, stirring occasionally, until the apples are lightly browned and slightly
softened. Put the apples aside while preparing the batter.

2. Combine the eggs and the milk in a large bowl and
whisk thoroughly. Sift the flour with the sugar and salt and
add to the eggs gradually, whisking constantly. Alternatively, combine all the ingredients in a food processor
and work until just smooth.

3. To cook the pancakes, melt 1 tbsp of butter over moderate heat in an 8 inch frying pan. Pour in about ½ cup of the
batter and swirl the pan from side to side so that the batter
covers the base.

4. Scatter over some of the filling and cook the pancake for

about 3 minutes.

5. Pour another ½ cup of the batter over the apples and
place under a preheated broiler for about 1-2 minutes, or
until the top is golden brown and firm to the touch.

6. Loosen the sides and the base of the pancake and slide
it onto a heated serving dish. Add 1 tbsp of butter to the pan
for each pancake. Just before serving, sprinkle the pancakes with the powdered sugar.

Step 3 Put the
batter into the
bottom of hot
frying pan and
swirl to coat the
base evenly.

Step 4 Scatter
some of the apple
filling evenly over
the pancake.

Cook's Notes

Time
Preparation takes about 30
minutes, cooking takes about
5-6 minutes per pancake, filling will take
about 10 minutes.

Variation
Grated rind of 1 lemon may be
added to the filling, if desired.
Add more or less sugar depending
upon the sweetness of the apples.

Serving Ideas
Accompany the pancakes
with whipped cream, pouring
cream or ice cream.

MAKES 1 CAKE

BEE STING CAKE

Sugar, butter and almonds combine to make a cake
sweet enough to please the bees, hence the name.
This is a favorite in pastry shops all over Germany.

Cake

1½ cups all-purpose flour with 1½ tsps baking powder
Salt
½ cup plus 2 tbsps butter or margarine
⅓ cup sugar
2 eggs
½ tsp vanilla extract
1-2 tbsps milk

Topping

¼ cup sugar
4 tbsps butter
1 tbsp milk
½ cup sliced almonds

Filling

¼ cup sugar
2 tbsps cornstarch
3 egg yolks
½ cup milk
⅓ cup heavy cream, whipped
¼ tsp vanilla or almond extract

1. Preheat the oven to 375°F. Sift the flour, baking powder
and pinch of salt into a large mixing bowl.

2. Cream the butter until light and fluffy and gradually add
the sugar, beating until the mixture is light and fluffy. Beat in
the eggs one at a time and add the vanilla.

3. Using a large spoon or rubber spatula, add the milk and
the flour, alternating between the two. Use enough milk to
bring mixture to thick dropping consistency.

4. Grease and flour a springform pan and spoon in the
cake mixture.

5. Combine the topping ingredients and heat long
enough to dissolve the sugar.

6. Sprinkle the top of the cake mixture lightly with flour and
pour on the topping.

7. Bake in the preheated oven for 25-30 minutes. The
topping will caramelize slightly as the cake bakes.

8. Meanwhile, prepare the filling. Combine the sugar,
cornstarch and egg yolks in a bowl and whisk until light.
Pour on the milk gently and gradually whisk into the egg
yolk mixture. Strain the mixture into a heavy-based
saucepan and cook over very gentle heat until the mixture
coats the back of a spoon. Add the vanilla or almond extract
and allow to cool. Place a sheet of damp wax paper or
plastic wrap directly over the top of the custard as it cools.
When the custard is completely cool, lightly whip the cream
and fold it in.

9. To assemble the cake, loosen it from the sides of the pan
turn the lock of the pan and push the cake out. Use a
spatula to lift the cake off the base of the pan and cut the
cake in half, horizontally through the middle. Fill the cake
and sandwich the layers together with the almond topping
uppermost. Chill thoroughly before serving. Cut the cake in
wedges to serve.

Step 6 Sprinkle
the top of the
cake mixture with
flour, and pour
over the topping.

Cook's Notes

Time
Preparation takes about 40
minutes in total. Cooking takes
about 25-30 minutes for the cake, 5
minutes for the topping and about 10
minutes for the filling.

Preparation
If the butter is creamed until
very soft, it is easier to
incorporate all the sugar. If the eggs are
added gradually, there is less chance
of the mixture curdling.

Watchpoint
Do not allow the topping to
become too hot. Heat just
long enough to dissolve the sugar. If
too hot when poured over the cake, it
will deflate the mixture.

MAKES 1 CAKE

ALMOND TORTE

Stop in at a konditorei or pastry shop in
Germany and this is one of the many fabulous
confections you will be able to sample.

½ cup dry breadcrumbs
½ cup milk
1 tbsp rum
6 tbsps butter or margarine
⅓ cup sugar
6 eggs, separated
¾ cup ground roasted almonds
2 cups heavy or whipping cream
2 tbsps sugar
1 tbsp rum
¼ cup roasted almonds, finely chopped
Whole blanched almonds, toasted, angelica or cherries
    for decoration

1. Preheat the oven to 350°F. Soak the breadcrumbs in milk and rum in a large bowl.

2. In a separate bowl, cream the butter until soft and beat in the sugar gradually until the mixture is light and fluffy. Beat in the egg yolks one at a time and then add to the crumb mixture. Beat the egg whites until stiff but not dry and fold into the crumb mixture along with the almonds.

3. Grease and flour three 8 inch round cake pans, placing a sheet of wax paper in the base, if desired. Divide the cake mixture among the three pans and bake for 30-40 minutes in the preheated oven. Allow to cool briefly in the pans, loosen the sides and remove the cakes to a rack to finish cooling.

4. Whip the cream and the sugar with the rum. Reserve one third of the cream for the top and fold the finely chop-

ped almonds into the remaining two thirds. Sandwich the cake layers together with the almond cream and spread a layer of plain cream on top, reserving some for piping.

5. Fill a pastry bag fitted with a rosette tube with the remaining cream and pipe out rosettes or other decorations on top of the cake. Decorate with the whole almonds and angelica or cherries.

Step 2 Fold the egg whites into the crumb mixture along with the almonds using a large spoon or a rubber spatula.

Step 4 Sandwich the layers of cake together with the almond cream, pressing down lightly so that the cream shows around the edge.

Cook's Notes

Time
Preparation takes about 30 minutes, cooking takes about 30-40 minutes.

Watchpoint
Over-whipped egg whites are difficult to incorporate into the cake mixture and also begin to liquify and loose volume.

Preparation
Almonds are usually available already ground, chopped, roasted or unroasted. Alternatively, buy whole blanched almonds and roast the total amount for the recipe all at once in a moderate oven. Turn them often for even roasting.

Cook's Tip
Cream that has been in the refrigerator for at least 2 hours before whipping produces a better result. If cream becomes slightly over whipped, stir in a few spoonfuls of milk.

SERVES 8-10

BLACK FOREST CAKE

Pastry Layer

½ quantity recipe for Apple, Pear or Plum Cake pastry
1 tbsp redcurrant jelly

Cake

½ cup plus 2 tbsps unsalted butter
6 eggs
1 tsp vanilla extract
1 cup sugar
½ cup unsweetened cocoa
½ cup all-purpose flour
Syrup

Filling and Topping

3 cups heavy cream
½ cup powdered sugar
4 tbsps kirsch
8oz fresh cherries, pitted (or canned, pitted cherries, drained)
Grated plain chocolate
Fresh cherries or cocktail cherries

1. First prepare the pastry according to the recipe for Apple, Pear or Plum Cake. Lightly grease a baking sheet and pat the pastry out into a round shape about ¼ inch thick. Prick lightly with a fork and bake in a preheated oven at 375°F. Cook until the pastry browns lightly around the edge and feels firm in the center. Cut a circle 7 inches in diameter while the pastry is still warm. Use a cake pan as a guide. Remove the excess pastry and allow the round to cool completely on a baking sheet after loosening it from the bottom.

2. Grease three 7 inch round cake pans and place a circle of wax paper in the bottom of each. Grease the surface of the paper and sprinkle the pans lightly with flour, tapping to knock out the excess.

3. Soften the butter until it runs easily from a spoon but is not melted. To do this leave the butter at room temperature for several hours and then beat vigorously with a wooden spoon, use a food processor or electric mixer.

4. Beat the eggs, vanilla and sugar together on high speed until the mixture is thick and fluffy.

5. Sift in the flour and cocoa 2 tbsps at a time, folding it into the egg mixture with a large metal spoon or rubber spatula. Finally fold in the soft butter. Divide the mixture between the cake pans and bake for about 10-15 minutes, or until a knife inserted in the middle of the cake comes out clean. Allow the cakes to cool in their pans for about 5 minutes and then loosen from the sides with a sharp knife. Turn the cakes out onto wire racks to cool completely. Gently peel off the paper.

6. While the cakes are baking, prepare the syrup. Combine the sugar and water in a heavy-based pan and bring to the boil over moderate heat, stirring only until the sugar dissolves. Raise the temperature and allow the syrup to boil rapidly for about 5 minutes. Remove the pan from the heat and allow the syrup to cool. Stir in the kirsch. Place a tray underneath the cooling rack and prick layers of cake with a fork. Pour syrup over cakes and leave to soak.

7. If using fresh cherries for the filling, place them in a pan with enough water to cover after they have been pitted. Bring them to the boil and then reduce the heat and allow to simmer for about 5 minutes, or until tender. Drain them and pat them dry with paper towels.

8. Beat the cream until it thickens slightly, add the sugar and continue beating until the cream forms peaks that hold their shape. Fold in the kirsch.

9. To assemble the cake, place the pastry layer on a serving plate and brush with 1 tbsp softened redcurrant jelly. Place one chocolate layer on top of the pastry and press down lightly to stick the two together. Spread one third of the whipped cream on top of the chocolate layer and cover with half of the cherries. Place another chocolate layer on top and press down slightly. Spread another third of the whipped cream on top and sprinkle over the remaining cherries. Press down the top layer and cover the top and sides with the plain whipped cream. Press grated chocolate around the sides of the cake to cover the cream evenly. Decorate the top with rosettes and sprinkle over any remaining grated chocolate. Decorate the rosettes with a fresh cherry or a cocktail cherry.

Cook's Notes

Time
Preparation takes about 45 minutes, cooking takes approximately 15 minutes for the pastry, 10-15 minutes for the cakes, 10 minutes for the syrup and 5 minutes for the cherries.

Preparation
Allow the chocolate to soften very slightly but not begin to melt before grating. This will produce larger, attractive-looking curls.

GREEK
COOKING

INTRODUCTION

Greek cookery has much in common with that of other countries which share the Mediterranean climate, and yet, it is different.

Herbs are used liberally – oregano and basil being the favorites – but the resulting taste is not Italian. Spices, such as cinnamon and coriander, figure prominently, but the taste is not Middle Eastern. Olives and olive oil are essential ingredients, but the taste is not Provençal. The taste is undeniably Greek, and reflects all the vitality of the country and the belief that food is part of life and to be enjoyed without pretensions.

Greek recipes rely on the freshest possible ingredients prepared to let the natural flavors shine through. Eggplant, zucchini and artichokes all speak of the warmth of the country, and are used in many delicious ways. Olive oil is an essential ingredient and lends its fragrant bouquet to all food, even sweets. Vegetables are usually cooked in it in preference to water. Lots of herbs and lemon juice offset any oiliness, and olive oil is both a health and flavor bonus since it is less fattening and more nourishing than most other cooking fats.

Walnuts, almonds, fresh figs and feta cheese – the list of ingredients that make Greek food special could go on and on. They all add up, though, to a cuisine as vibrant and colorful as the country itself.

SERVES 6-8

SALTED ALMONDS AND CRACKED OLIVES

Olives take on a special flavor when prepared in this way.
Served with crisp toasted almonds, they make a perfect snack.

1lb almonds, unskinned
1 tbsp citric acid
4 tbsps cold water
1 tbsp salt
1lb green olives
2oz coarse salt
1 clove garlic, peeled and left whole
2 sprigs of fresh dill
1 bay leaf
1 sprig thyme
1 tbsp chopped oregano
Vine leaves

1. Spread the almonds in a large roasting pan. Mix the citric acid with the water and sprinkle over the almonds. Stir them around to coat evenly and leave for 10 minutes. Remove them, rinse out the pan and dry it.

2. Place the almonds back into the pan, spread them out and sprinkle with the salt. Shake the pan to coat evenly in salt and then spread the almonds out in an even layer.

3. Cook in a preheated 350°F oven for about 30 minutes, stirring frequently until brown and crisp. Allow them to cool completely before sealing tightly in jars for storage.

4. Hit the green olives gently with a meat mallet or rolling pin to crack the flesh. Alternatively, cut a cross in one side of each olive with a small, sharp knife. Rinse the olives and place them in storage jars. Cover with water and divide the ingredients between the jars. Cover the surface of the olives with the vine leaves.

Step 1 Put the almonds into a large roasting pan and spread into an even layer. Pour the citric acid mixture over the top and stir them to coat evenly.

Step 4 Crack the skin on the olives by gently hitting with a meat mallet or rolling pin.

Step 4 Alternatively, make a small cross on the side of each olive with a sharp knife.

5. Seal the jars to keep in a cool, dark place for 3-4 weeks. To serve, remove the olives and sprinkle with chopped oregano, if desired. Serve with the salted almonds.

Cook's Notes

Preparation
When cracking the olives, take care not to crack the stones. Taste the olives after about 2 weeks; if they have absorbed enough flavor from the various ingredients, they are ready to use.

Cook's Tip
In Greece raw olives are used. If using olives that have already been preserved in brine, they will not need to be stored as long. Use half the quantity of coarse salt.

Time
Preparation takes about 20 minutes, with 3-4 weeks storage time for the olives. Cooking time for the almonds is about 30 minutes.

SERVES 4

FRIED SQUID

Serve this sweet and delicious seafood
as an appetizer or main course. It's
easier to prepare than you think!

1½lb fresh squid
½ cup all-purpose flour
Salt and pepper
Oil for deep-frying
Lemon wedges and parsley for garnishing

1. Hold the body of the squid with one hand and the head with the other and pull gently to separate. Remove the intestines and the quill, which is clear and plastic-like. Rinse the body of the squid inside and outside under cold running water.

2. Cut the tentacles from the head, just above the eye. Separate into individual tentacles.

3. Remove the brownish or purplish outer skin from the body of the squid and cut the flesh into ¼ inch rings.

4. Mix the flour, salt and pepper together on a sheet of paper or in a shallow dish. Toss the rings of squid and the tentacles in the flour mixture to coat. Heat the oil to 350°F and fry the squid, about 6 pieces at a time, saving the tentacles until last. Remove them from the oil when brown and crisp with a draining spoon and place on paper towels.

Step 2 Cut the tentacles from the head just below the eye and separate them into individual pieces.

Step 3 Remove the outer skin from the body of the squid and cut the body into thin rings.

Sprinkle lightly with salt and continue with the remaining squid. The pieces will take about 3 minutes to cook. Place on serving dishes and garnish each dish with a wedge of lemon and some parsley.

Cook's Notes

Time
Preparation takes about 25 minutes, cooking takes 3 minutes per batch of 6 pieces.

Serving Ideas
Sprinkle the squid with chopped fresh oregano just before serving.

Preparation
Do not coat the pieces of squid too soon before frying or they will become soggy.

Watchpoint
Once the squid is added to the hot oil, cover the fryer as the oil will tend to spatter.

Cook's Tip
If the squid must be re-heated, spread the pieces on wire cooling racks covered with paper towels and place in a slow oven for about 10 minutes. Do not re-fry, as this toughens the squid.

SERVES 4

FRIED EGGPLANT WITH TZATZIKI

The fresh taste of cucumber, mint and yogurt is the
perfect complement to rich, fried eggplant slices.

4 small or 2 medium sized eggplants
½ cup all-purpose flour
Salt and pepper
Vegetable oil for frying

Tzatziki

¼ cucumber, finely chopped or grated
Salt and pepper
1 tbsp olive oil
1 tsp white wine vinegar
1 clove garlic, crushed
½ cup natural yogurt
2 tsps chopped fresh mint
Whole mint leaves for garnishing

1. Wash the eggplants and dry them. Cut into ¼ inch
rounds and lightly score the sides with a sharp knife.
Sprinkle both sides with salt and leave to drain in a colander
or on paper towels for 30 minutes before using.

2. Sprinkle the cucumber lightly with salt and leave in a
colander, slightly weighted down, to drain.

3. Rinse both the eggplant slices and cucumber to
remove the salt, pat the eggplant slices dry on paper towels
and squeeze excess moisture from the cucumber.

4. Mix the salt and pepper together with the flour and coat
the eggplant slices well. Heat the oil to 350°F and fry the
eggplant slices a few at a time. Remove them with a
draining spoon to paper towels and sprinkle lightly with salt.
Continue with the remaining slices.

5. Meanwhile, mix the oil and vinegar until well blended
and add the crushed garlic. Mix in the yogurt and add the

Step 1 Score the
eggplant slices on
both sides,
sprinkle lightly
with salt and
leave to drain in a
colander or on
paper towels.

Step 3 Rinse the
cucumber and
squeeze, or press
between two
plates to remove
excess moisture.

Step 4 Coat the
eggplant slices in
seasoned flour
and fry them, a
few at a time, in
hot oil until they
turn golden
brown. Remove
with a draining
spoon.

drained cucumber. To serve, arrange the eggplant slices on
individual plates or one large plate and add the Tzatziki.
Garnish with mint leaves.

Cook's Notes

Cook's Tip
Sprinkling eggplant and
cucumber with salt before
using draws out excess moisture and
bitter juices. Sprinkling deep-fried food
lightly with salt while it stands helps to
draw out excess fat.

Variation
Zucchini may be used instead
of eggplant. Top and tail the
zucchini and slice them into 3-4 lengthwise
slices. Zucchini do not have to be
sprinkled with salt and left to stand.

Time
Preparation takes about 30
minutes, cooking time takes
about 2-3 minutes per batch of
eggplant slices.

SERVES 6

EGG AND LEMON SOUP

This is one of the best known of all
Greek soups. Diced chicken can be
added to make a more filling soup.

5 cups chicken stock
2 eggs, separated
2 lemons
2oz rice, rinsed

1. Bring the stock to the boil in a large saucepan. When boiling, add the rice and cook for about 10 minutes. Meanwhile, beat the eggs with 1 tbsp cold water for about 3 minutes, or until lightly frothy. Squeeze the lemons for juice and add to the eggs, straining out any seeds. Beat for about 1 minute to blend well.

2. Beat a few spoonfuls of the hot stock into the egg mixture.

Step 1 Squeeze the lemons for juice and add to the egg yolks, straining out any seeds. Beat for about a minute to blend well.

Step 2 Beat a few spoonfuls of the hot stock into the egg mixture.

Step 3 Pour the egg mixture back into the stock in a thin, steady stream, stirring continuously. Do not allow to boil.

3. Gradually add that back to the stock, stirring continuously. Put the soup back over very low heat for about 1-2 minutes, stirring constantly. Do not allow the soup to boil. Serve immediately.

Cook's Notes

Variation
The soup may be served without rice, if desired.

Watchpoint
If the stock boils once the egg is added, it will curdle and the soup will be spoiled.

Time
Preparation takes about 15 minutes, longer if making stock from scratch. Cooking takes about 12-13 minutes. Home made stock will take about 1-1½ hours to make.

Serving Ideas
Sprinkle the soup with chopped fresh oregano or parsley. Also, slice a lemon thinly and float one slice on the top of each serving bowl.

MAKES 1 OMELET

FRESH TOMATO OMELET

For a summer appetizer or lunch, don't forget
about omelets. This one is especially
summery with its ripe tomatoes and fresh herbs.

1lb tomatoes
½ tsp chopped fresh oregano or basil
Salt and pepper
4 eggs, lightly beaten
3 tbsps oil

1. To make the tomatoes easier to peel, drop them into boiling water and leave them for about 5 seconds. Remove them with a draining spoon and put immediately into ice cold water. Peel with a sharp knife.

2. Cut the tomatoes in half and remove the seeds and juice with a teaspoon. Cut the tomato halves into thin strips.

3. Beat the eggs with the herbs, salt and pepper and heat

Step 1 Dropping tomatoes in boiling water for about 5 seconds will make them easier to peel.

Step 1 Put the tomatoes immediately into cold water to stop the cooking, and loosen the peels with a small, sharp knife.

Step 2 Remove the seeds and juice from the tomatoes by cutting them in half and scooping the flesh out with a small teaspoon.

the oil in a large frying pan. When the oil is hot, pour in the eggs and stir with a spatula for about 2-3 minutes, or until the eggs are cooked but not completely set. Sprinkle over the tomato strips and cook until just heated through. Sprinkle with chopped parsley, if desired, before serving.

Cook's Notes

Time
Preparation takes about 25 minutes, cooking about 2-3 minutes.

Preparation
Tomatoes may be prepared well in advance and kept in the refrigerator, tightly covered.

Serving Ideas
This omelet is usually served in the frying pan it was cooked in. Alternatively, cut into wedges to serve.

Variation
One clove of garlic, crushed, may be added to the egg mixture if desired.

SERVES 4

TARAMASALATA

This is a classic Greek appetizer, luxurious
in taste and texture. It is also a
delicious dip for vegetable crudités.

2oz smoked cod's roe
6 slices white bread, crusts removed
1 small onion, finely chopped
1 lemon
6 tbsps olive oil
Black olives and chopped parsley for garnishing

1. Cut the cod's roe in half and scrape the center into a bowl, food processor or blender. Discard the skin. Soak the bread in a bowl of water to soften.

2. Squeeze most of the water from the bread and add it to the roe. Squeeze the lemon and add the juice to the roe and bread, straining to remove the seeds. Add the onion and process until the ingredients form a smooth paste, or beat very well with a wooden spoon.

3. Gradually beat in the oil a drop at a time as if making mayonnaise. If using a blender, it is best to make the Taramasalata in two batches.

4. When all the oil has been added, spoon the Taramasalata into a bowl and chill slightly before serving. Sprinkle with chopped parsley and garnish with black olives.

Step 1 Remove the soft insides of the smoked cod's roe by cutting it in half and scraping with a spoon. Discard the skin.

Step 2 Squeeze the bread to remove excess moisture.

Step 3 Add the oil gradually, drop by drop, beating well continuously, or with the blender or food processor running.

Cook's Notes

Time
Preparation takes about 15 minutes using a blender or food processor and about 25 minutes if beating by hand.

Preparation
If prepared in advance, remove from the refrigerator about 20 minutes before serving.

Watchpoint
Do not add the oil too quickly or the mixture will curdle. If it does, add a bit more soaked bread and it should come together.

Cook's Tip
Home-made taramasalata is not as pink as that bought commercially.

Variation
If desired, substitute garlic for the onion.

Serving Ideas
Warm pitta bread or toast makes a good accompaniment.

SERVES 6-12

SPINACH AND CHEESE PIE

Traditionally made at Easter, this classic
Greek pie is now enjoyed all year round.
Packaged pastry makes it simplicity itself.

1lb package fyllo pastry
1 cup butter, melted
2lbs fresh spinach
3 tbsps olive oil
2 onions, finely chopped
3 tbsps chopped fresh dill
Salt and pepper
3 eggs, slightly beaten
2 cups feta cheese, crumbled

1. Preheat the oven to 375°F. Unfold the pastry on a flat surface and cut it to fit the size of the baking dish to be used. Keep the pastry covered.

2. Tear the stalks off the spinach and wash the leaves well. Shred the leaves with a sharp knife.

3. Heat the oil in a large sauté pan and cook the onions until soft. Add the spinach and stir over a medium heat for about 5 minutes. Turn up the heat to evaporate any moisture.

4. Allow the spinach and onions to cool. Mix in the dill, eggs, salt, pepper, and cheese.

5. Melt the butter and brush the baking dish on the bottom and sides. Brush top sheet of fyllo pastry and place it in the dish. Brush another sheet and place that on top of the first. Repeat to make 8 layers of pastry.

6. Spread on the filling and cover the top with 6 or 7 layers

Step 2 Before washing the spinach, cut off the stalks by holding the leaves firmly and pulling the stems backwards.

Step 5 To assemble the pie, butter the base and sides of the dish and then brush each layer of pastry before stacking them up in the dish.

of pastry, brushing each layer with melted butter. Brush the top layer well and score the pastry in square or diamond shapes. Do not cut through to the bottom layer.

7. Sprinkle with water and bake for 40 minutes or until crisp and golden.

8. Leave the pie to stand for about 10 minutes and then cut through the scoring completely to the bottom layer. Lift out the pieces to a serving dish.

Cook's Notes

Serving Ideas
Serve hot or cold. If serving cold, use olive oil to brush the pastry instead of butter. Serves 6 as a main course, 12 as first course.

Buying Guide
Pastry is available fresh or frozen in large supermarkets or specialty shops.

Time
Preparation takes about 25 minutes, cooking about 40 minutes.

Preparation
The pie can be cooked in advance and reheated for 10 minutes to serve hot.

Cook's Tip
Pastry will go a little soggy when prepared more than a day in advance.

SERVES 6

SAVORY FILLED PIES

Packaged pastry makes these pies very
easy. They make excellent appetizers,
snacks or light meals with a salad.

8oz package fyllo pastry
¾ cup butter, melted
8oz sprue (thin asparagus)
4oz feta cheese
½ cup plain yogurt
2 eggs, beaten
3 green onions, finely chopped
1 tbsp chopped mint
Salt and pepper

1. Use a patty tin with 12 spaces or use 12 ramekin dishes. Cut the pastry in squares large enough to fill the pans or dishes, with enough to overlap the tops by about 1 inch.

2. Layer 3 sheets of pastry, each brushed with melted butter. Cut into 3 inch squares and stack 3 squares, turning each slightly to make a frilled edge. Carefully push the pastry into buttered patty tins or ramekins and keep covered while preparing the filling.

3. Cut the sprue into 1 inch pieces, leaving the tips whole. Cook in boiling salted water until just tender. Rinse under cold water and allow to drain completely. Mix together thoroughly the cheese, yogurt, eggs, onions, mint, salt and pepper. Stir in the drained sprue and fill the pastry to within ½ inch of the top.

4. Bake in a preheated 375°F oven for about 25 minutes or until the pastry is crisp and golden and the filling is set and risen. Allow to cool for about 10 minutes and then remove to a serving dish.

To chop spring onions quickly, cut several into quarters lengthwise and then cut crosswise into small pieces using a very sharp knife.

Step 2 Fill patty tins or ramekin dishes with the prepared pastry to form tartlet cases.

Step 3 The cheese should still be fairly chunky when all the filling ingredients are mixed.

Cook's Notes

Variation
Use spinach instead of asparagus. Cook the spinach briefly and drain it well before combining with the filling ingredients. Substitute other herbs for mint, if desired.

Time
Preparation takes about 30 minutes, cooking takes about 25 minutes.

Cook's Tip
If prepared in advance, reheat for about 5 minutes to serve. The pies can also be served cold.

SERVES 6-8

DOLMADES

In Greece, stuffed vine leaves are not
served with a tomato sauce. Try a light
egg-lemon sauce or plain yogurt instead.

8oz fresh vine leaves or leaves packed in brine
6oz long-grain rice, cooked
8 green onions, finely chopped
1½ tbsps chopped fresh dill
3 tbsps chopped fresh mint
1 tbsp chopped fresh parsley
½ cup pine nuts
½ cup currants
Salt and pepper
½ cup olive oil
Juice of 1 lemon

1. If using fresh vine leaves, put them into boiling water for
about 1 minute. Remove them and drain. If using preserved
vine leaves, rinse them and then place in a bowl of hot water
for 5 minutes to soak. Strain and pat dry.

2. Mix together all the remaining ingredients except the
olive oil and lemon juice. Taste the filling and adjust the
seasoning if necessary.

3. Spread the vine leaves out on a flat surface, vein side
upwards. Cut off the stems and place about 2 tsps of filling
on each leaf, pressing it into a sausage shape.

4. Fold the sides of the leaves over to partially cover the
stuffing and roll up as for a jelly roll. Place the rolls seam side
down in a large saucepan. Pour over the olive oil and lemon
juice.

Step 3 Spread
the leaves out on
a flat surface.
Place spoonfuls of
stuffing on the
leaves and make
into a sausage
shape.

Step 4 Fold the
sides over the
filling and roll up
the leaves.

5. Pour hot water over the rolls until it comes about halfway
up their sides. Place a plate on top of the rolls to keep them
in place, cover the pan and cook slowly for about 40
minutes.

6. Remove the Dolmades to a serving plate and accompany with lemon wedges, black olives and plain yogurt if
desired.

Cook's Notes

 Time
Preparation takes about 30
minutes, cooking takes about
40 minutes.

 Serving Ideas
Dolmades may be served
either hot or cold, and are
ideal for picnics.

 Variation
Other ingredients may be
used in the filling. Substitute
chopped olives, almonds or chopped
cooked lamb.

 **Preparation**
Dolmades may be prepared a
day before serving. Leave in
their liquid in the refrigerator and reheat
just before serving.

SERVES 4

GREEK COUNTRY SALAD

Lettuce is cut finely for salads
in Greece. In fact, the finer the shreds of lettuce
the better the salad is considered to be.

2 tbsps olive oil
1 tbsp lemon juice
Salt and ground black pepper
1 clove garlic, crushed
1 Romaine lettuce, well washed
3 tomatoes, sliced
3oz black olives
1 cup feta cheese, diced
½ red pepper, seeded, cored, and sliced
6 peperonata
Fresh or dried oregano

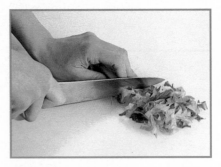

Step 2 To shred the lettuce leaves more quickly, stack them up and use a sharp knife to shred 5 or 6 leaves at a time.

Step 3 Use a serrated fruit knife or a bread knife to make the tomatoes easier to slice and the slices neater looking.

Step 1 If a thick dressing is desired, first whisk the lemon juice, salt, pepper and garlic together in a small bowl and then add the oil gradually, whisking constantly.

1. Whisk the oil, lemon juice, salt, pepper and garlic together until well emulsified. A blender or food processor may be used for this.

2. Stack up 5 or 6 lettuce leaves and shred them finely with a sharp knife.

3. Place the lettuce in the bottom of a serving dish and arrange the other ingredients on top. Spoon over the dressing and sprinkle on the oregano.

Cook's Notes

$ **Buying Guide**
Peperonata are small whole peppers preserved in brine. They can be bought bottled in delicatessens and some supermarkets.

Variation
Substitute green pepper for red pepper if desired. Other varieties of lettuce may also be used.

 Time
Preparation takes about 10-15 minutes.

SERVES 4

STUFFED TOMATOES

In Greece, stuffed vegetables are
often cooked in olive oil and no
other liquid except the natural juices.

4 large beefsteak tomatoes
6oz cooked rice
2 tsps chopped oregano
1 clove garlic, crushed
2 hard-boiled eggs
4 tbsps feta cheese, grated
1oz black olives, chopped
Salt and pepper
Olive oil

1. Preheat the oven 375°F. Choose tomatoes with nice looking stems and leaves. Cut about 1 inch off the top of each tomato on the stem end. Reserve the tops. Scoop out the pulp and seeds with a small teaspoon into a strainer. Sieve and reserve the juice and pulp.

2. Chop the egg using an egg slicer or a food processor. Mix all the stuffing ingredients together and add some of the reserved tomato pulp and juice.

3. Stuff the tomatoes and place on the caps, leaving some stuffing showing around the edges. Place the tomatoes in a baking dish.

4. Drizzle olive oil over the tops of the tomatoes and bake for about 20 minutes, depending on the ripeness of the tomatoes. Transfer to a serving dish and serve hot or cold.

Step 1 Cut the top off of each tomato on the stem end. Scoop out the pulp and seeds with a small teaspoon or use a serrated grapefruit knife.

Step 2 To chop an egg using an egg slicer, place the egg in the slicer and cut down into rounds.

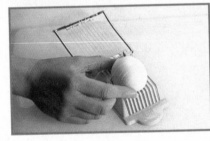

Step 2 Carefully remove the egg, replace it in the slicer and cut down lengthwise.

Cook's Notes

Variation
Mix the filling ingredients with oil and lemon juice. Stuff the tomatoes and serve them cold.

Time
Preparation takes about 30 minutes, cooking takes about 20 minutes.

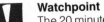

Watchpoint
The 20 minute cooking time is just a guide. Watch the tomatoes carefully – they will fall apart easily if overcooked.

Cook's Tip
Keep the hard-boiled eggs in cold water until ready to use. This prevents a grey ring from forming around the yolk.

STUFFED ZUCCHINI

When stuffed vegetables are served with a sauce
in Greece, it is usually a lemon-egg mixture.
Try the sauce with peppers or vine leaves, too.

4 medium-sized zucchini
2 tbsps butter or margarine
1 small onion, finely chopped
4oz ground lamb or beef
1 tsp ground cumin
1 tsp chopped oregano
2 tsps chopped fresh parsley
2 tsps chopped fresh fennel
2oz cooked long-grain rice
2 tbsps grated cheese
Salt and pepper

Egg and Lemon Sauce

2 egg yolks
1 lemon
Salt and pepper

Step 1 Once the zucchini are washed, topped and tailed, cut off a thin strip of skin lengthwise, then hollow out zucchini using a swivel vegetable peeler.

Step 4 Pile the stuffing into the hollowed-out zucchini using a teaspoon.

1. Wash the zucchini well and top and tail them. Using a swivel vegetable peeler, apple corer or a small baller, scoop the middle out of the zucchini, being careful not to damage the outer skins. Leave a thin margin of flesh on the inside for support. Alternatively, slice lengthwise and scoop out the middle.

2. Place the zucchini in boiling salted water and parboil for about 2 minutes. Rinse immediately in cold water and leave to drain. Meanwhile, chop parsley using a large, sharp knife.

3. Prepare the stuffing by softening the onions in half of the butter until they are just transparent. Add the meat and cook until just beginning to brown. Chop up reserved zucchini flesh and add it to the meat. Mix with the remaining stuffing ingredients.

4. Mix the stuffing well and fill the hollow in each zucchini using a small teaspoon.

5. Melt the remaining butter in a large frying pan or sauté pan and, when foaming, place in the zucchini in a single layer. Add water to the pan to come halfway up the sides of the vegetables and cover the pan. Cook over gentle heat for about 20 minutes, basting the zucchini occasionally. Add more water during cooking as necessary.

6. When the zucchini are tender, remove them to a serving dish and keep them warm. Reserve about 4-6 tbsps of the liquid in the pan.

7. To prepare the sauce, beat the egg yolks and the lemon juice together until slightly thickened. Add some of the hot cooking liquid to the eggs and lemon juice and then return the mixture to a small saucepan. Cook over gentle heat, whisking constantly until slightly thickened. Strain over the zucchini before serving. Garnish with sprigs of fresh herbs if desired.

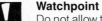

Cook's Notes

Serving Ideas
Stuffed vegetables may be served as a first dish or side dish. The zucchini may be served cold without the sauce.

Watchpoint
Do not allow the sauce to boil once the eggs have been added; it will curdle.

Time
Preparation takes about 30 minutes, cooking takes about 20 minutes.

SERVES 4
STUFFED EGGPLANT

In Greece eggplant are hollowed out from
one end and stuffed. Our recipe employs the
easy method of cutting them in half.

2 small eggplants
2 tbsps butter or margarine
1 small onion, finely chopped
1 clove garlic, crushed
5oz long-grain rice, cooked
2 tsps oregano
Pinch cinnamon
Salt and pepper
4oz tomatoes, peeled, seeded and
    coarsely chopped

1. Preheat oven to 350°F. Wrap eggplants in paper or foil
and bake for 20 minutes to soften. Allow to cool, cut in half
and scoop out the pulp leaving a ½ inch border to form a
shell.

2. Melt butter or margarine and add the onion and garlic.

Step 1 Cut the
cooked eggplants
in half and scoop
out the pulp with
a spoon or melon
baller.

Step 1 Leave a
layer of pulp on
the inside of the
skin to form a
shell.

Step 2 Chop the
pulp roughly
before adding to
the onions.

Cook to soften slightly. Chop the eggplant pulp roughly
and add to the pan. Cook for about 5 minutes and then add
the remaining ingredients.

3. Fill the eggplant shells and place them in an ovenproof
dish or on a baking sheet. Bake an additional 20 minutes in
the oven. Garnish with chopped parsley or other herbs if
desired.

Cook's Notes

Time
Preparation takes about 25
minutes, cooking takes about
40 minutes.

Preparation
Pre-cooking the eggplant
makes it easier to remove
the pulp.

Variation
The eggplants may be
sprinkled with dry
breadcrumbs and drizzled with olive oil
before baking. Add cheese to the filling
if desired.

Serving Ideas
Serve the eggplants hot or
cold as a first course or a
vegetable side dish.

SERVES 4

STUFFED PEPPERS

Stuffed vegetables are very popular in Mediterranean countries. The addition of lamb to the stuffing makes these a meal in themselves.

4 medium-sized red or green peppers
½ cup olive oil
1 small onion, finely chopped
8oz ground lamb or beef
1 tbsp chopped fresh dill
2 tsps chopped fresh coriander
2 tsps lemon juice
Grated rind of half a lemon
Salt and pepper
½ cup grated cheese
4oz long-grain rice, cooked

1. Wash the peppers and place them in a pan of boiling water. Parboil for about 3 minutes and allow to drain and cool.

2. Cut about 1 inch off the tops and remove the core and seeds. Trim the bottoms of the peppers so that they will stand upright.

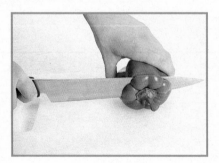

Step 2 Cut the tops off the peppers, but leave the stems attached.

Step 2 Remove the core and seeds, with a teaspoon or small knife. If necessary, rinse to remove all the seeds.

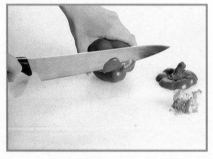

Step 2 Slice a thin piece off the bottoms of the peppers so that they will stand level while cooking.

3. Heat 2 tbsps of the oil and cook the onions briefly. Add the lamb and cook until beginning to brown. Add the remaining filling ingredients and stuff the peppers. Put on the tops.

4. Stand the peppers upright close together in a baking dish. Pour over the remaining oil and add enough water to come halfway up the sides of the peppers. Cook 40-45 minutes or until the peppers are tender, basting often. Remove the peppers to a serving dish with a slotted spoon.

Cook's Notes

Preparation
Parboiling the peppers helps to speed up their cooking and makes it easier to remove the core and seeds.

Serving Ideas
Serve the peppers either hot or cold, as a first course or a vegetable side dish.

SERVES 4

OKRA CASSEROLE

This vegetable has always been popular in
Mediterranean cookery and is becoming easier
to find in supermarkets and greengrocers.

4 tbsps olive oil
1 small onion, sliced
8oz okra
6 ripe tomatoes, peeled and quartered
Juice of half a lemon
Salt and pepper
Chopped parsley

1. Heat the olive oil in a sauté pan and cook the onion until soft but not colored.

2. Remove just the stems from the okra, but leave on the tops and tails.

To slice onions, peel and cut in half lengthwise. Place cut side down on chopping board and use a sharp knife to cut across in thin slices.

Cook the onion in the olive oil until soft and transparent.

Step 2 Trim the stems from the tops of the okra, but do not top and tail.

3. Add the okra to the pan and cook for 10 minutes. Add remaining ingredients and cook to heat the tomatoes through. Spoon into a serving dish and serve hot or cold with lamb or chicken.

Cook's Notes

Variation
Substitute canned okra, but drain and rinse before use. Cut the cooking time in half. Green beans may be used instead of okra.

Preparation
If too much liquid is left at the end of cooking, remove the vegetables and boil to reduce the sauce.

Cook's Tip
Okra only needs brief cooking or it will become soggy.

SERVES 4

ZUCCHINI AND RED PEPPER SALAD

Salad dressing in Greece is most commonly made from olive oil and lemon juice instead of vinegar.

1½ lbs very small zucchini
1 red pepper, cored, seeded and thinly sliced
6 tbsps olive oil
Juice and zest of 1 small lemon
Fresh basil
Salt and pepper
Pinch sugar
Whole basil leaves for garnish

1. Top and tail the zucchini. Use a cannelle knife to remove strips of peel from the zucchini. Cut the zucchini in half. If using baby zucchini, top and tail, but leave whole.

2. Place the zucchini and red pepper in boiling salted water and cook for 2 minutes. Allow to drain.

3. Strip the zest from the lemons with a zester. Alternatively, use a swivel peeler to take off strips and then cut the peel in very fine shreds. Blanch for 2 minutes.

4. Mix the oil, lemon juice, chopped basil, salt and pepper and sugar, if desired. Pour over the vegetables while they are still warm and sprinkle with the lemon zest. Garnish with whole basil leaves.

Step 3 Use a lemon zester to make thin strips of lemon peel.

Step 3 As an alternative method, use a swivel peeler to remove thin strips of peel and then cut into thin shreds.

Step 4 Mix the oil, lemon juice, basil, sugar, salt and pepper together well and pour over the warm vegetables.

Cook's Notes

Cook's Tip
If serving the salad cold, rinse the vegetables under cold running water and leave to drain thoroughly

Time
Preparation takes about 25 minutes, cooking takes about 2 minutes.

Serving Ideas
Serve as a side salad, first course, or part of an hors d'oeuvre selection.

SERVES 4

CAULIFLOWER AND OLIVES

Kalamata, where this dish is said to
have originated, is an area of Greece
well known for its black olives.

1 large cauliflower
4 tbsps olive oil
1 onion, cut in rings
½ cup water
Juice of half a lemon
3 tbsps tomato paste
Salt and pepper
3oz black olives
2 tbsps chopped parsley

1. Trim the leaves from the cauliflower and remove the core. Cut into medium sized pieces.

2. Heat the oil and sauté the cauliflower for 1-2 minutes. Remove to a plate and add the onion to the pan. Cook to soften and add the water and lemon juice. Bring to the boil and return the cauliflower to the pan. Cook until tender.

Step 1 Trim the leaves from the cauliflower and remove the core with a small, sharp knife. Cut the flowerets into even-sized pieces

Step 2 When cutting an onion into rings, pierce with a fork and hold the handle to keep the onion steady while slicing.

Step 4 To pit olives, use a cherry pitter or roll them firmly on a flat surface to loosen the stones, then use a swivel peeler to remove them.

3. Remove the cauliflower to a serving dish and add the tomato paste to the liquid and boil to reduce.

4. Pit the olives, chop them roughly and add to the pan. Pour the sauce over the cauliflower and sprinkle with chopped parsley to serve.

Cook's Notes

Cook's Tip
A bay leaf may be added to the water while cooking the cauliflower. This reduces the cauliflower smell.

Variation
Add strips of tomato pulp with the olives if desired. Green olives may be substituted for black.

Time
Preparation takes about 25 minutes, cooking takes about 20 minutes.

SERVES 4-6

PEAS AND ARTICHOKES

Fresh peas are a springtime delicacy in
Greece. They are well worth the effort
of shelling for their taste and texture.

2lbs fresh peas
Juice of 1 lemon
Pinch sugar
2 tbsps chopped fresh dill
2 tbsps olive oil
1 small bunch green onions
1 can artichoke hearts, drained
Salt and pepper

1. Shell the peas and put them into boiling salted water with the lemon juice, a pinch of sugar and the dill. Cover and cook for about 20 minutes, or until the peas are tender. Drain and keep warm.

2. Trim the root ends from the green onions and trim down

Step 1 To shell peas, break off stem ends and pull down strings.

Step 1 Press open the pods and push out the peas with finger or thumb.

Step 2 Trim the root ends from the green onions and about 1 inch of the green tops. If the onions are very large, cut in half lengthwise.

the green tops leaving about 1 inch green attached. Heat the olive oil in a saucepan or sauté pan and cook the onions to soften. Cut the artichoke hearts into halves or quarters and add to the onions.

3. Add the peas, salt and pepper and cook for 5 minutes. Serve immediately.

Cook's Notes

Variation
Add peeled and seeded tomatoes, roughly chopped, during the last 5 minutes of cooking. Frozen peas may be substituted for fresh ones, and the cooking time reduced by half.

Cook's Tip
A pinch of sugar added to peas while cooking brings out their flavor.

Serving Ideas
Serve as a vegetable side dish with chicken or lamb.

SERVES 4-6

LEMON CHICKEN

Chicken, lemon and basil is an ideal flavor combination
and one that is used often in Greek cookery.

3lb chicken, jointed
2 tbsps olive oil
2 tbsps butter or margarine
1 small onion, cut in thin strips
2 sticks celery, shredded
2 carrots, cut in julienne strips
1 tbsp chopped fresh basil
1 bay leaf
Juice and grated rind of 2 small lemons
½ cup water
Salt and pepper
Pinch sugar (optional)
Lemon slices for garnishing

1. Heat the oil in a large sauté pan. Add the butter or margarine and, when foaming, place in the chicken, skin side down, in one layer. Brown and turn over. Brown the other side. Cook the chicken in two batches if necessary. Remove the chicken to a plate and set aside.

2. Add the vegetables and cook 2-3 minutes over a moderate heat. Add the basil, bay leaf, lemon juice and rind, water, salt and pepper and replace the chicken. Bring the mixture to the boil.

3. Cover the pan and reduce the heat. Allow to simmer about 35-45 minutes or until the chicken is tender and the juices run clear when the thighs are pierced with a fork.

4. Remove the chicken and vegetables to a serving dish and discard the bay leaf. The sauce should be thick, so boil

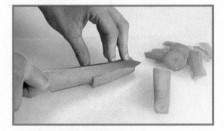

To cut the onion in thin strips, first cut in half through the root end. Using a sharp knife, follow the natural lines in the onion and cut through neatly to the flat base. Cut off the root end and the onion will fall apart in strips.

To make the carrots easier to cut into julienne strips, first cut them into rectangular blocks.

Cut the carrot blocks into thin slices and then stack them up to cut into strips quickly.

to reduce if necessary. If the sauce is too tart, add a pinch of sugar. Spoon the sauce over the chicken to serve and garnish with the lemon slices.

Cook's Notes

Watchpoint
Pat the chicken with paper towels to make sure it is really dry or it will spit when browning.

Variation
Use limes instead of lemons and oregano instead of basil.

Serving Ideas
There is a flat, square shaped pasta in Greece that is often served with chicken dishes. Rice is also a good accompaniment, along with a green salad.

Time
Preparation takes about 30 minutes, cooking takes about 45-55 minutes total, including browning of chicken.

SERVES 4-6

CHICKEN WITH OLIVES

This is a chicken sauté dish for
olive lovers. Use more or less of
them as your own taste dictates.

3lb chicken, jointed
2 tbsps olive oil
2 tbsps butter or margarine
1 clove garlic, crushed
½ cup white wine
½ cup chicken stock
Salt and pepper
2 tbsps chopped parsley
20 pitted black and green olives
4 zucchini, cut in ½ inch pieces

1. Heat the oil in a large sauté pan and add the butter or margarine. When foaming, add the chicken skin side down in one layer. Brown one side of the chicken and turn over to brown the other side. Cook the chicken in two batches if necessary.

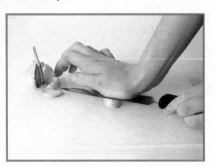

To peel a garlic clove easily, first crush it gently with the side of a large knife. The peel will split, making it easier to remove.

To cut the zucchini quickly into chunks, first top and tail them, then cut them in half if small, or quarters if large, lengthwise. Gather the strips together and cut crosswise into chunks of the desired size.

Step 1 Cook the chicken, skin side down first, until golden brown.

2. Turn the chicken skin side up and add the garlic, wine, stock, salt and pepper. Bring to the boil, cover the pan and allow to simmer over gentle heat for about 30-35 minutes.

3. Add the zucchini and cook 10 minutes. Once the chicken and zucchini are done, add the olives and cook to heat through. Add the parsley and remove to a dish to serve.

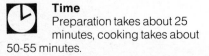

Cook's Notes

Time
Preparation takes about 25 minutes, cooking takes about 50-55 minutes.

 Serving Ideas
Serve with rice or pasta and tomato salad.

 Variation
Artichoke hearts may be used in place of the zucchini.

SERVES 4

MARINATED CHICKEN WITH WALNUT SAUCE

Offer your guests a walnut sauce that tastes
delicious and is very easy to make.

2 2lb chickens, cut in half
½ cup olive oil
Juice and grated rind of 2 lemons
1 tbsp chopped fresh oregano
Pinch ground cumin
1 tbsp chopped fresh parsley
2 tsps chopped fresh thyme
Salt and pepper
Pinch sugar

Walnut Sauce

2 cloves garlic, peeled and roughly chopped
4 slices bread, crusts removed and soaked in water for 10
　　minutes
2 tbsps white wine vinegar
Salt and pepper
4-5 tbsps olive oil
1-2 tbsps water (optional)
¾ cup ground walnuts

Step 1 Remove the backbone from the chickens using a pair of sharp poultry shears or a cleaver.

Step 1 Cut away some of the ribcage to make the chickens easier to flatten with a meat mallet or rolling pin.

1.　Remove the backbones from the chickens with poultry shears. Bend the legs backwards to break the ball and socket joint. Cut away some of the ribcage with a sharp knife. Flatten the chickens slightly with a meat mallet or rolling pin. Mix together the marinating ingredients in a large, shallow dish or a large plastic bag. Place in the chicken and turn to coat. If using a plastic bag, fasten securely and place in a dish to catch any drips. Refrigerate for at least 4 hours or overnight.

2.　Place the chicken on a broiler pan and cook under low heat for about 30 minutes, basting frequently. Raise the

heat and cook for a further 10 minutes, skin side up, to brown nicely.

3.　Meanwhile, place the garlic in a food processor and squeeze the bread to remove the water. Add the bread to the food processor along with the vinegar. With the machine running, pour the oil through the funnel in a thin, steady stream. Add water if necessary to bring the sauce to coating consistency. Add salt and pepper and stir in the walnuts by hand. When the chicken is cooked, remove it to a serving dish and pour over any remaining marinade. Serve with the walnut sauce.

Cook's Notes

Cook's Tip
If broiler does not have an adjustable setting, pre-cook the chicken in the oven for about 30 minutes and then broil for the remaining time until done.

Serving Ideas
Garnish with lemon wedges and sprigs of parsley or other fresh herbs, if desired. Serve with rice and a green or tomato salad.

Time
Preparation takes about 30 minutes plus marinating time, cooking takes about 40 minutes.

SERVES 4-6

MOUSSAKA

There are many different recipes for this casserole dish. This one is light, with no potatoes and a soufflé-like topping.

2 large eggplant, thinly sliced
Oil for frying
2 tbsps butter or margarine
2 onions, thinly sliced
1 clove garlic, crushed
1lb ground lamb
14oz canned tomatoes
2 tbsps tomato paste
Salt and pepper
2 tsps chopped oregano
¼ tsp ground cinnamon
¼ tsp ground cumin

White Sauce

4 tbsps butter or margarine
4 tbsps flour
2 cups milk
Salt and white pepper
2 tbsps grated cheese
2 eggs, separated

Topping

4 tbsps finely grated cheese
4 tbsps dry breadcrumbs

Step 5 To assemble the Moussaka, layer up the meat and eggplants, ending with an even layer of eggplants on top.

their juice, tomato paste, oregano, spices, salt and pepper. Bring to the boil, cover the pan and allow to simmer over gentle heat for 20 minutes.

3. To prepare the white sauce, melt the butter in a deep saucepan and stir in the flour off the heat. Gradually pour in the milk and add a pinch of salt and pepper. Whisk or beat well and return the pan to the heat. Cook over moderate heat, stirring continuously until thickened. Add the cheese and allow the sauce to cool slightly. Beat the egg yolks with one spoonful of the hot sauce and then gradually add to the sauce.

4. Whip the egg whites until stiff peaks form and fold a spoonful into the hot sauce mixture. Make sure it is thoroughly incorporated and then gently fold in the remaining egg whites.

5. Layer the meat mixture and the eggplant slices in an ovenproof casserole, ending with a layer of eggplant. Spoon the white sauce on top and sprinkle on the topping of cheese and breadcrumbs. Cook for about 45 minutes to 1 hour or until the topping has risen slightly and formed a golden crust on top. Allow to stand for about 5 minutes before serving to make cutting easier.

1. Preheat the oven to 350°F. Heat the oil in a large frying pan and fry the eggplant slices for about 3 minutes. Remove them and drain on paper towels.

2. Pour the oil from the pan and melt the butter or margarine. Fry the onion and garlic for about 4 minutes, or until golden brown. Add the lamb and cook for about 10 minutes, breaking up well with a fork. Add the tomatoes and

Cook's Notes

Cook's Tip
If preparing and assembling the moussaka in advance, add whole eggs to the white sauce and omit the separate whisking of egg whites.

Economy
Use left-over roast lamb, minced in a food processor or cut into small dice by hand.

Time
Preparation takes about 30 minutes, cooking takes about 45 minutes to 1 hour.

SERVES 4

LAMB KEBABS

Meat kebabs are the typical Greek dish and these have all the characteristic flavors — oregano, garlic, lemon and olive oil.

1½lbs lean lamb from the leg or neck fillet
Juice of 1 large lemon
6 tbsps olive oil
1 clove garlic, crushed
1 tbsp chopped fresh oregano
1 tbsp chopped fresh thyme
Salt and pepper
2 medium-sized onions
Fresh bay leaves

1. Trim the meat of excess fat and cut it into 2 inch cubes. Mix together the remaining ingredients except the bay leaves and the onions. Pour the mixture into a shallow dish or into a large plastic bag.

2. Place the meat in the dish or the bag with the marinade and turn to coat completely. If using a bag, tie securely and place in a dish to catch any drips. Leave to marinate for at least four hours, or overnight.

Step 1 Cut the meat into even-sized cubes.

Step 2 Marinade may be poured into a plastic bag. Add the meat, tie the bag securely and shake gently to coat the meat completely. Place the bag in a dish to catch any drips.

Step 3 Thread the meat and bay leaves onto skewers and slip the onion rings over the meat.

3. To assemble the kebabs, remove the meat from the marinade and thread onto skewers, alternating with the fresh bay leaves.

4. Slice the onions into rings and slip the rings over the meat on the skewers.

5. Place the kebabs on the broiler pan and broil for about 3 minutes per side under a preheated broiler. Baste the kebabs often. Alternatively, grill over hot coals. Pour over any remaining marinade to serve.

Cook's Notes

Time
Preparation takes about 20 minutes plus marinating time. Cooking takes about 3 minutes per side, but will vary according to desired doneness.

Variation
Rump or sirloin steak may be used in place of the lamb. The cooking time will have to be increased, but cook until desired doneness is reached.

Serving Ideas
A Greek country salad and rice make good accompaniments. Kebabs may also be served with stuffed vegetables.

SERVES 6-8

LAMB WITH PASTA AND TOMATOES

Lamb appears in many different guises in Greek cuisine;
this recipe offers a delicious blend of subtle tastes.

1 leg or shoulder of lamb
2 cloves garlic, peeled and cut into thin slivers
4 tbsps olive oil
1lb fresh tomatoes or 14oz canned tomatoes
1 tbsp chopped fresh oregano
Salt and pepper
2 cups lamb or beef stock or water
8oz pasta shells, spirals or other shapes
Finely grated Parmesan cheese

1. Cut slits at about 2 inch intervals all over the lamb. Insert small slivers of garlic into each slit. Place the lamb in a large baking dish and rub the surface with the olive oil.

2. Cook in a preheated oven at 425°F for about 50 minutes, basting occasionally.

3. Meanwhile, parboil the pasta for about 5 minutes and rinse in hot water to remove the starch.

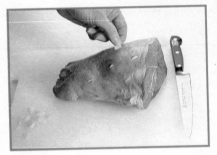

Step 1 Cut slits at intervals all over the lamb with a small, sharp knife. Insert slivers of garlic into each cut.

Step 4 Mix the tomatoes with oregano, salt and pepper and pour over the lamb.

Step 4 Once the pasta is added to the lamb, take the dish out of the oven occasionally and stir so that the pasta cooks evenly.

4. Turn the meat over and add the stock or water, pasta and additional seasoning. Mix the tomatoes with the oregano, salt and pepper and pour over the lamb. Stir well. Cook an additional 20-30 minutes, stirring the pasta occasionally to ensure even cooking.

5. When the pasta is completely cooked, turn the lamb over again and sprinkle with cheese to serve. Serve directly from the dish or transfer to a large, deep serving plate.

Cook's Notes

Cook's Tip
If the meat reaches desired doneness before the pasta is cooked, remove it to a serving plate and keep it warm. Continue cooking the pasta, covering the dish to speed things up.

Variation
The dish can be made without tomatoes, if desired. Beef can be substituted for the lamb and the cooking time increased.

Time
Preparation takes about 20 minutes, cooking takes about 1 hour 35 minutes.

SERVES 4

FRIED FISH WITH GARLIC SAUCE

Fish in such an attractive shape makes an
excellent first course.

2lbs fresh anchovies or whitebait
1 cup of all-purpose flour
4-6 tbsps cold water
Pinch salt
Oil for frying

Garlic Sauce

4 slices bread, crusts trimmed, soaked in water for 10
   minutes
4 cloves garlic, peeled and roughly chopped
2 tbsps lemon juice
4-5 tbsps olive oil
1-2 tbsps water (optional)
Salt and pepper
2 tsps chopped fresh parsley
Lemon wedges for garnishing (optional)

1. Sift the flour into a deep bowl with a pinch of salt.
Gradually stir in the water in the amount needed to make a
very thick batter.

2. Heat enough oil for frying in a large, deep pan. A deep-
sided sauté pan is ideal.

3. Take 3 fish at a time and dip them into the batter together.
Press their tails together firmly to make a fan shape.

4. Lower them carefully into the oil. Fry in several batches
until crisp and golden. Continue in the same way with all the
remaining fish.

Step 3 Dip three
fish at a time into
the batter and
when coated
press the tails
together firmly to
form a fan shape.

Step 4 Lower the
fish carefully into
the hot oil to
preserve the
shape.

5. Meanwhile, squeeze out the bread and place in a food
processor with the garlic and lemon juice. With the processor running, add the oil in a thin, steady stream. Add
water if the mixture is too thick and dry. Add salt and pepper
and stir in the parsley by hand. When all the fish are cooked,
sprinkle lightly with salt and arrange on serving plates with
some of the garlic sauce and lemon wedges, if desired.

Cook's Notes

Time
Preparation takes about 30
minutes, cooking takes about
3 minutes per batch for the fish.

Preparation
Coat the fish in the batter just
before ready for frying.

Cook's Tip
The fish should be eaten
immediately after frying. If it is
necessary to keep the fish warm, place
them on a wire cooling rack covered
with paper towels in a slow oven with
the door open. Sprinkling fried food
lightly with salt helps to absorb excess
fat.

Variation
Fish may be dipped in the
batter and fried singly if
desired. Other fish, such as smelt or
sardines, may also be used. Use thin
strips of cod or halibut as well. Vary the
amount of garlic in the sauce to your
own taste.

SERVES 4
BAKED RED MULLET WITH GARLIC AND TOMATOES

This is a fish that appears often in Mediterranean cookery.

4 even-sized red mullet
3 tbsps olive oil
3 tbsps dry white wine
1 lemon
2 cloves garlic, crushed
Salt and pepper
12oz fresh tomatoes, thinly sliced or 14oz canned
    tomatoes, strained
Sprigs of fresh dill for garnish

1. Preheat the oven to 375°F. First scale the fish by running the blunt edge of a large knife over the skin of the fish going from the tail to the head.

2. Using a filleting knife, cut along the belly of the fish from just under the head to the vent, the small opening near the tail. Clean out the cavity of the fish, leaving in the liver if desired. Rinse the fish well inside and out and pat dry.

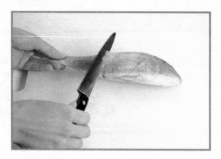

Step 1 To scale the fish, hold it by the tail and run the blunt side of a knife down the length of the body from the tail to the head.

Step 2 To gut the fish, cut with a filleting knife from just under the head to the vent and remove the insides of the fish.

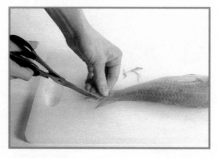

Step 3 Rinse the fish well under cold running water and, using kitchen scissors, trim the tail and fins.

3. Trim the fins and neaten the tail with kitchen scissors. Place the fish head to tail in an ovenproof dish. Mix the oil and the wine together and squeeze the juice from one of the lemons. Add the garlic, salt and pepper and pour over the fish. Place on the tomato slices or if using canned tomatoes, crush them slightly and spoon over. Bake for about 25 minutes, basting frequently until the fish is tender. Garnish with dill.

Cook's Notes

Variation
Add thinly sliced fennel to the fish before baking, in addition to the tomatoes. Substitute other fish such as sea bass, gray mullet, or fish steaks such as cod or halibut.

Time
Preparation takes about 20 minutes, cooking takes about 25 minutes.

Cook's Tip
Red mullet spoils quickly, so use on the day of purchase.

SERVES 4

GRILLED FISH

Grilling fish with herbs and lemon is one of
the most delightful ways of preparing it, and
is particularly common in the Greek Islands.

2 large bream or other whole fish
Fresh thyme and oregano
Olive oil
Lemon juice
Salt and pepper
Lemon wedges
Vine leaves

1. Preheat a broiler. Gut the fish and rinse it well. Pat dry
and sprinkle the cavity with salt, pepper and lemon juice.
Place sprigs of herbs inside.

2. Make 3 diagonal cuts on the sides of the fish with a
sharp knife. Place the fish on the broiler rack and sprinkle
with olive oil and lemon juice.

3. Cook on both sides until golden brown and crisp. This
should take about 8-10 minutes per side, depending on the
thickness of the fish.

To make perfect
lemon wedges,
first cut the ends
off the lemons,
then cut in 4 or 8
wedges and
remove the
membrane and
seeds.

Step 1 Open the
cavity of the fish
and sprinkle with
salt, pepper and
lemon juice.

Step 2 Use a
sharp knife to
make diagonal
cuts on both sides
of each fish.

4. If using vine leaves preserved in brine, rinse them well.
If using fresh vine leaves, pour over boiling water and leave
to stand for about 10 minutes to soften slightly. Drain and
allow to cool. Line a large serving platter with the vine leaves
and when the fish is cooked place it on top of the leaves.
Serve surrounded with lemon wedges.

Cook's Notes

Time

Preparation takes about 20
minutes, cooking takes about
16-20 minutes, depending upon the
size of the fish.

Cook's Tip
When broiling large whole
fish, slit the skin on both sides
to help the fish cook evenly.

Variation

The fish may be wrapped in
vine leaves before broiling.
This keeps the fish moist and adds
extra flavor. Other fish suitable for
cooking by this method are red mullet,
trout, sea bass, gray mullet, sardines,
herring or mackerel.

Preparation
If desired, the fish may be
cooked on an outdoor
barbecue grill. Wait until the coals have
white ash on the top and be sure to oil
the racks before placing on the fish, or
use a special wire cage for cooking
fish.

SERVES 4

FIGS AND CURRANTS WITH ORANGE

Fruit is the most popular sweet in Greece, and fresh figs are a favorite choice.

---

4 fresh figs
Small bunches of fresh redcurrants
6 oranges
1 tsp orange flower water

---

1. Cut the stalks off the tops of the figs but do not peel them.

2. Cut the figs in quarters but do not cut completely through the base. Open the figs out like flowers and stand them on their bases on serving dishes. Arrange small bunches of redcurrants on the figs. Squeeze the juice from 2 of the oranges. Peel and segment the other 4 and arrange segments around each fig.

Step 2 Peel the oranges and cut into segments.

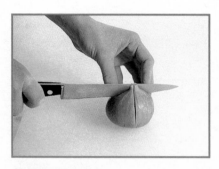

Step 2 With a small, sharp knife, cut the figs into quarters, but not all the way through the base.

Step 2 Open the figs out like flowers.

3. Pour over the orange juice mixed with the orange flower water and chill before serving.

Cook's Notes

Variation
Orange flower water may be omitted if desired.
Blackcurrants may be substituted for the redcurrants.

Serving Ideas
Yogurt and honey may be served as an accompaniment.

Time
Preparation takes about 15 minutes.

SERVES 6-8

BAKLAVA

Fyllo pastry is used for sweet dishes as well as savory ones. Serve baklava in small portions; it is buttery and rich.

Syrup

1½ cups granulated sugar
6 tbsps liquid honey
1½ cups water
1 tbsp lemon juice
1 tbsp orange flower water

Pastry

1lb package fyllo pastry
1 cup unsalted butter, melted
1 cup chopped walnuts, almonds or pistachio nuts
½ tsp ground cinnamon
1½ tbsps sugar

1. First make the syrup by combining all the ingredients in a heavy-based saucepan. Place over low heat until the sugar dissolves. Stir occasionally. Once the sugar is dissolved, raise the heat and allow the syrup to boil until it is thick enough to coat a spoon. This should take about 2 minutes. Allow the syrup to cool and then chill thoroughly.

2. Preheat the oven to 350°F. Brush a rectangular baking dish, about 12x18 inches, with some of the melted butter. Place about 8 of the pastry sheets in the dish, brushing the top of each with melted butter.

3. Mix the nuts, sugar and cinnamon together and spread half of the mixture over the top of the pastry. Place two more layers of the buttered pastry on top and then cover with the remaining nuts. Layer up the remaining pastry, brushing each layer with butter.

Step 1 Cook the syrup slowly until the sugar dissolves and the liquid looks clear.

Step 1 Bring the syrup to a rapid boil and allow to boil for about 2 minutes, until thick enough to coat a spoon.

4. With a sharp knife, score a diamond pattern in the top. Sprinkle the pastry with water to keep it moist and prevent curling. Bake for 30 minutes and then raise the oven temperature to 425°F. Continue baking for 10-15 minutes longer, or until the pastry is cooked and the top is golden brown and crisp.

5. Remove the pastry from the oven and immediately pour over the syrup. Leave the pastry to cool and when thoroughly cold, cut into diamond shapes to serve.

Cook's Notes

Time
Preparation takes about 30 minutes, cooking takes about 40-45 minutes. Preparation time does not include chilling the syrup or the pastry.

Cook's Tip
Baklava may be made several days in advance and kept in the refrigerator. Leave at room temperature for about 20 minutes before serving.

Watchpoint
When boiling the syrup, watch it constantly. Sugar syrups can turn to caramel very quickly. If this happens, discard the syrup and begin again.

HONEY SHORTBREAD

Sweets in a honey syrup are quite common
in Greece. Use hymettus honey, which is
dark and fragrant, for authenticity.

3 cups all-purpose flour, sifted
1 tsp baking powder
1 tsp bicarbonate of soda
1 cup olive oil
¼ cup sugar
½ cup brandy
4 tbsps orange juice
1 tbsp grated orange rind
½ cup chopped walnuts
1 tsp cinnamon

Syrup

1 cup honey
½ cup sugar
1 cup water

1. Preheat the oven to 350°F. Sift flour, baking powder and soda together.

2. Combine oil, sugar, brandy, orange juice and rind in a large bowl or food processor. Gradually add the dry ingredients, running the machine in short bursts. Work just until the mixture comes together.

Step 2 Add the dry ingredients to the liquid ingredients gradually, combining well after each addition.

Step 3 Flour hands well and shape mixture into ovals. Place well apart on baking sheets.

Step 5 Dip the shortbread into the syrup and sprinkle on nuts and cinnamon while still wet.

3. Grease and flour several baking sheets. Shape the shortbread mixture into ovals about 3 inches long. Place well apart on prepared baking sheets and cook about 20 minutes. Cool on the baking sheet.

4. Mix the syrup ingredients together and bring to the boil. Boil rapidly for 5 minutes to thicken. Allow to cool.

5. Dip the cooled shortbread into the syrup and sprinkle with nuts and cinnamon. Allow to set slightly before serving.

Cook's Notes

Freezing
Do not dip the biscuits in syrup. Wrap them well, label and store for up to 2 months. Defrost thoroughly before coating with syrup, nuts and cinnamon.

Watchpoint
If the mixture is overworked it becomes too soft to shape and will spread when baked. Chill in the refrigerator to firm up.

Time
Preparation takes about 20 minutes, cooking takes 10 minutes for the syrup to boil and about 20 minutes for the biscuits to bake.

POLISH COOKING

INTRODUCTION

From what we hear of the food situation in Poland today, it is hard to believe that the cuisine of this land was once thought to be extravagant and excessive. Consider Christmas Eve dinner, for example. This feast was made up of 21 courses. The preparation of some of the dishes began months before the celebration and the cooking for that evening began in the early hours of the morning. In the midst of this conspicuous consumption, the Poles did not lose sight of the hospitality of the season. There was always a place set on Christmas Eve for an unexpected guest.

This hospitality extended to everyday visits as well as holiday celebrations. The Polish proverb — A guest in the home is God in the home — was taken to heart and even an unexpected guest would find tea or coffee and pastries. Our recipe for Crullers is just one traditional favorite.

Polish cuisine has throughout the nation's history been greatly influenced by the political climate. Kings and princes who ruled the land often married foreign princesses and noblewomen who brought their own ideas on food with them. Even so, there were the same traditional staples in every well-stocked Polish pantry. A look inside would have revealed kasha, or cereal grain, buckwheat being the favorite and the foundation for both sweet and savory dishes. There would be wheat and rye flours, fried and pickled mushrooms, smoked sausages, game, butter, eggs, cheese and honey for sweetening and for making mead. There would be fresh and pickled pickles, fresh cabbage and sauerkraut, beets, turnips, onions, carrots and potatoes. Supplies of parsley, caraway and poppyseed would be on the shelves alongside fresh and preserved apples, cherries and plums to use for puddings and as accompaniments to meat and game. From these ingredients, the people prepared the characteristic dishes that were part of the culture they had always known and loved.

SERVES 4

STUFFED EGGS

An inexpensive appetizer, these can also be a snack
or canapé. The filling is delicious cold, too,
so they are perfect for summer parties and picnics.

4 hard-boiled eggs
8oz cooked ham, ground
4 tbsps grated mild cheese
4 tbsps sour cream
2 tsps mustard
Pinch salt and pepper
2 tsps chopped fresh dill or chives
Dry breadcrumbs
Melted butter

1. Using a pin or egg pricker, make a small hole in the larger end of each egg.

2. Lower the eggs gently into boiling water.

3. As the eggs come back to the boil, roll them around with the bowl of a spoon for about 2-3 minutes. This will help set yolk in the middle of the whites. Allow the eggs to cook 9-10 minutes after the water re-boils.

4. Drain and place the eggs under cold running water. Allow to cool completely and leave in the cold water until ready to peel.

5. Peel the eggs, cut them in half lengthwise and remove the yolks. Combine yolks and all the remaining ingredients except the breadcrumbs and melted butter and mix well.

6. Pipe or spoon the mixture into each egg white and mound the top, smoothing with a small knife. Sprinkle on the breadcrumbs, covering the filling and the edge of the whites completely. Place the eggs in a heatproof dish and drizzle with melted butter. Place under a preheated broiler for about 3 minutes, or until crisp and golden brown on top.

Step 1 Using an egg pricker or making a small hole with a pin in the large end of the egg will help prevent the shell from cracking.

Step 3 Use the bowl of the spoon to roll the eggs around in the boiling water to set the yolk.

Step 6 Pipe or spoon the mixture onto each egg white and mound the top.

Cook's Notes

Cook's Tip
Keeping hard-boiled eggs in water until ready to use helps prevent a gray ring from forming around the yolk.

Time
Preparation takes about 20 minutes, cooking takes about 9-10 minutes for the eggs to boil and 3 minutes for broiling.

Watchpoint
Do not broil the eggs too long. Overheating will toughen the whites.

SERVES 6

SPRING SALAD

Don't save this salad just for green — the ingredients are available all year round. Try it as a spread for sandwiches or a topping for canapes, too.

12-14oz cottage cheese
1 carrot, coarsely grated
8 radishes, coarsely grated
2 green onions, thinly sliced
Pinch salt and pepper
1 tsp chopped fresh dill or marjoram
½ cup sour cream or thick yogurt
Lettuce leaves (red oak leaf lettuce, curly endive or radicchio)

1. If cottage cheese is very liquidy, pour into a fine strainer and leave to stand for about 15-20 minutes for some of the liquid to drain away. Alternatively, cut down on the amount of sour cream.

2. Peel the carrots and shred them using the coarse side of the grater or the coarse shredding blade in a food processor. Make sure the carrots are shredded into short strips.

Step 2 Using the coarse side of a grater, grate the carrots into short strips.

Step 3 Trim the root ends from the green onions and any part of the green tops that looks damaged.

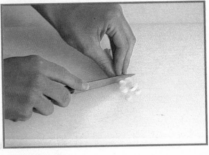

Step 3 Use a large, sharp knife to slice through both onions at once to save time.

3. Shred the radishes with the grater and cut the onion into thin rounds with a large, sharp knife.

4. Mix all the ingredients together, except the lettuce leaves, and chill for about 20 minutes to blend all the flavors.

5. To serve, place lettuce leaves on individual plates and mound the cottage cheese salad mixture on top. If desired, sprinkle with more chopped fresh dill.

Cook's Notes

Variation
Add finely chopped red or green pepper or cucumber to the salad. If using cucumber, grate and sprinkle with salt. Leave to stand 30 minutes, rinse and pat dry.

Serving Ideas
Serve with thinly sliced whole-wheat or rye bread, lightly buttered. The salad may also be served with French bread.

Time
Preparation takes about 20 minutes and salad requires 15-20 minutes refrigeration.

SERVES 6-8

PIG'S TROTTERS IN ASPIC

Pigs were an important source of food in Poland
and no part of them was wasted. The trotters or
feet produce a stock which jells naturally.

1½lbs pig's trotters, cleaned and skinned
8oz pork or uncooked gammon, left whole
2 carrots, peeled
4 sticks celery
1 onion, quartered
2 bay leaves
5 black peppercorns
3 allspice berries
Pinch salt
6 tbsps white wine vinegar
2 egg whites
2 egg shells

1. Place the trotters, meat, carrots, celery and onion into a large stockpot.

2. Tie the bay leaves, peppercorns and allspice berries in a muslin bag and add to the pot.

3. Pour in enough water to come 2 inches above the ingredients. Bring to the boil and then simmer, covered, for 2 hours. Add more water as necessary during cooking. Skim off any foam that collects on the surface during cooking. Add salt and vinegar and cook a further 2 hours and then strain, reserving about 3 pints of the liquid.

4. Discard the muslin bag, remove meat and carrots and discard celery and onion.

5. Take the meat off the trotters and dice it along with the pork or gammon. Slice the carrot and set it aside. Strain the stock into a clean pan and add the egg whites and shells.

6. Bring to the boil, whisking constantly until a thick foam forms on top.

Step 6 Bring the liquid to the boil, whisking constantly with a large balloon whisk until a thick foam forms.

Step 7 Allow the liquid to boil up the sides of the pan and then subside. Repeat twice more.

7. Allow the stock to boil up the sides of the pan, remove from the heat and allow to subside. Allow to boil up and subside twice more, but do not whisk.

8. Strain into a clean bowl through a clean, scalded tea towel or piece of muslin. Let the foam fall into the towel and allow liquid to drain slowly through. Do not allow the crust to fall into the liquid. When the aspic is drained through, chill until syrupy.

9. Dampen a mold and pour in a thin layer of aspic. Chill in the refrigerator until firm. Place slices of carrot in a decorative pattern on top and spoon on more aspic to set the carrot. Chill again until set. Mix the meat and the remaining aspic and fill up the mold. Chill until firm, at least 4 hours. Turn out and garnish the plate with parsley if desired.

Cook's Notes

Cook's Tip
The aspic may be softened by gentle re-heating. Place the bowl in another bowl or pan of hot water. Do not stir too much or bubbles will form.

Watchpoint
If the aspic does not set when the first layer is chilled, add about 1 tbsp gelatine and re-heat. Use as indicated in the recipe.

Time
Preparation takes about 45 minutes with about 4 hours chilling. Cooking takes about 4½ hours.

SERVES 6-8

CHRISTMAS BORSCH WITH PIEROZKI

Borsch was served at both Christmas and Easter celebrations
in Poland.

Dough

2 cups all-purpose flour
Pinch salt
5oz butter or margarine
1 egg
1 tbsp yogurt or sour cream

Filling

Mushroom from the borsch
1 tbsp butter or margarine
1 small onion, finely chopped
1-2 tbsps fresh breadcrumbs
1 small egg
Salt and pepper

Borsch

1 celeriac
3 parsley roots or 12 parsley stalks
4 carrots, peeled and roughly chopped
3 leeks
1 onion, thinly sliced
3lbs uncooked beets
10 black peppercorns
2 whole allspice berries
1 bay leaf
2-3oz dried mushrooms
Juice of 1-2 lemons
⅓ cup dry red wine
1 clove garlic, crushed

1. First prepare the Pierozki dough. Sift the flour with a pinch of salt into a large bowl. Cut the butter into small pieces and rub into the flour until the mixture resembles fine breadcrumbs.

2. Mix the egg and the yogurt or sour cream together and combine with the flour and butter to make a firm dough. Knead the dough together quickly into a bowl, wrap well and chill for 30 minutes.

3. Peel the celeriac root with a swivel vegetable peeler and chop the root roughly. Chop the parsley roots or slightly crush the stalks.

4. Cut the leeks in half lengthwise and rinse well under cold running water. Chop the leeks roughly and place all the vegetables, except beets, in a large stockpot. Add the black peppercorns, allspice berries and bay leaf and cover the vegetables with water. Cover and bring to the boil. Reduce the heat and allow to simmer, partially covered, for about 45 minutes.

5. Place the dried mushrooms in a small saucepan and cover with 2 cups water. Cover and bring to the boil. Allow to simmer until the mushrooms soften. Strain and add liquid to vegetable stock. Chop the mushrooms finely.

6. Melt 1 tbsp butter for the filling in a small pan and add the onion and chopped mushrooms. Cook briskly to evaporate moisture, and blend in the egg and breadcrumbs. Add enough crumbs to help the mixture hold its shape. Set the filling aside to cool completely. Roll out dough thinly on a well-floured surface. Cut into circles about 3 inches in diameter. Fill with a spoonful of filling, seal the edges with water and fold over to seal. Crimp with a fork, if desired. Bake on greased baking sheets in a pre-heated 425°F oven for about 10-15 minutes, or until brown and crisp.

7. After the vegetable stock has cooked 45 minutes, add peeled, grated beets, lemon juice, red wine and garlic, and cook a further 15-20 minutes, or until a good red color. Strain and serve immediately with the pierozki.

Cook's Notes

Buying Guide
Celeriac is a root vegetable with a strong taste of celery. If unavailable, substitute one head of celery, washed and roughly chopped. Include the celery leaves.

Variation
If dried mushrooms are unavailable, substitute 4oz fresh button mushrooms. Cook until the mushrooms are very soft.

Time
Preparation takes about 40 minutes, cooking takes about 1 hour.

SERVES 6-8

DUMPLING SOUP

Dumplings with a variety of fillings are very
popular in Poland. Use fewer dumplings per
serving for an appetizer, more for a filling soup.

6 cups home-made beef stock

Filling

6oz ground beef or pork
1 tsp chopped fresh marjoram
1 small onion, grated or very finely chopped
Salt and pepper

Dough

2 cups all-purpose flour, sifted
Pinch salt
1-2 eggs
4 tbsps water
Chopped parsley

1. Combine all the filling ingredients, mixing very well.

2. Prepare the dough by sifting the flour with a pinch of salt
into a large bowl. Make a well in the centre and add the
eggs and water. Use only one egg if they are large.

3. Using a wooden spoon, beat the ingredients together,
gradually incorporating flour from the outside until the
dough becomes too stiff to beat.

Step 3 If
preparing dough
by hand, use a
wooden spoon to
gradually incor-
porate the liquid
and dry ingredients.

Step 5 Place a
small spoonful of
filling on top of
each dough circle
and brush the
edges with water.

Step 6 Press
together to seal
well and crimp
the edges with a
fork if desired.

4. Knead the dough by hand until firm but elastic. Roll out
the dough very thinly on a floured surface and cut into 3
inch rounds.

5. Place a small spoonful of filling on each dough circle
and brush the edges with water.

6. Press the edges together to seal well, and crimp with a
fork if desired.

7. Bring stock to the boil and add the dumplings. Cook
about 10 minutes, or until all have floated to the surface.

8. Add parsley to the soup, adjust the seasoning and serve
in individual bowls or from a large tureen.

Cook's Notes

Time
Home-made stock takes
approximately 1 hour to cook.
Dumplings take about 25 minutes to
prepare and about 10 minutes to cook
in the stock.

Serving Ideas
The dumplings may be
cooked for the same length of
time in water and dried and tossed with
melted butter. Serve with sour cream
and fresh dill or chives.

Variation
Chicken may be used in the
dumpling filling in place of the
beef or pork, and chicken stock
substituted for beef stock.

SERVES 4-6

MUSHROOMS IN SOUR CREAM

This very old recipe originally called for freshly gathered forest mushrooms.

1lb button mushrooms, quartered
2 tbsps butter or margarine
6 green onions, thinly sliced
1 tbsp flour
1 tbsp lemon juice
2 tbsps chopped fresh dill or 1 tbsp dried dill
Pinch salt and pepper
⅓ cup sour cream
Paprika

1. Rinse the mushrooms and pat dry well. Trim the stalks level with the caps before quartering. Melt the butter in a sauté pan and add the mushrooms and onions. Sauté for about 1 minute and stir in the flour.

2. Add the lemon juice and all the remaining ingredients

Step 1 Sauté mushrooms and onions in the butter or margarine to soften.

Step 2 Add flour, lemon juice, herbs and seasoning and cook for 1 minute, stirring occasionally.

Step 3 Stir in the sour cream and heat through without boiling.

except the sour cream and paprika and cook slowly for about 1 minute.

3. Stir in the sour cream and adjust the seasoning. Heat through for about 1 minute. Spoon into individual serving dishes or on top of buttered toast. Sprinkle with paprika and serve immediately.

Cook's Notes

 Watchpoint
Sour cream will curdle if boiled, although the addition of flour to the sauce will help to stabilize it somewhat.

 Serving Ideas
Use as an appetizer or a side dish with meat, poultry or game. Prepare double quantity and serve with a salad and bread as a light lunch.

 Time
Preparation takes about 20 minutes, cooking takes about 5-7 minutes.

SERVES 6

BEANS AND CARROTS POLISH STYLE

Breadcrumbs browned in butter are often
called a Polish sauce.

8oz green beans
8oz baby carrots with green tops
4 tbsps butter or margarine
4 tbsps dry breadcrumbs
½ tsp chopped fresh dill or marjoram
Salt and pepper

1. Top and tail the beans. This is easier done in several large bunches.

2. Leave some of the green tops on the carrots and peel them using a swivel vegetable peeler.

3. Place the carrots in cold salted water, cover the pan and bring to the boil. Cook for 10-15 minutes after the water comes to the boil. The beans may be added during the last 5 minutes of cooking time or they may be cooked separately.

Step 1 Top and tail the green beans. Gather them together in bunches and cut through with a sharp knife or trim off the ends with kitchen scissors.

Step 2 Cut off the green tops of the carrots, leaving a tiny amount of the stem, if desired. Peel with a swivel vegetable peeler or scrape with a small, sharp knife.

Step 4 Cook the breadcrumbs slowly in butter until golden brown. Stir frequently with a wooden spoon.

4. Melt the butter for the topping in a small saucepan and, when foaming, add the breadcrumbs, herbs, salt and pepper. Cook over low heat, stirring constantly until brown and crisp.

5. Drain the vegetables and mix them together. Sprinkle on the topping and serve.

Cook's Notes

Time
Preparation takes about 20 minutes and cooking time a total of about 20 minutes.

Preparation
The topping may be prepared ahead of time and tossed with the hot vegetables just before serving.

Serving Ideas
Serve the vegetables as a side dish with meat, fish, poultry or game.

Watchpoint
The breadcrumbs can burn easily so keep stirring them as they brown.

Variation
Frozen vegetables may be used instead, and the cooking times altered according to package directions.

SERVES 6

NOODLES WITH POPPY SEEDS AND RAISINS

Christmas Eve dinner in Poland traditionally had up
to 21 courses, of which this was but one!

8oz noodles or other pasta shapes
Pinch salt
1 tbsp oil
½ cup heavy cream
6 tbsps black poppy seed, ground
2 tbsps honey
6 tbsps raisins

1. Bring lots of water to the boil in a large saucepan with a pinch of salt. Add the oil and the noodles or other pasta shapes and bring back to the boil. Cook, uncovered, until tender, about 10-12 minutes.

2. Drain and rinse the pasta under hot water. If using immediately, allow to drain dry. If not, place in a bowl of water to keep.

3. Place the cream in a deep, heavy-based saucepan and

Step 3 Pour the poppy seeds, honey and raisins into the cream, mixing very well.

Step 3 The poppy seed mixture should be thick when ready, but still fall from the spoon easily.

Step 3 Cream is at scalding point when it begins to bubble round the edges. Remove quickly from heat, it can boil over.

bring almost to the boil. When the cream reaches the scalding point, mix in the poppy seeds, honey and raisins. Cook slowly for about 5 minutes. The mixture should become thick but still fall off a spoon easily. Use a food processor or spice mill to grind the poppy seeds.

4. Toss the poppy seed mixture with the noodles and serve hot.

Cook's Notes

Serving Ideas
Serve as a course on its own in a Polish Christmas Eve dinner or as a side dish to duck, pork or gammon.

Time
Preparation takes about 15 minutes and cooking takes about 15-17 minutes.

Variation
Use currants or golden raisins.

SERVES 4-6

CAULIFLOWER POLISH STYLE

A crunchy almond and golden fried breadcrumb topping
brightens up a plain boiled cauliflower.

1 large head cauliflower
4 tbsps butter or margarine
4 tbsps finely chopped blanched almonds
4 tbsps dry breadcrumbs
2 hard-boiled eggs
Chopped parsley and fresh dill

1. Remove the large coarse green leaves from the outside of the cauliflower. If desired, leave the fine pale green leaves attached.

2. Trim the stem and wash the cauliflower well.

3. Place the whole cauliflower in boiling water right side up. Add salt and bay leaf to the water and bring back to the boil. Cook the cauliflower for 12-15 minutes, or until just tender.

4. Melt the butter in a small frying pan and add the almonds. Cook slowly to brown. Stir in the breadcrumbs and cook about 1 minute or until crisp.

Step 1 Cut away the coarse green leaves with a sharp knife

Step 3 Place right side up in a pan of boiling water.

Step 4 Melt the butter in a small pan and add the almonds. Cook slowly to brown, stir in the bread-crumbs and cook for 1 minute, or until crisp.

5. Peel the eggs and cut them in half. Remove the yolks and cut the whites into thin strips. Press the yolks through a strainer.

6. When the cauliflower is cooked, drain it and place on serving dish. Spoon the breadcrumbs and almond topping over the cauliflower. Arrange the sliced egg white around the base of the cauliflower and sprinkle the egg yolks over the breadcrumb topping. Sprinkle over chopped parsley and dill. Serve immediately.

Cook's Notes

 Time
Preparation takes about 20 minutes, cooking takes about 12-15 minutes.

Cook's Tip
Adding a bay leaf to the water when cooking cauliflower helps to neutralize the strong smell.

 Watchpoint
Do not overcook cauliflower. It becomes watery very quickly.

SERVES 6

CUCUMBER SALAD

In Polish this salad is known by the name Mizeria
– quite a gloomy word for such a refreshing,
delicious and versatile salad and side dish.

1 large cucumber
½ cup sour cream
2 tsps white wine vinegar
1 tsp sugar
1 tbsp chopped fresh dill
Salt and pepper

1. Wash the cucumber well. Trim off the thin ends of the cucumber.

2. Using a cannelle knife or the prongs of a fork, score the skin of the cucumber in long strips.

3. Cut the cucumber into thin slices and place in a colander. Sprinkle with salt and leave for 30 minutes.

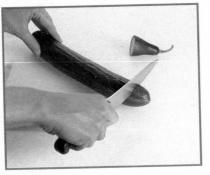

Step 1 Trim the ends of the cucumber so that the slices will all be even in size.

Step 2 Use a cannelle knife or a fork to make a decorative pattern in the skin of the cucumber.

Step 3 Sprinkle with salt. When the cucumber has been standing for 30 minutes, a lot of liquid will have been drawn out.

4. Place the colander in a bowl to collect the cucumber liquid. Rinse the cucumber well and pat dry.

5. Mix the remaining ingredients together in a large bowl and toss with the cucumber slices.

6. Arrange the cucumber in a serving dish and serve chilled.

Cook's Notes

 Preparation
Sprinkling cucumber lightly with salt and leaving it to stand will help draw out the moisture and keep the dressing from becoming watery. This also makes cucumbers easier to digest.

Variation
Other chopped herbs may be used instead of, or in addition to, the dill.

 Time
Preparation takes about 30 minutes.

SERVES 4-6

POLISH STYLE LETTUCE SALAD

Polish style in this case means the use of sour cream and hard-boiled egg in a dressing that really livens up plain lettuce salads.

1 head iceberg lettuce or 2 heads Webb or round lettuce
1 clove garlic
½ cup sour cream
Juice and grated rind of ½ lemon
½ tsp sugar
Salt and pepper
2 tsps chopped parsley
2 hard-boiled eggs

1. Break the lettuce into leaves and wash them well. Dry on paper towels or on a clean tea towel.

2. Peel a clove of garlic and crush it with the side of a large knife. Rub the clove of garlic on the inside of a salad bowl.

3. Tear the lettuce into bite-sized pieces and place in the salad bowl.

4. Mix together the remaining ingredients, except the

Step 2 Slightly crush the clove of garlic with the flat side of a knife or a fish slice.

Step 5 Chop the egg whites finely.

Step 6 Place egg yolks in a sieve and push through over a bowl.

hard-boiled eggs, and pour over the lettuce.

5. Cut the hard-boiled eggs in half, remove the yolks and chop the whites finely. Scatter the white over the top of the dressing.

6. Place the yolks in a small sieve and hold it over a bowl. Using the back of the spoon or your fingers, push the yolk through the holes in the sieve and sprinkle yolks over the salad. Serve immediately.

Cook's Notes

Cook's Tip
If hard-boiling eggs in advance, keep them submerged in cold water. This will prevent a gray ring from forming around the yolks.

Variation
Add other ingredients such as sliced cucumber, grated carrot or diced peppers to the salad.

Time
Preparation takes about 20 minutes. Hard-boiled eggs take about 9-10 minutes to cook.

SERVES 4

FRIED CARP

Carp is a favorite fish in Poland
and is prepared in numerous ways. This
dish is popular on Christmas Eve.

1 cleaned, filleted carp weighing about 2-3lbs
Salt
Flour
1-2 eggs, lightly beaten
Dry breadcrumbs
Butter and oil for frying

Cabbage and Mushrooms Polish Style

1lb canned sauerkraut
2-3oz dried mushrooms
2 tbsps butter or margarine
1 onion, thinly sliced or finely chopped
1½ tbsps flour
Salt and pepper

1. Cut the cleaned and scaled carp into even-sized portions and sprinkle lightly with salt. Leave to stand for half an hour. Skin, if desired.

2. Place the sauerkraut in a heavy-based saucepan and add 1 cup water. Bring to the boil and then allow to simmer until tender.

3. Place the mushrooms in a separate pan and add enough water to cover. Cook over gentle heat until softened. Slice the mushrooms and reserve them and their cooking liquid.

4. Melt the butter in a frying pan and, when foaming, add the onion. Cook in the butter until golden brown. Sprinkle

Step 8 Place crumbs on wax paper and lift the sides to toss the crumbs over the fish.

over the flour and mix thoroughly.

5. When the sauerkraut is tender, strain the cooking liquid over the butter mixture. Stir very well and bring to the boil. Cook until thickened and add to the sauerkraut, along with the sliced mushrooms and their liquid. Stir thoroughly and set aside to keep warm.

6. Dredge the carp lightly with flour, shaking off the excess.

7. Coat with beaten egg using a pastry brush, or dip the pieces into the egg using two forks.

8. Coat the fish with the crumbs, shaking off the excess. Heat the butter and oil together in a large frying pan until very hot. Place in the fish and cook on both sides until golden brown – about 5 minutes per side. Make sure the oil and butter come half way up the sides of the fish.

9. Drain fish on paper towels and serve immediately with the cabbage and mushrooms.

Cook's Notes

Time
Sauerkraut needs about 20-25 minutes to cook until tender. Fish will take about 10 minutes for both sides. It may be necessary to cook the fish in several batches, depending on the size of frying pan.

Preparation
To make coating the fillets easier, spread the crumbs out on a sheet of wax paper and place on a piece of fish coated with egg and lift the paper to toss the fillet from side to side to coat evenly.

Cook's Tip
After coating several pieces of fish, breadcrumbs may clump together with the egg. Sift the breadcrumbs through a strainer and discard the eggy bits.

SERVES 4

POLISH STYLE HERRING

Herring, prepared in any form, is a national
favorite in Poland. These fish can be prepared
well in advance and stored in their marinade.

4 even-sized herring, cleaned
2 onions, thinly sliced
10 black peppercorns
5 whole allspice berries
2 bay leaves
1 lemon, sliced
Juice of 3 lemons
½ cup cream
½ tsp sugar
4 potatoes, peeled and sliced
Salt, pepper and caraway seed
6 tbsps vegetable oil
Lemon wedges and chopped parsley to garnish

1. Place fish open end downward on a chopping board. Press along the backbone with the heel of your hand to loosen the bone.

2. Turn over and carefully pull out the main bone.

3. Cut the fillets in half and skin them using a filleting knife, beginning at the tail end and working up to the head end using a sawing motion, with the knife at an angle to the skin.

4. Layer up the fillets in a deep casserole, placing onion slices, spices, bay leaves and lemon slices between each layer.

5. Mix lemon juice and sugar together and pour over the fish. Place a sheet of wax paper directly over the top of the fish and cover with the casserole lid. Store in the refrigerator for 24 hours. Remove the fillets and strain the liquid. Mix 4

Step 2 Turn over and carefully pull out the bone.

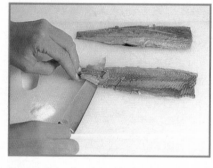

Step 3 Cut fillets in half and skin them using the same knife held at a slight angle. Dip fingers in salt to grip the fish skin more easily.

tbsps of the liquid with the cream and pour over the fillets to serve.

6. Layer the potatoes in an ovenproof serving dish and sprinkle salt, pepper, and caraway seeds in between each layer and on top. Spoon the oil over the top of the potatoes and bake, uncovered, in a preheated 400°F oven for about 30-40 minutes or until golden and cooked through. Serve with the herring. Garnish the dish with chopped parsley and lemon wedges.

Cook's Notes

Time
Herring takes about 25 minutes to prepare and must marinate in the refrigerator for 24 hours. Potatoes take about 15 minutes to prepare and 30-40 minutes to cook.

Preparation
To make the fish easier to skin, dip fingers in salt for a better grip on slippery skin.

Buying Guide
A fishmonger will clean and fillet the herrings for you if required.

SERVES 4-6

STUFFED FISH

A whole baked fish makes an impressive main course for a dinner party. The stuffing makes the fish go further and with no bones it's easy to serve and eat.

2-3lb whole fish such as carp, sea bass or salmon trout
2 tbsps melted butter

Stuffing

1 tbsp butter or margarine
1 small onion, finely chopped
4oz mushrooms, roughly chopped
1 hard-boiled egg, peeled and roughly chopped
¾ cup fresh breadcrumbs, white or whole-wheat
Pinch salt and pepper
2 tsps chopped fresh dill
2 tsps chopped fresh parsley
Pinch nutmeg

Sauce

½ cup sour cream
Pinch sugar
Grated rind and juice of ½ lemon
Pinch salt and white pepper
Lemon slices and parsley sprigs to garnish

1. Ask the fishmonger to gut and bone the fish for you, leaving on the head and tail. Sprinkle the cavity of the fish with salt and pepper and set it aside while preparing the stuffing.

2. To chop the onion finely, peel it and cut it in half lengthwise. Place the onion cut side down on a chopping board. Using a large, sharp knife, make four cuts into the onion, parallel to the chopping board, but not completely through to the root end. Using the pointed tip of the knife,

Step 2 Slice the onion crosswise into individual dice.

make four or five cuts into the onion lengthwise, following the natural lines in the onion and not cutting through to the root end. Next, cut the onion crossways into thin or thick slices as desired and the onion should fall apart into individual dice. Keep fingers well out of the way when slicing.

3. Melt the butter or margarine in a medium-sized saucepan and add the chopped onion and mushrooms. Cook briefly to soften the vegetables and set aside. Stir in the remaining stuffing ingredients.

4. Spread the stuffing evenly into the cavity of the fish and place the fish in lightly buttered foil or in a large baking dish. Sprinkle the top with melted butter and bake in a preheated 350°F oven for about 40 minutes, basting frequently. If the fish begins to dry out too much on top, cover loosely with aluminum foil.

5. When the fish is cooked, combine the sauce ingredients and pour over the fish. Cook a further 5 minutes to heat the sauce, but do not allow it to bubble. Remove the fish to a serving dish and garnish with lemon and parsley.

Cook's Notes

Cook's Tip
Cover the head and tail of the fish with lightly greased foil about halfway through cooking time . This will prevent the fish from drying out and improve the appearance of the finished dish.

Time
Preparation takes about 20 minutes. If boning the fish yourself, add a further 30 minutes. Cooking takes approximately 45 minutes.

Variation
Other vegetables, such as grated carrot, finely chopped green or red pepper or peeled, seeded and chopped tomatoes may be added to the stuffing.

SERVES 8-10

CABBAGE ROLLS

In Polish these are called Golabki, which translates
as 'little pigeons.' They make a tasty, inexpensive
supper dish, and you can improvise with different fillings.

1 head white cabbage or 2 heads green cabbage
6oz rice
4 tbsps butter or margarine
1 large onion, chopped
10oz ground pork, veal or beef
Salt and pepper
1 egg

Sauce

2 tbsps butter or margarine
2 tbsps flour
2lbs canned tomatoes
1 clove garlic, crushed
½ cup chicken stock
1 tsp chopped fresh thyme or ½ tsp dried thyme
Pinch sugar
Salt and pepper
2 tbsps tomato paste
4 tbsps chopped parsley

1. Cut the core out of the cabbage completely. Place cabbage in boiling salted water and cook for 15-20 minutes for green cabbage and 25-30 minutes for white cabbage. Remove and drain in a colander or on paper towels and leave to cool.

2. Cook the rice in boiling salted water for about 10 minutes or until almost tender. Drain and rinse under hot water to remove the starch. Leave in a colander and make five or six wells with the handle of a wooden spoon to allow the rice to drain thoroughly. Leave to dry.

3. Melt 4 tbsps butter or margarine in a large frying pan and cook the onion for about 3 minutes, or until slightly softened. Add the meat and cook slowly just until the meat

Step 5 Fold in the sides around the filling and then roll up the leaves from the thick end to the thin end.

loses its pink color. Break the meat up with a fork as it cooks. Add salt, pepper, rice and egg and set aside to cool.

4. Separate the cabbage leaves and trim down the spines with a small, sharp knife. Place all the leaves out on a clean work surface and divide the filling evenly among all the leaves.

5. To roll up, fold in the sides around the filling and roll up from the thick end to the thin end.

6. Place all the cabbage rolls in a tightly fitting casserole. It may be necessary to have two layers of rolls and possibly three. Pour water into the casserole to come about half way up the rolls. Cover the casserole tightly and cook in a preheated 375°F oven for 30 minutes.

7. To prepare the sauce, put 2 tbsps butter or margarine in a heavy-based pan and stir in the flour. Cook for 1-2 minutes and add all the remaining ingredients except the chopped parsley. Bring to the boil, stirring continuously. Partially cover the pan and cook for 20 minutes over low heat. Break up the tomatoes with a fork as the sauce cooks.

8. Check the level of liquid in the casserole. Pour away all but ½ cup. Pour on the tomato sauce and cook, uncovered, for a further 20 minutes, or until the cabbage is tender. Sprinkle with chopped parsley before serving.

Cook's Notes

Time
Preparation takes about 30 minutes, cooking takes about 15-20 minutes to pre-cook the cabbage and 50 minutes to cook the cabbage rolls.

Variation
Substitute mushrooms for the meat in the recipe or add chopped, cooked ham and chopped hard-boiled eggs.

Preparation
Trimming the spines of the cabbage leaves makes them easier to roll up.

SERVES 6

STUFFED ROAST BEEF

The roasting is done on top of the stove instead
of in the oven. This means a succulent piece
of meat with a moist stuffing.

2lb beef joint
Flour
1 cup beef stock
1 bay leaf
1 blade mace

Stuffing

4 tbsps butter or margarine
3 medium onions, peeled and finely chopped
3-4 slices bread, made into crumbs
Grated rind and juice of ½ lemon
2 tsps chopped parsley
1 tsp chopped thyme
1 egg
Pinch paprika
Salt and pepper

Step 6 Spread the stuffing between each slice.

Step 6 Press the joint back into shape and return to the pan.

1. Melt half of the butter in a large saucepan. Coat the meat with flour and brown the meat in the butter on all sides.

2. Pour the stock into the casserole and add the bay leaf, blade mace and a pinch of pepper. Cover the pan and cook on top of the stove over low heat for about 45 minutes, turning the joint from time to time and adding more water or stock if necessary.

3. Remove the joint from the casserole and place it on a cutting board to stand for 10-15 minutes.

4. Melt the remaining butter in a saucepan and add the chopped onions. Cook until the onions are tender, but not brown. Add the breadcrumbs and remaining stuffing in-gredients, beating well to mix thoroughly.

5. Slice the joint thinly, but without cutting completely through the meat.

6. Spread an even amount of stuffing between each slice of meat and press the joint back into shape. Return the joint to the casserole for a further 35-40 minutes. When the meat is tender, remove it to a serving dish and boil the pan juices rapidly until of syrupy consistency. Pour some over the joint and serve the rest separately.

Cook's Notes

Time Preparation takes about 30 minutes, and cooking time about 1 hour 15 minutes.	**Variation** If rare roast beef is desired, cook for only 20 minutes after stuffing.	**Serving Ideas** Serve with mashed potatoes and red cabbage.

SERVES 8

HUNTER'S STEW

The tradition of this stew — bigos in Polish — goes back
centuries. It was kept in supplies in well-stocked larders,
taken on long road journeys and eaten on feast days.

4 tbsps oil
¾lb stewing steak, pork or venison cut in 2 inch pieces
1 onion
2 cloves garlic, crushed
4 tbsps flour
2 tbsps mild paprika
4 cups light stock
4oz smoked ham, cut in 2 inch pieces
4oz smoked sausage, cut in 2 inch pieces
1 tsp marjoram
1 tsp chopped thyme
1 tsp chopped parsley
Salt and pepper
Pinch cayenne pepper (optional)
2 tbsps tomato paste
1 head white cabbage, chopped
2 apples, cored and chopped
2 carrots, thinly sliced
8 pitted prunes, roughly chopped
3 tomatoes, peeled and roughly chopped
⅓ cup red wine or Madeira
Pinch sugar (optional)

1. Heat the oil in a large, flameproof casserole. Slice onion
thickly and add with the garlic and cook 2-3 minutes.
Remove and set aside.

2. Add the meat in four small batches, cooking over high
heat to brown.

3. When all the meat is browned, return it to the casserole
with the onions and garlic. Sprinkle over the flour and cook
until light brown.

Step 1 To slice an onion, peel and cut in half. Leave the root end on to hold the onion together and place cut side down on a chopping board.

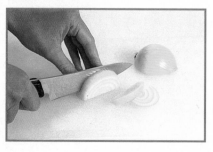

Step 1 Using a large, sharp knife, slice the onion, keeping the fingers out of the way. Alternatively, hold with a fork.

4. Add paprika and cook 1-2 minutes, stirring constantly.

5. Pour on the stock gradually and bring to the boil. Turn
down the heat to simmering and add the smoked meats,
herbs, salt, pepper, cayenne and tomato purée.

6. Stir well, cover and cook over low heat for 45 minutes.
Stir occasionally and add more liquid if necessary during
cooking.

7. When the meat is almost tender, add cabbage, apples,
carrots and prunes. Cook a further 20 minutes.

8. Add the tomatoes, wine or Madeira and a pinch of
sugar, if desired. Cook a further 10 minutes, adjust the
seasoning and serve immediately.

Cook's Notes

Time
Preparation takes about 25
minutes and cooking takes
about 1 hour 25 minutes in total.

Serving Ideas
Accompany with rice, mashed
potatoes or bread. The stew
may be eaten hot or cold.

Variation
Use a combination of beef,
pork and venison if desired.

SERVES 4

FILLED BEEF ROLLS

Zrazy, thin slices of tender beef, go back to the 14th century in Polish cuisine. There are different kinds of zrazy and many different stuffings for the rolled variety.

8 thin frying steaks, trimmed
2 dill pickles, cut in thin strips
4oz cooked ham steak, cut in thin strips
2 green onions, shredded
Mustard
4 tbsps oil
2 tbsps flour
1 cup beef stock
4 tbsps white wine
1 tbsp tomato paste
Salt and pepper
4 tbsps sour cream or thick yogurt
Chopped parsley

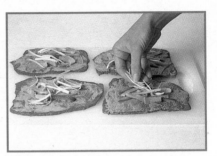

Step 4 Divide the filling ingredients among all the pieces of meat and fold in the sides.

Step 4 Roll the ends of the meat over the filling to cover completely and secure with string or wooden picks.

1. Place each steak between two sheets of damp wax paper and bat out with a meat mallet or rolling pin to flatten.

2. Cut the dill pickles, ham and green onions into even-sized lengths.

3. Spread the meat thinly with the mustard and divide the dill pickles, ham and onions among all the slices.

4. Fold in the sides of the meat about ½ inch. Roll the meat around the filling and secure with wooden picks or tie with fine string.

5. Heat the oil in a large sauté pan and when hot, brown the beef rolls. It may be necessary to brown them in two batches. Remove the meat and set aside.

6. Add the flour to the pan and allow to cook until light brown. Gradually stir in the stock and add the wine, tomato paste, salt and pepper. Bring to the boil and allow to simmer for one minute.

7. Return the beef rolls to the pan and spoon over some of the sauce. Cover and cook over low heat for 45 minutes to 1 hour. Add more liquid as necessary during cooking.

8. When the beef rolls are cooked, transfer them to a serving dish and remove the wooden picks or string. Spoon over the sauce and top with the sour cream and chopped parsley to serve.

Cook's Notes

Variation
Other filling ingredients such as mushrooms, sauerkraut, herbs and breadcrumbs or horse-radish and breadcrumbs bound with egg may be used.

Time
Preparation takes about 25 minutes, cooking takes about 1 hour.

Serving Ideas
Serve with pasta, rice or mashed potatoes.

SERVES 6-8

ROAST PORK IN WILD GAME STYLE

The love of game is part of Polish culinary history, so even meat from domestic animals was often given the same treatment.

3lb boneless pork roast
Paprika
4 tbsps lard or dripping
¾ cup sour cream or thick yogurt
1 tsp flour
1 tbsp chopped fresh dill

Marinade

1 carrot, finely chopped
2 celery sticks, finely chopped
1 bay leaf
5 black peppercorns
5 allspice berries
2 sprigs thyme
10 juniper berries, slightly crushed
2 onions, sliced
½ cup dry white wine
Juice and grated rind of 1 lemon

Beet Accompaniment

4 tbsps butter or margarine
2 tbsps flour
1 onion, finely chopped
1 clove garlic, crushed
½ cup chicken or vegetable stock
2lbs cooked beet, peeled and grated or cut into small dice
White wine vinegar
Sugar, salt and pepper

1. First combine the marinade ingredients in a small saucepan and bring to the boil. Allow to cool. Place the pork in a casserole dish or bowl and pour over the marinade. Cover and refrigerate for two days, turning the

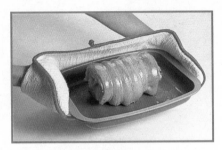

Step 2 Heat the fat in a roasting pan and brown the pork joint on all sides in the hot fat.

meat frequently. Remove the meat from the marinade and wipe it dry with paper towels. Reserve the marinade.

2. Heat the lard or dripping in a roasting pan. Sprinkle the fat side of the pork with paprika, and brown the pork on all sides in the hot fat. Pour over marinade after one hour's cooking. Cook, uncovered, in a preheated 375°F oven for 2 hours and 15 minutes. Baste frequently with the pan juices.

3. Remove the pork from the pan and set aside. Skim any fat from the surface of the sauce and strain the vegetables and meat juices into a saucepan. Mix the flour, sour cream, and dill together and add to the pan. Bring just to the boil, turn down the heat and allow to simmer for 1-2 minutes.

4. Grate the beet or cut it into small dice. Melt the butter in a heavy-based saucepan and add the flour and onion. Stir well and cook over moderate heat until light brown. Add the garlic and stir in the stock gradually.

5. Bring to the boil, add beet, sugar, vinegar, salt and pepper to taste and cook for ten minutes over moderate heat. Stir occasionally to prevent sticking.

6. To serve, slice the pork and pour over the sauce. Serve with the beet. Crackling can be removed and sliced separately to make carving easier.

Cook's Notes

Time
The beet takes approximately 10 minutes to cook. The pork should be roasted for 30 minutes to the pound and 30 minutes over.

Watchpoint
Beet will lose its color if overcooked or reheated. Make the beet accompaniment just before serving.

SERVES 6

ROAST PORK WITH CARAWAY SEEDS

In old Poland, pork was the most popular meat because there was such an abundance of wild boar in the forests.

2lb pork roast
Salt
Marjoram
2 tsps caraway seed
1½ tbsps lard or oil
2 onions, sliced
1 cup stock

Potato Kopytka

2lbs potatoes, peeled and cooked
1 large egg
1lb all-purpose flour
Salt

Step 2 Score the fat in a chequerboard pattern, and sprinkle with salt, marjoram and caraway seeds.

1. Remove the crackling, leaving most of the fat on the joint. Place crackling in a shallow pan, brush lightly with oil and sprinkle with salt.

2. Score the fat of the joint in a checkerboard pattern. Sprinkle with salt, a pinch of marjoram and the caraway seeds at least one hour before cooking.

3. Heat the lard in a roasting pan and brown the meat, fat side down first. Cook on all sides and then turn over fat side down again. Add the onions and the stock.

4. Roast in a preheated 425°F oven for 30 minutes. Turn over and continue roasting for 45 minutes or until the juices run clear, basting frequently with the cooking liquid. Cook the crackling at the same time, turning it over halfway through the cooking time.

5. Meanwhile, cook the potatoes, drain them, place back

in the pan and toss over high heat to dry completely. Push them through a sieve into a large bowl. Beat in the egg and gradually add the flour with a good pinch of salt. It may not be necessary to add all the flour, but the mixture should be very stiff.

6. Turn the mixture out onto a floured surface and knead until a smooth dough forms.

7. Divide the dough into 4-6 pieces and roll each into a sausage shape about 1 inch thick. Cut into diagonal pieces about 2 inches long.

8. Drop the dough pieces into boiling salted water and cook until they float to the surface and are slightly firm.

9. Drain the dumplings and keep warm. Carve the joint into slices or bring to the table whole. Skim the fat from the surface of the pan juices and reduce them slightly if necessary by boiling over high heat. Pour around the meat to serve.

10. Crumble the crackling over the Kopytka and serve with the pork.

Cook's Notes

Variation
Serve Kopytka with butter instead of crackling. They may be served with other roast meats, poultry or game.

Time
Preparation takes about 35-40 minutes, cooking takes about 1 hour 15 minutes.

Serving Ideas
Add a green vegetable or serve with cucumber salad.

SERVES 2

ROAST PIGEON WITH JUNIPER SAUCE

This sauce goes as well with
venison as it does with game birds.

2 pigeons, dressed
4oz chicken liver pâté
1 tbsp brandy
6 strips bacon

Sauce

2oz smoked bacon, chopped
1 onion, finely chopped
½ carrot, finely chopped
1 stick celery, finely chopped
1 tbsp juniper berries
2 tbsps flour
1 cup stock
½ cup white wine
1 tsp tomato paste (optional)
Salt and pepper

Step 1 Remove pin feathers with tweezers or singe the pigeons over an open flame.

Step 5 Cook the vegetables and juniper berries in the bacon fat until they begin to brown lightly.

1. Pluck any pin feathers from the pigeons with tweezers or singe them over a gas flame.

2. Mix pâté and brandy together and spread on the insides of each pigeon.

3. Tie the bacon on the pigeons to cover the breasts and roast them in a preheated 400°F oven for 35-40 minutes.

4. Meanwhile, place chopped bacon in a heavy-based saucepan over low heat. Cook slowly to render the fat.

5. Add the vegetables and juniper berries and cook until the vegetables begin to brown lightly.

6. Add the flour and cook until golden brown.

7. Pour on stock gradually, stirring continuously. Bring to the boil and reduce the heat to simmer. Partially cover the pan and cook slowly for about 20-25 minutes. Add more stock or water as necessary.

8. Skim the fat from the roasting pan and discard it. Add pan juices to the sauce and pour in the juices from the cavity of each pigeon.

9. Strain the sauce into a clean pan and add the wine and tomato paste, if using.

10. Bring to the boil for about 3 minutes to reduce slightly. Season with salt and pepper and serve with the pigeons.

Cook's Notes

Variation
Use pheasant when in season. Hen pheasants are more tender than cock pheasants. If using cock pheasants, increase the cooking time to 40-50 minutes.

Serving Ideas
Accompany with noodles or potatoes. Serving and eating are easier if the pigeons are cut in half first.

Watchpoint
Do not allow the vegetables to get too brown before adding the flour or the sauce will taste bitter.

SERVES 4

CHICKEN POLISH STYLE

Choose small, young chickens for a truly Polish
style dish. A dried white roll was originally
used for stuffing, but breadcrumbs are easier.

2 chickens, weighing approximately 2lbs each
2 chicken livers
1 tbsp butter or margarine
6 slices bread, made into crumbs
2 tsps chopped parsley
1 tsp chopped dill
1 egg
Salt and pepper
½ cup chicken stock

1. Remove the fat from just inside the cavities of the chickens and discard it. Melt the butter in a small frying pan. Pick over the chicken livers and cut away any discolored portions. Add chicken livers to the butter and cook until just brown. Chop and set aside.

2. Combine the breadcrumbs, egg, herbs, salt and pepper and mix well. Mix in the chopped chicken livers.

3. Stuff the cavities of the chickens and sew up the openings. Tie the legs together.

4. Place the chickens in a roasting pan and spread the breasts and legs lightly with more butter. Pour the stock

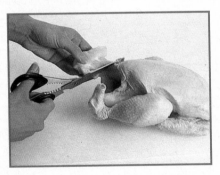

Step 1 Remove the fat from the inside of the cavity of each chicken and discard it.

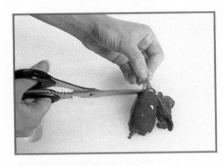

Step 1 Pick over the chicken livers and remove any discolored parts.

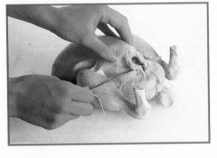

Step 3 Fill the chickens and sew up the opening with fine thread using a trussing needle.

around the chickens and roast in a preheated 375°F oven for about 40-45 minutes. Baste frequently with the pan juices during roasting.

5. To check if the chickens are done, pierce the thickest part of the thigh with a skewer or small, sharp knife. If the juices run clear the chickens are ready. If the juices are pink, return to the oven for another 5-10 minutes.

6. When the chickens are done, remove them from the roasting pan, remove the strings and keep them warm. Skim any fat from the surface of the pan juices. If a lot of liquid has accumulated, pour into a small saucepan and reduce over high heat. Pour the juices over the chicken to serve.

Cook's Notes

Serving Ideas
Serve with a cucumber salad
or a Polish style lettuce salad
and new potatoes tossed with butter
and dill.

Variation
Chopped mushrooms or
onions may be added to the
stuffing, if desired.

Time
Preparation takes about 20
minutes and cooking takes
about 45 minutes.

SERVES 2-3

DUCK IN CAPER SAUCE

A sweet-sour sauce with the tang of
capers is a perfect accompaniment to
a rich meat such as duck.

4½lb whole duck, giblets removed
1 clove garlic, crushed
Salt and pepper
1 tbsp oil
3 tbsps butter or margarine
1 cup chicken stock
4 tbsps sugar
½ cup water
1 tbsp vinegar or lemon juice
6 tbsps capers
4 tsps cornstarch mixed with 2 tbsps water

1. Rub the cavity of the duck with the crushed garlic and sprinkle in salt and pepper. Leave to stand 1-2 hours but do not refrigerate.

2. Heat the oil in a heavy frying pan or roasting pan and when hot add the butter or margarine. Prick the duck skin all over with a sharp fork and brown the duck on all sides in the butter or oil. Transfer the duck to a saucepan or flameproof casserole.

3. Pour over the stock, cover and simmer over medium heat for about 1 hour 40 minutes, or until the duck is tender.

4. Meanwhile, heat the water and sugar together slowly in a small, heavy-based saucepan until the sugar dissolves.

5. Once the sugar is dissolved, turn up the heat and allow the syrup to boil rapidly until it caramelizes. Remove from the heat and pour in the vinegar or lemon juice. It will splutter. Add several spoonfuls of the cooking liquid from the duck and set the caramel over medium heat. Allow mixture to come to the boil, stirring constantly.

Step 2 Brown the duck in a mixture of oil and butter over brisk heat.

Step 4 Combine the sugar and the water in a heavy-based saucepan and cook to dissolve the sugar and make a clear syrup.

6. When the duck is tender, remove it to a heated serving dish. Skim off the fat from the cooking liquid and discard. Mix the water and cornstarch together and add several spoonfuls of the duck cooking liquid. Return to the rest of the liquid and bring to the boil. Add the capers and stir over high heat until the sauce clears and thickens. Add the caramel and stir until the sauce is thick.

7. Cut the duck into portions or serve whole and spoon over some of the sauce. Serve the rest of the sauce separately.

Cook's Notes

Cook's Tip
Pricking the duck skin with a sharp fork allows the fat to run out as the duck cooks. Use this method when roasting or pot roasting to produce duck that is not fatty.

Watchpoint
Keep a close eye on the caramel as it browns. It can burn very quickly. Use an oven glove when adding the vinegar or hot liquid to the caramel as it will splutter.

Time
Preparation takes about 20 minutes with 1-2 hours standing time for the duck. Cooking takes about 1 hour.

SERVES 4

ROAST QUAIL

Quail are delicate, very elegant birds that are
perfect as a dinner party dish. They are also easy to
prepare and quick to cook – a bonus when entertaining.

8 dressed quail
8 thin slices pork fat or 8 strips bacon
Fresh sage leaves
4oz butter
8 slices white bread, crusts removed
Whole cranberry sauce or blueberry preserves with the
  juice of ½ lemon

1. Remove any pin feathers from the birds and wash them under cold running water. Dry thoroughly inside and out. Salt lightly inside and place a fresh sage leaf inside each quail.

2. Tie the pork fat or bacon strips around each bird.

3. Melt the butter over a low heat and brush over each bird before placing them in a preheated 400°F oven for about 20-25 minutes. Baste the quail from time to time with the melted butter and the pan juices.

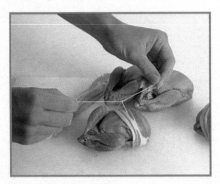

Step 2 Using fine string, tie the pork fat or bacon strips around each quail.

Step 4 Cut the slices of bread about the same size as the quails. Cut in rectangles or ovals with a pastry cutter.

Step 4 Cook the bread in melted butter until nicely browned on both sides.

4. Put the remaining butter in a large frying pan and place over fairly high heat. When hot, add slices of bread which have been cut to a size to fit the quail. Brown them on both sides in the butter and remove to paper towels to drain.

5. When the quail are cooked, remove the threads and take off the bacon or pork fat, if desired. The fat or bacon may be served with the quail. Place each quail on a piece of fried bread and serve with whole cranberry sauce or the blueberry preserves mixed with the lemon juice. Spoon some of the pan juices over each quail before serving.

Cook's Notes

 Variation
Frozen quail may be used in place of fresh quail. Allow to defrost completely before roasting. If neither are available, use pigeons or poussins and increase the cooking time to 35-40 minutes.

Time
Preparation takes about 20-25 minutes and cooking takes about 20 minutes.

 Serving Ideas
Serve with new potatoes and fresh peas.

SERVES 8

SWEET PIEROZKI

In Polish cuisine, dumplings can be sweet as well
as savory. Surprisingly, these are often eaten as
a side dish to meat or as a main dish by themselves.

Dough

Full quantity dough recipe for Christmas Borsch with
  Pierozki
Oil for Frying

Cheese Filling

8oz dry cottage cheese
1 egg yolk
2 tbsps sugar
2 tsps finely chopped candied orange peel
2 tbsps currants

Plum Filling

4-6 purple plums, halved, stoned and chopped
1/3 cup sugar
Sour cream
Grated nutmeg or cinnamon

1. Prepare the dough as for the Pierozki in the Christmas
Borsch recipe. Roll out very thinly on a well-floured surface
and cut into circles about 3 inches in diameter.

2. For the cheese filling, beat the cottage cheese, egg yolk
and sugar together until smooth. Stir in the peel and the
currants by hand. Place a spoonful of the filling on half of the

Step 2 Place the
dough circles out
on a clean sur-
face. Fill half with
cheese and half
with plums.

Step 4 Drop the
filled and sealed
pierozki into
boiling water and
cook until they
float to the
surface.

Step 5 Cook the
drained pierozki in
oil until lightly
browned on both
sides.

dough circles and moisten the edges with water. Fold over
the top and seal the edges well, crimping with a fork if
desired.

3. On the remaining half of the dough circles, place on
some of the chopped plums and sprinkle with sugar. Seal
the edges as before.

4. To cook the Pierozki, drop a few at a time into boiling
water. Simmer for 2-3 minutes or until they float to the top. Lift
out of the water with a slotted spoon and drain on paper
towels.

5. When all the Pierozki are done, heat about 4 tbsps oil in
a frying pan and cook the Pierozki over brisk heat for about
3-4 minutes, or until lightly browned on both sides. Place
the Pierozki on a serving plate and top with sour cream
sprinkled with nutmeg or cinnamon.

Cook's Notes

Time
Preparation takes about 50-60
minutes, cooking takes about
2-3 minutes per batch of Pierozki and
3-4 minutes for frying.

Variation
Other fruit such as pitted
cherries, apricots or peaches,
stoned and chopped, may be used.

Preparation
Pierozki can be cooked in
advance and fried just before
serving.

MAKES 2 ROLLS

POPPY SEED CAKE

This is the Christmas version of an ever popular
Polish cake. As a symbol of holiday generosity, more
poppy seeds were used than in the everyday recipe.

Pastry Dough

6 cups all-purpose flour
¾ cup sugar
1½ sticks butter or margarine
2 eggs
⅓-½ cup milk
3 tbsps yeast
Pinch salt

Filling

8oz poppy seeds
1½ cups milk
⅓ cup butter or margarine
½ cup honey
4 tbsps ground walnuts
3oz raisins
2 tbsps finely chopped candied peel
2 eggs
½ cup sugar
⅓ cup brandy

Step 8 Roll up the dough as for a jelly roll.

1. To prepare the dough, cream the butter with the sugar until light and fluffy and gradually add the eggs, beating well in between each addition. Add a pinch of salt and heat the milk until lukewarm. Dissolve the yeast in the milk and add to the other ingredients. Sift in the flour and knead the dough until smooth and elastic.

2. When kneading dough, be sure to stretch it well and work on a lightly- floured surface. If necessary, flour hands if the dough tends to stick.

3. To test if the dough has been sufficiently kneaded, press lightly with two fingers. If the dough springs back fairly quickly, it is ready to leave to rise.

4. Place the dough in a lightly greased bowl, cover with a cloth or lightly greased plastic wrap and leave for about 1 hour, or until doubled in bulk. Keep in a warm place.

5. Bring the milk for the filling to the boil and mix with the poppy seeds. Cook over low heat for about 30 minutes, stirring frequently. Drain the poppy seed well and blend to a paste in a food processor or liquidizer.

6. Melt the butter and add the honey, walnuts, raisins and peel. Add the poppy seed and cook for about 15 minutes, stirring frequently over moderate heat.

7. Beat the eggs with the sugar until light and fluffy and combine with the poppy seed mixture. Cook over gentle heat, stirring constantly to thicken. Add the brandy and set the filling aside.

8. When the dough has doubled in bulk, knock it back and knead for a further 2-5 minutes. Divide dough in half. Roll each half out thinly on a floured surface, shaping into rectangles. Spread the filling evenly over each piece and roll up as for a jelly roll. Roll up tightly, pressing the ends together to seal. Place on a lightly buttered baking sheet curving into a horse shoe. Bake in a preheated 375°F oven for 45-50 minutes, or until golden brown. Serve with or without icing.

Cook's Notes

Watchpoint
Do not mix the yeast into milk that is too hot. This can kill the yeast and the dough will not rise as it should.

Variation
1 tsp almond or vanilla extract may be used instead of the brandy.

Time
Preparation takes about 1 hour, cooking takes about 45-50 minutes.

MAKES 36

CRULLERS

These are crisp, light biscuits that are fried like fritters. They are best eaten on the day they are made and are lovely with coffee or tea.

2 egg yolks
1 whole egg
4 tbsps sugar
4 tbsps whipping cream
1¼ cups all-purpose flour
Pinch salt
Powdered sugar
Oil for deep frying

1. Beat yolks and whole egg together until thick and lemon colored, about 10 minutes. Add the sugar and beat well to dissolve. Sift the flour with a pinch of salt and whisk half of it into the egg mixture, alternating with the cream. Fold in the remaining flour. Leave to stand 30 minutes in a cool place.

2. Turn the dough out onto a well-floured surface and knead with floured hands. Dough will be sticky at first.

3. Roll out until very thin with a well-floured rolling pin on a well-floured surface.

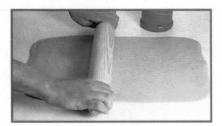

Step 4 Roll out dough paper thin and cut strips with a pastry wheel.

Step 5 Cut slits in the lower half of each strip.

Step 6 Pull one end of each strip through the slit before frying in hot oil.

4. Using a fluted pastry wheel, cut into strips about 3x1½ inches.

5. Cut a slit in the lower half of each piece.

6. Pull one end through the slit. Deep fry at 350°F until golden brown on both sides, about 3-4 minutes. Drain on paper towels and sprinkle with powdered sugar before serving.

Cook's Notes

Time
Preparation takes about 45 minutes and cooking takes about 3-4 minutes per batch.

Serving
Serve as an accompaniment to fruit or ice cream, or serve with coffee or tea.

Preparation
Cook a maximum of 6 crullers at a time.

SERVES 8

ROYAL MAZUREK

Mazureks are flat pastry cakes and there are many different recipes for these. The dough needs careful handling, but the result is well worth the effort.

1½ sticks butter or margarine
4 tbsps sugar
6 tbsps blanched almonds, finely chopped
½ tsp grated lemon rind
2½ cups all-purpose flour
Yolks of 2 hard-boiled eggs, sieved
1 raw egg yolk
Pinch salt
Pinch cinnamon
Apricot and raspberry or cherry preserves
Powdered sugar

1. Cream the butter and the sugar together until light and fluffy. Stir in the almonds, lemon rind, flour and egg yolks by hand. Add the egg yolk and a pinch of salt and cinnamon, and mix all the ingredients into a smooth dough. This may be done in a food processor. Wrap well and leave in the refrigerator for about 1 hour.

2. Roll out ⅔ of the dough and place on a baking sheet. If dough cracks, press back into place. Keep remaining ⅓ of the dough in the refrigerator.

Step 1 Cream the butter and sugar together until light and fluffy

Step 2 Roll out the dough on a well-floured surface with a well-floured rolling pin. Alternatively, roll directly onto the baking sheet.

Step 3 Arrange the strips in a latticework pattern on top of the pastry base, pressing edges together well.

3. Roll out the remaining dough and cut into thin strips about ¼ inch thick. Arrange these strips on top of the dough in a lattice pattern and press the edges to seal.

4. Brush the pastry with a mixture of 1 beaten egg with a pinch of salt. Bake in a preheated 375°F oven for about 20-30 minutes, or until light golden brown and crisp. Loosen the pastry from the baking sheet but do not remove until completely cool. Place the pastry on a serving plate and spoon some of the preserves into each of the open spaces of the lattice work. Alternate the two flavors of preserves. Sprinkle lightly with powdered sugar before serving.

Cook's Notes

Time
Preparation takes about 30 minutes with 1 hour chilling for the pastry. Cooking takes about 20-30 minutes.

Variation
Use other finely chopped nuts in the pastry and other varieties of preserves.

Cook's Tip
If lattice strips break, press ends together and they will stick together again.

MAKES 2 CAKES

SAFFRON BABAS

This is a traditional Easter cake. Cooks spoke in whispers when these cakes were cooling since loud noise was believed to damage the delicate texture!

2½ cups all-purpose flour
1½ cups lukewarm milk
3 envelopes dry yeast
¾ cup sugar
8 egg yolks
4 egg whites
Rind of 1 lemon
3 tbsps brandy
Pinch saffron powder
7½ cups all-purpose flour
Pinch salt
1½ sticks melted butter, slightly cooled
1 cup golden raisins
2 tbsps candied peel

1. First prepare a batter with 2½ cups flour. Combine the milk and yeast and pour into a well in the center of the flour. Mix with a wooden spoon and cover the bowl.

2. Leave in a warm place for about 1 hour, covered with a cloth or plastic wrap, until it doubles in bulk and the top becomes bubbly.

3. Combine the sugar together with the egg yolks, egg whites, lemon rind, brandy and saffron. Mix with the yeast mixture and add the remaining flour and salt. Knead the

Step 1 Sift the flour into a bowl and make a well in the center. Pour in the milk and yeast mixture and stir to form a dough.

Step 2 Leave in a warm place until doubled in bulk and bubbly on top.

Step 4 Leave the dough to rise a second time in the baking dish until it is filling it completely.

dough by hand for about 30 minutes in the bowl or on a very well-floured surface.

4. Place the dough back in the bowl and add the butter, raisins and peel. Knead the dough by hand until it is smooth and elastic and does not stick. Divide in 2 equal portions. Butter 2 10 inch round cake pans very thickly and place in the dough, patting out evenly. Cover with lightly-oiled plastic wrap and put in a warm place to rise until it fills the pan. Bake in a pre-heated 400°F oven for about 60 minutes.

5. Test with a metal skewer. If the skewer comes out clean when inserted into the center of the babas the cakes are done. Leave to cool in the pans for about 10-14 minutes and then remove to a cooling rack. Sprinkle with sugar or drizzle with icing.

Cook's Notes

 Watchpoint
Do not mix the yeast with milk that is too hot. This can kill the yeast and the cakes will not rise as they should.

 Time
Preparation takes about 2 hours, cooking takes about 1 hour.

SERVES 6-8

BUCKWHEAT AND RAISIN PUDDING

Of all the cereals or kashas used in Polish cooking,
buckwheat was the most highly prized.

3 cups milk
1 vanilla pod
6 tbsps butter or margarine
1 cup buckwheat
4 eggs, separated
¾ cup sugar
1-1¼ cups raisins
Grated rind of half a lemon
Red cherry preserves

1. Boil the milk with the vanilla pod in a large saucepan.

2. Stir in 4 tbsps of the butter until melted. Reserve remaining butter.

3. Pick over the buckwheat and add it to the milk, stirring well.

4. Cook, uncovered, over low heat, stirring occasionally to prevent sticking.

5. When the mixture thickens, transfer it to an ovenproof dish with a tight fitting lid. Bake in a preheated 375°F oven for 45 minutes. Remove the vanilla pod and allow the

Step 2 Boil milk with the vanilla pod in a large saucepan and stir in 4 tbsps of the butter.

Step 6 Beat the egg yolks with the sugar until light and fluffy.

Step 7 Whisk the egg whites just until stiff peaks form.

mixture to cool slightly.

6. Beat the egg yolks with the sugar until light and fluffy. Add lemon rind, mix with the buckwheat, and stir in the raisins.

7. Whisk egg whites until stiff peaks form and fold into the buckwheat mixture.

8. Smooth the top of the pudding and dot with the remaining butter. Bake a further 30 minutes at 375°F.

9. Serve topped with cherry preserves and cream, if desired.

Cook's Notes

Variation
Substitute golden raisins, currants or mixed peel for the raisins if desired.

Cook's Tip
Vanilla pods and cinnamon sticks may be used several times. Rinse and dry after use and store air tight.

Time
Preparation takes about 20 minutes, cooking takes a total of 1 hour 25 minutes.

SPANISH
COOKING

INTRODUCTION

Spanish cuisine has been a very well kept secret for a long time, and it is only recently that people have begun to discover that there is a lot to like about Spanish food, and that the old myths about the food being fiery-hot and very oily are untrue. While the food is flavorful, this comes mostly from a subtle blend of herbs and spices rather then a heavy-handed use of chili peppers. Olive oil is the usual choice for frying, sautéeing and salad dressing, but there is no oil more fragrant.

Spanish cuisine is made up of foods that most of us know and like, and ones that are easy to find. It is the different combinations of those familiar ingredients that truly reflect Spanish flavor.

Although the style of eating in Spain is evolving just as it is everywhere else, and food is getting lighter, it still maintains a connection with culinary tradition. The recipes we have included reflect both the traditions and the new trends that make up the best of Spanish cuisine.

SERVES 6-8

GAZPACHO

A typically Spanish soup, this is the. perfect summer first course. The recipe comes from Andalusia, in southern Spain.

1 medium green pepper, seeded and roughly chopped
8 medium tomatoes, peeled, seeded and roughly chopped
1 large cucumber, peeled and roughly chopped
1 large onion, roughly chopped
3-5oz French bread, crusts removed
3 tbsps red wine vinegar
3 cups water
Pinch salt and pepper
1-2 cloves garlic, crushed
3 tbsps olive oil
2 tsps tomato paste (optional)

Garnish

1 small onion, diced
½ small cucumber diced, but not peeled
3 tomatoes, peeled, seeded and diced
½ green pepper, seeded and diced

1. Combine all the prepared vegetables in a deep bowl and add the bread, breaking it into small pieces by hand. Mix together thoroughly.

2. Add the vinegar, water, salt, pepper and garlic.

3. Pour the mixture, a third at a time, into a blender or food processor and purée for about 1 minute, or until the soup is smooth.

4. Pour the purée into a clean bowl and gradually beat in the olive oil using a whisk. Add enough tomato paste for a good red color.

5. Cover the bowl tightly and refrigerate for at least 2 hours, or until thoroughly chilled. Before serving, whisk the soup to make sure all the ingredients are blended and then pour into a large chilled soup tureen or into chilled individual soup bowls. Serve all the garnishes in separate bowls to be added to the soup if desired.

Step 2
Add the liquid, seasoning and garlic and stir the mixture well.

Step 4
After puréeing the soup, pour back into a bowl and whisk in the olive oil by hand.

Cook's Notes

 Time
Preparation takes about 20 minutes and the soup must chill for at least 2 hours.

Preparation
Gazpacho may be prepared a day in advance and kept overnight in the refrigerator. To quickly chill the soup, omit 1 cup water from the recipe and use crushed ice instead. Leave refrigerated for 30 minutes, stirring frequently to melt the ice.

Variation
Use only enough garlic to suit your own taste, or omit if desired. Vary the garnishing ingredients by using croûtons, chopped green onions, or red onions, red or yellow peppers.

SERVES 6
ANCHOVY STUFFED EGGS

A perfect 'tapa' or hors d'oeuvre with cocktails or
wine, these also make good picnic food.

6 eggs
6 anchovy fillets
½ fresh red chili, finely chopped
2 tsps finely chopped parsley or coriander
1 tbsp lemon juice
3-4 tbsps heavy cream
Salt
6 black olives, pitted

Step 3
Use the bowl of a large spoon to roll the eggs in the hot water to set the yolks in the middle of the whites.

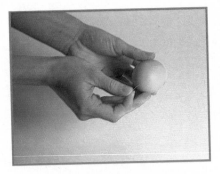

Step 1
Use an egg pricker or needle to make a small hole in the rounded end of each egg to prevent cracking.

Step 5
To fill the eggs, use a small teaspoon or a pastry bag.

1. Prick the rounded end of each egg with a sharp needle or an egg pricker. Lower the eggs carefully into boiling water and bring back to the boil.

2. Using a large metal spoon, roll the eggs around in the pan, gently, while the water comes up to the boil to set the yolk in the middle of the white. Once the water is boiling, allow the eggs to cook for about 9-10 minutes.

3. When the eggs are cooked, pour off the hot water and rinse them under cold running water. Leave in the cold water until ready for use.

4. Chop the anchovies finely and set them aside in a bowl. When the eggs have cooled, peel them and cut them in half lengthwise. Scoop out the yolks and add these to the anchovies. Add all the remaining ingredients, except the olives, and mix thoroughly. Do not over mix. The filling should not be a uniform color.

5. Spoon or pipe the filling back into the hollow of each egg white and top with half a black olive. Serve chilled.

Cook's Notes

Time
Preparation takes about 20 minutes and cooking takes 9-10 minutes.

Variation
Decorate the tops of the eggs in various different ways. Use stuffed green olives, small pieces of red or green pepper or capers, for example.

Serving Ideas
Serve as a tapa. The eggs are also perfect for picnics.

SERVES 6

WHITE GAZPACHO

Often called Ajo Blanco, this soup is
prepared in much the same way as the
Gazpacho based on tomatoes.

6oz blanched almonds
1lb loaf white bread
1-2 cloves garlic, crushed
2 eggs
1 cup olive oil
½ cup white wine vinegar
Pinch of salt and white pepper
1 small bunch of seedless white grapes

Step 6
Beat the reserved
water into the
soup gradually.

Step 3
Purée the
almonds and the
garlic to form a
smooth paste.

Step 5
Squeeze the
bread to remove
all the water.

1. Place the almonds in a bowl and cover with boiling
water. Leave to soak for about 30-45 minutes.

2. Cut the crusts from the bread and cut the bread into
slices or cubes. Place in a bowl and cover with 4 cups cold
water.

3. Drain the almonds and place them in a food processor
or blender with the garlic. Process to a smooth paste.

4. Add the eggs and blend well. With the machine running, add the oil in a thin, steady stream.

5. Drain the bread, wringing it out with your hands, and reserve the water. Add the bread to the other ingredients in
the food processor or blender and purée. Add vinegar, salt
and white pepper and transfer the mixture to a bowl.

6. Gradually add the water, stirring constantly to the
desired consistency. The soup should be as thick as light
cream. Cover the soup and chill for at least 4 hours or
overnight in the refrigerator. Garnish the soup with halved
grapes to serve.

Cook's Notes

Time
Preparation takes about 25
minutes, with 4 hours
minimum chilling time.

Variation
Use other light colored fruit
such as melon, apples, pears
or pineapple for garnish. Peeled
cucumber, cut into small dice, may also
be used. Vary the amount of garlic to
suit your taste.

Cook's Tip
Be sure to add the oil in a thin.
steady stream. If added too
quickly, the soup may curdle. Adding
extra bread will sometimes bring the
mixture back together.

SERVES 4-6

TORTILLA
(SPANISH POTATO OMELET)

Unlike the usual French omelet, this
one isn't folded, so it's easier to prepare.

½ cup olive oil
½lb potatoes, peeled and thinly sliced
1 large onion, peeled and thinly sliced
Salt and pepper
4 eggs
2 tomatoes, peeled, seeded and roughly chopped or
   sliced
2 green onions, chopped

Step 4
Push the eggs
and potatoes
back from the
sides of the pan
using a fork.

Step 3
Pour the potato,
onion and egg
mixture into a
large frying pan.

Step 5
Slide pan under a
preheated broiler
to brown the top
of the omelet.

1. Heat the oil in a large frying pan and add the potatoes. Sprinkle lightly with salt and pepper and cook over medium heat until golden brown and crisp.

2. Add the onion once the potatoes begin to brown slightly. Turn the potatoes and onions over occasionally so that they brown evenly. They should take about 20 minutes to soften and brown.

3. Beat the eggs with a pinch of salt and pepper and stir the potatoes and onions into the eggs and pour the mixture back into the pan.

4. Cook over gentle heat until the bottom browns lightly.

5. Invert a large plate over the top of the pan and carefully turn the omelet out onto it.

6. Slide the omelet back into the pan so the uncooked side has a chance to brown. Cook until the eggs are set. Garnish with the tomatoes and green onions and serve warm.

Cook's Notes

 Time
Preparation takes about 30 minutes, cooking takes about 30-40 minutes.

Preparation
As the potatoes cook, turn them frequently to prevent them sticking together. They will, however, stick slightly, which is not a problem.

 Serving Ideas
The omelet may be cut into small squares and served as a tapa. It can also be served with a salad and bread for a light lunch or supper. Serve hot or cold.

SERVES 4

AVOCADO, ORANGE AND BLACK OLIVE SALAD

A light and colorful salad combining three of
Spain's abundant ingredients.

2 oranges, peeled and segmented
2 avocados
20 black olives, pitted
Basil leaves
½ small red onion, thinly sliced

Dressing

1 tbsp white wine or sherry vinegar
4 tbsps olive oil
½ tsp mustard
Pinch of salt and pepper

Step 1
Hit the stone with
the sharp edge of
a large knife and
twist to remove it.

Step 1
To peel the av-
ocado, lightly
score the skin in
two or three
places, place the
half cut side down
on a chopping
board and gently
pull back the
peel.

Step 1
Cut the avocados
in half and twist to
separate.

1. Make sure all the white pith is removed from each segment of orange. Cut the avocados in half and remove the
stone. Peel them and cut into slices.

2. Cut the olives in half and slice them thinly or chop them.

Use kitchen scissors to shred the basil leaves finely.

3. Arrange the orange segments, avocado slices, sliced
onion and olives on serving plates and sprinkle over the
shredded basil leaves. Mix the dressing ingredients
together well and pour over the salad to serve.

Cook's Notes

Time
Preparation takes about 30
minutes.

Cook's Tip
Do not peel the avocados
more than 30 minutes before
serving time unless you prepare the
dressing beforehand and coat the
avocados with it to prevent
discoloration.

Variation
Green onions may be used
instead of the red onions. Use
different varieties of herbs. Substitute
grapefruit for the orange.

SERVES 6

CARROT AND ZUCCHINI SALAD

This salad couldn't be easier. It is colorful, inexpensive
and can be made almost all year round.

12oz carrots, peeled
12oz zucchini, topped and tailed
Grated rind and juice of 2 oranges
3 tbsps olive oil
Salt and pepper
4 tbsps unblanched almonds, chopped

Step 2
Grate the zucchini
coarsely and add
to the carrots.

Step 1
Grate the carrots
on the coarse
side of a grater.

Step 3
When grating
oranges or other
citrus fruit, use a
pastry brush to
remove all the
zest from holes in
grater.

1. Shred the carrots on the coarse side of a grater or use
the coarse grating blade of a food processor. Place in a
large bowl.

2. Grate the zucchini in the same way and add to the
carrots.

3. Grate the orange on the fine side of the grater and then
cut in half to squeeze the juice. Mix the juice and rind with

the olive oil and salt and pepper. Pour over the carrots and
the zucchini and stir well. Leave to marinate for about 15
minutes.

4. Sprinkle over the almonds and toss just before serving.

Cook's Notes

Time
Preparation takes about 15-25
minutes. Vegetables should
marinate for about 15 minutes.

Preparation
The salad may be prepared in
advance and left to stand
longer than 15 minutes. Cover well and
refrigerate.

Serving Ideas
Serve in individual bowls with
a selection of other tapas.
Spoon on to lettuce leaves for a first
course or serve as a side salad.

SERVES 6

ROAST PEPPER SALAD

Charring the peppers makes the skins
easier to remove and gives a slightly
smoky taste that is very pleasant.

6 red peppers
6 tbsps olive oil
1 clove garlic, roughly chopped
2 tbsps red or white wine vinegar
Salt and pepper
1 green onion, diagonally sliced

Step 3
Broil the lightly-
oiled peppers
until the skins are
very charred.

Step 2
Flatten the
peppers by
pushing down
with the palm of
the hand.

Step 4
Use a small,
sharp knife to
peel away the
skin.

1. Preheat a broiler and cut the peppers in half, removing the seeds, stems and cores.

2. Flatten the peppers with the palm of your hand and brush the skin side of each pepper lightly with oil. Place the peppers under the broiler.

3. Broil the peppers until the skins are well charred on top. Do not turn the peppers over.

4. Wrap the peppers in a clean towel and leave to stand for about 15-20 minutes.

5. Unwrap the peppers and peel off the skin using a small, sharp knife. Cut the peppers into strips or into 1 inch pieces. Mix the remaining oil with the vinegar, salt and pepper. Place the peppers in a serving dish and pour over the dressing. Sprinkle over the garlic and green onion and leave the peppers to stand for about 30 minutes before serving.

Cook's Notes

Time
Preparation takes about 20 minutes. Broiling time for the peppers is approximately 10-12 minutes.

Preparation
The peppers must be well charred for the skin to loosen easily. Wrapping peppers in a tea towel creates steam, which helps to loosen the skin more easily.

Serving Ideas
Serve as a tapa or mix with cooked cold rice for a more substantial salad.

SERVES 4

SALMON AND VEGETABLE SALAD

The fish in this salad 'cooks' in the refrigerator in its vinegar marinade. Insist on very fresh fish for this recipe.

12oz salmon or salmon trout fillets
2 carrots, peeled and diced
1 large zucchini, peeled and diced
1 large turnip, peeled and diced
Chopped fresh coriander
3 tbsps tarragon or sherry vinegar
Salt and pepper
Pinch cayenne pepper
3 tbsps olive oil
Whole coriander leaves to garnish

Step 2
Cut all the vegetables into 1 inch dice.

Step 1
Place the salmon in a bowl with the vinegar and stir to coat well.

Step 3
When the salmon has marinated, it will become opaque and look cooked. Mix with the other ingredients.

1. Skin the salmon fillet and cut the fish into 1 inch pieces. Place in a bowl and add the vinegar, stirring well. Leave to stand for at least 2 hours.

2. Cut the vegetables into ½ inch dice and place the carrots in boiling water for about 5 minutes. Add the

zucchini and turnip during the last minute of cooking time.

3. Add the coriander, oil, salt and pepper and pinch cayenne pepper to the fish. Combine with the vegetables, mixing carefully so the fish does not break up. Chill briefly before serving, and garnish with coriander.

Cook's Notes

Time
Preparation takes about 30 minutes, with 2 hours for the salmon to marinate.

Cook's Tip
Fish allowed to marinate in vinegar, lemon or lime juice will appear opaque and 'cooked' after standing for about 2 hours.

Serving Ideas
Serve as a tapa or as a first course.

SERVES 6

FISH ESCABECH

Originally, this method of marinating sautéed fish in vinegar was simply a way of preserving it. All kinds of fish and even poultry and game were prepared this way.

3lb monkfish
6 tbsps flour
Pinch salt and pepper
1 medium carrot, peeled and thinly sliced
1 medium onion, thinly sliced
1 bay leaf
2 sprigs parsley
¼-½ fresh red chili, finely chopped
1½ cups white wine vinegar
6 cloves garlic, peeled and thinly sliced
Olive oil

1. Peel the brownish membrane from the outside of the monkfish tails.

2. Cut along the bone with a sharp filleting knife to separate the flesh from it.

3. Cut the monkfish into slices about 1 inch thick. Mix the salt and pepper with the flour and dredge the slices of monkfish, shaking off the excess. Fry in olive oil until golden brown. Remove and drain on paper towels.

4. Add the carrot and onion and fry gently for about 5 minutes. Add the bay leaf, parsley, vinegar, chili pepper and 1 cup water. Cover and simmer gently for about 20 minutes.

5. Place the fish in a shallow casserole dish and pour over the marinade. Sprinkle on the sliced garlic and cover well. Refrigerate for 24 hours, turning the fish over several times.

6. To serve, remove the fish from the marinade and arrange on a serving plate. Pour the marinade on top of the fish and garnish with parsley, if desired.

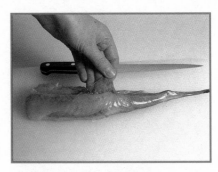

Step 1
Remove the brownish membrane from the outside of the monkfish tails.

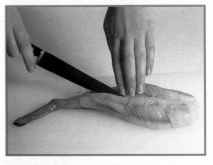

Step 2
Using a sharp filleting knife, cut along the bone to separate one side of the tail. Repeat with the other side.

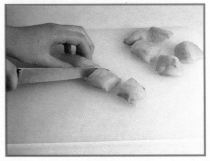

Step 3
Slice the tails into 1 inch thick pieces.

Cook's Notes

Time
Preparation takes about 25 minutes, with 24 hours refrigeration, cooking takes about 25 minutes.

Variation
Other fish, such as whole small trout or trout fillets, or fish steaks such as cod or salmon, may be used.

Serving Ideas
Serve as a first course or for a light lunch with a salad and bread.

SERVES 6

PAELLA

This dish has as many variations as Spain
has cooks! Fish, meat and poultry combine with
vegetables and rice to make a complete meal.

12 mussels in their shells
6 clams (if not available use 6 more mussels)
6oz cod, skinned and cut into 2 inch pieces
12 large shrimp
3 chorizos or other spicy sausage
2lb chicken cut in 12 serving-size pieces
1 small onion, chopped
1 clove garlic, crushed
2 small peppers, red and green, seeded and shredded
1lb long grain rice
Large pinch saffron
Salt and pepper
4 cups boiling water
5oz frozen peas
3 tomatoes, peeled, seeded and chopped or shredded

1. Scrub the clams and mussels well to remove beards
and barnacles. Discard any with broken shells or those that
do not close when tapped. Leave the mussels and clams to
soak in water with a handful of flour for 30 minutes.

2. Remove the heads and legs from the shrimp, if desired,
but leave on the tail shells.

3. Place the sausage in a saucepan and cover with water.
Bring to the boil and then simmer for 5 minutes. Drain and
slice into ¼ inch rounds. Set aside.

4. Heat the oil and fry the chicken pieces, browning evenly
on both sides. Remove and drain on paper towels.

5. Add the sausage, onions, garlic and peppers to the oil in
the frying pan and fry briskly for about 3 minutes.

6. Combine the sausage mixture with uncooked rice and
saffron and place in a special Paella dish or a large oven-
and flame-proof casserole. Pour on the water, season with
salt and pepper and bring to the boil. Stir occasionally and
allow to boil for about 2 minutes.

7. Add the chicken pieces and place in a preheated 400°F
oven for about 15 minutes.

8. Add the clams, mussels, shrimp, cod and peas and
cook a further 10-15 minutes or until the rice is tender,
chicken is cooked and mussels and clams open. Discard
any that do not open. Add the tomatoes 5 minutes before
the end of cooking time and serve immediately.

Step 5
Cook the saus-
ages, onions
garlic and
peppers briefly in
oil.

Step 6
Combine the
sausage mixture,
rice and water in
a special Paella
dish or flame-
proof casserole.

Cook's Notes

 Time
Preparation takes about 30-40
minutes, cooking takes about
35-40 minutes.

 Variation
Vary the ingredients to suit
your own taste. Use other
kinds of fish and shellfish. Omit chicken
or substitute pork for part of the
quantity. Use red or green onions if
desired and add more sausage.

 Watchpoint
Do not stir the Paella once it
goes into the oven.

SERVES 4

MUSSELS IN RED WINE

Red wine makes an unusual, but very pleasant,
combination with seafood. This recipe is equally
good with clams or cockles.

3lb mussels, well scrubbed
1 cup dry red wine
6 tbsps olive oil
4 cloves garlic, finely chopped
2 bay leaves
2 tbsps fresh thyme, chopped
6 tbsps red wine vinegar
1 tsp paprika
Grated rind and juice of 1 lemon
Salt and pepper
Pinch cayenne pepper
Pinch sugar (optional)
Chopped parsley

1. Prepare the mussels as in the recipe for Paella. Place the wine in a large saucepan and bring to the boil. Add the mussels, cover the pan and cook briskly for about 4-5 minutes, stirring frequently, until the shells open. Discard any that do not open.

2. Transfer the mussels to a bowl and pour the cooking liquid through a fine strainer and reserve it.

3. In a clean saucepan, heat the oil and fry the garlic over gentle heat until golden brown. Add the bay leaves, thyme, vinegar, paprika, lemon juice and rind, salt, pepper and cayenne pepper. Pour on the wine, add sugar, if using, and bring to the boil. Cook to reduce to about ⅔ cup. Allow to cool completely.

4. Remove the mussels from their shells and add them to the liquid, stirring to coat all the mussels. Cover and place in the refrigerator for at least 2 hours. Allow to stand at room temperature for about 30 minutes before serving. Sprinkle with parsley.

Step 1
Cook the mussels over high heat, stirring frequently, until the shells begin to open.

Step 2
Transfer the mussels to a plate and pour the liquid through a fine strainer or through muslin.

Step 4
Remove the mussels from their shells with your fingers or by using a small teaspoon.

Cook's Notes

 Time
Preparation takes about 30 minutes and cooking takes about 9-10 minutes.

Serving Ideas
Serve in small dishes as tapas. To serve as a more formal first course, place lettuce leaves on individual plates and spoon on the mussels. Sprinkle with chopped parsley, if desired.

 Variation
Shelled mussels, purchased from a fishmonger, or frozen mussels may be used instead. If using frozen mussels, allow a further 2-3 minutes cooking time.

SERVES 4

Broiled Fish with Romescu

Romescu is a sauce that evolved from a fish stew recipe
and is still often considered a dish on its own. It is
simple to make and has a strong, pungent taste.

2lbs whole fish such as trout, red mullet, herring, sardines
    or mackerel, allowing 1-4 fish per person, depending
    on size.
Bay leaves
Salt and pepper
Olive oil
Lemon juice

Romescu (Almond and Hot Pepper Sauce)

1 tomato, peeled, seeded and chopped
3 tbsps ground almonds
½ clove garlic, crushed
½ tsp cayenne pepper
Pinch salt
3 tbsps red wine vinegar
⅔ cup olive oil

with a wire whisk or a wooden spoon. Make sure each
addition of oil is absorbed before adding more. Once about
half the oil is added, the remainder may be poured in in a
thin, steady stream. Adjust the seasoning and set the sauce
aside.

3. Wash the fish well, sprinkle the cavities with salt and
pepper and place in a bay leaf. Brush the skin with olive oil
and sprinkle with lemon juice. Place under a preheated
broiler and cook for about 2-5 minutes per side, depending
on the thickness of the fish. Brush with lemon juice and olive
oil while the fish is broiling. Serve with the sauce and lemon
or lime wedges if desired.

Step 2
Transfer the paste
to a bowl and
whisk in the wine
vinegar.

Step 1
Mix all the
ingredients
together into a
smooth paste
using a mortar
and pestle.

Step 2
Once half the oil
has been added,
add the remain-
der in a thin,
steady stream,
whisking by hand.

1. To prepare the sauce, combine all the ingredients,
except the olive oil and vinegar, in a mortar and pestle and
work to a smooth mixture.

2. Transfer to a bowl, whisk in red wine vinegar and add
the oil gradually, a few drops at a time, mixing vigorously

Cook's Notes

Time
Preparation takes about 20
minutes and cooking takes
about 10-20 minutes.

Preparation
The sauce may be made
several days in advance and
stored tightly sealed in the refrigerator.
Allow the sauce to come to room
temperature and whisk again before
serving.

Serving Ideas
Serve with boiled or fried
potatoes and a salad.

SERVES 6

SEAFOOD STEW

This makes the most of the delicious
and varied fish and shellfish found
off Spain's beautiful coastline.

24 clams or mussels in the shell
3 squid
2lb firm whitefish, filleted into 2 inch pieces
3 medium-sized tomatoes, peeled, seeded and chopped
½ green pepper, seeded and chopped
1 small onion, chopped
1 clove garlic, finely chopped
1 cup dry white wine
Salt and pepper
½ cup olive oil
6 slices French bread
3 tbsps chopped parsley

1. Scrub the clams or mussels well to remove the beards and barnacles. Discard any shellfish with broken shells or ones that do not close when tapped. Place the mussels or clams in a large saucepan or heatproof casserole. scatter over about half of the vegetables and garlic and spoon over 4 tbsps of the olive oil.

2. To clean the squid, hold the tail section in one hand and the head section in the other to pull the tail away from the head.

3. Cut the tentacles free from the head just above the eyes. Discard the head, entrails and ink sack.

4. Remove the quill from the body of the squid and peel away the reddish-purple outer skin.

5. Slice the tail into strips about ½ inch thick. Cut the tentacles into individual pieces.

6. Scatter the squid and the prepared whitefish over the vegetables in the pan and top with the remaining vegetables. Pour over the white wine and season with salt and

pepper. Bring to the boil over high heat and then reduce to simmering. Cover the pan and cook for about 20 minutes or until the clams open, the squid is tender and the fish flakes easily. Discard any clams or mussels that do not open.

7. Heat the remaining olive oil in a frying pan and when hot, add the slices of bread, browning them well on both sides. Drain on paper towels.

8. Place a slice of bread in the bottom of a soup bowl and ladle the fish mixture over the bread. Sprinkle with parsley and serve immediately.

Step 2
To clean the squid, separate the head from the tail by pulling them in opposite directions

Step 4
Remove the quill from the tail and peel the reddish-purple skin from the outside.

Cook's Notes

Time
Preparation takes about 35 minutes and cooking takes about 20 minutes.

Preparation
Fry the bread while the fish stew is cooking. The stew must be served immediately and not reheated.

Variation
Different kinds of fish, such as haddock, cod, halibut or sea bass can be used.

SERVES 4

MARINATED TROUT WITH EGG SAUCE

This recipe came from Navarre, an area famous for its brook trout.
The simply-prepared sauce allows the flavor of the fish to shine through.

4 even-sized trout, gutted but heads and tails left on
6 tbsps red wine
3 tbsps olive oil
3 tbsps water
1 clove garlic, crushed
2 sprigs fresh mint, 1 sprig fresh rosemary, 1 sprig fresh thyme, 1 small bay leaf, crumbled
6 black peppercorns
Pinch salt
3 egg yolks, lightly beaten
1 tbsp fresh herbs
Lemon or lime slices to garnish

1. Place the fish in a roasting pan and pour over the wine, oil, water and add the garlic and herbs. Sprinkle over the peppercorns and the salt and turn the fish several times to coat them thoroughly with the marinade. Leave at room temperature for about 30 minutes.

2. Place the roasting pan with the fish on top of the stove and bring the marinade just to the simmering point. Cover the pan and place in a preheated 350°F oven and cook for about 20 minutes or until the fish is firm.

3. Transfer the fish to a serving dish and peel off the skin on one side. Cover and keep warm.

4. Strain the fish cooking liquid into a bowl or the top of a double boiler and discard the herbs and garlic. Mix about 3 tbsps of the liquid into the egg yolks and then return to the bowl or double boiler.

5. Heat slowly, whisking constantly until the sauce thickens. Do not allow the sauce to boil. Add the chopped herbs and adjust the seasoning.

6. Coat the sauce over the skinned side of each trout and garnish the plate with lemon or lime wedges. Serve the rest of the sauce separately.

Step 2
Bring the marinade and fish to the simmering point on top of the stove. Allow to boil.

Step 3
When the fish is cooked, transfer to a serving dish and peel off one side of the skin on each fish.

Step 5
Cook the strained marinade and egg yolks slowly in a double boiler, whisking constantly until the sauce thickens.

Cook's Notes

Time
Preparation takes about 30 minutes, cooking takes about 20 minutes for the fish and about 5 minutes to finish the sauce.

 Variation
The sauce may be made with white wine instead of red wine if desired.

 Serving Ideas
A classic accompaniment is boiled potatoes.

SERVES 4-6

CHORIZO SAUSAGES WITH PEAS AND MINT

Spicy sausages are a perfect foil for the mild flavor of peas
and the cooling tang of mint in this informal dish.

4 chorizos
4oz salt pork, finely diced
1 small onion, finely chopped
½ clove garlic, finely chopped
¾ cup white wine
¾ cup water
1 bay leaf
Pinch salt and pepper
2 tsps chopped fresh mint
1lb shelled fresh peas or frozen peas

Step 3
Cook the onions and garlic until soft but not colored.

Step 2
Cook the bacon in its own fat until crisp and golden brown.

Step 4
Add all the ingredients and cook, uncovered, until tender.

1. Place the chorizo sausages in a saucepan or frying pan and add enough water to cover completely. Bring to the boil and then reduce the heat to simmering. Cook, uncovered, for about 5 minutes and drain on paper towels. Set the sausages aside.

2. Cook the bacon slowly in a frying pan or saucepan until the fat is rendered. Then turn up the heat and cook until crisp and golden brown. Place on paper towels to drain.

3. Add the onion and garlic to the bacon fat in the pan and cook until the onions are softened but not browned. Add the wine, water, bay leaf, bacon, mint, salt and pepper. Bring to the boil over high heat and then reduce to simmering. Add the sausages and cook, partially covered, for about 20 minutes.

4. If using fresh peas, add with the sausages. If using frozen peas, add during the last 5 minutes of cooking time. Remove sausages and slice. Add to the peas and re-heat if necessary. Using a draining spoon, place a serving on each plate.

Cook's Notes

Time
Preparation takes about 20 minutes, or slightly longer if shelling fresh peas. Cooking takes about 35 minutes.

Variation
Lima beans or green beans may be used instead of the peas.

Serving Ideas
Serve as a side dish to meat, poultry or fish. Add rice to serve as a main course.

SERVES 4

SWEETBREADS WITH PEPPERS AND SHERRY

Rich, velvety sweetbreads are perfectly complemented by the sweet-sour taste of honey and vinegar.

2.2lbs lamb or calf sweetbreads
1 slice lemon
1 small red pepper, seeded and sliced
1 small green pepper, seeded and sliced
1 medium onion, peeled and thinly sliced
2 tbsps olive oil
1 tbsp butter or margarine
4 tbsps dry sherry
2 tbsps tarragon vinegar
1 cup chicken or veal stock
1 tbsp lemon juice
2 tbsps clear honey
Salt and pepper

1. Soak the sweetbreads in enough water to cover with the lemon slice for at least 2 hours. Transfer the sweetbreads to a saucepan and pour over clean water to cover.

2. Bring to the boil and cook for 10 minutes. Drain the sweetbreads and rinse them under cold water. Place drained sweetbreads on a plate and cover with another plate to weight down slightly. Leave to stand for 15 minutes.

3. Using a small, sharp knife, peel away the outer membrane from the sweetbreads.

4. Heat the oil, add the butter and, when foaming, fry the sweetbreads until golden brown. Remove them to a plate.

5. Cook the peppers and onions until softened and set them aside with the sweetbreads. Pour off any remaining fat in the pan.

6. Add the sherry and vinegar to the pan and boil. Pour on the stock and boil rapidly to reduce by half. Add the lemon juice and honey and return the sweetbreads and vegetables to the pan. Heat through and serve immediately.

Step 1
Soak the sweetbreads with a slice of lemon in enough cold water to cover.

Step 2
Once the sweetbreads have boiled, place them between two plates to weight down slightly.

Step 3
Use a small, sharp knife to pull away the outer membrane from the sweetbreads to keep them from shrinking and toughening.

Cook's Notes

Time
Preparation takes about 45 minutes, with 2 hours soaking time for the sweetbreads. Cooking takes about 25 minutes.

Preparation
The method for preparing sweetbreads is designed to allow the outer membrane to be removed fairly easily. This prevents the sweetbreads from shrinking and toughening.

Buying Guide
Sweetbreads are the thymus or pancreas of lambs and calves. Lamb sweetbreads are more readily available and are less expensive. Sweetbreads have a mild flavor much like chicken.

SERVES 6

PORK WITH TOMATO AND BLACK OLIVE SAUCE

A recipe like this one is often served in a small amount
as one of a selection of tapas — hors d'oeuvres.

3lb pork tenderloin, cut into ½ inch slices
Salt and pepper
4 tbsps flour
3 tbsps olive oil
1 medium-sized onion, thinly sliced
1lb canned tomatoes, drained and juice reserved
6 tbsps white wine
¾ cup light stock
3 slices cooked ham, shredded
1 hard-boiled egg
10-12 black olives, pitted and sliced
2 tbsps chopped parsley or coriander

Step 1
Place pieces of
pork in a sieve
with the flour and
shake to coat
evenly.

1. Mix the salt and pepper with the flour and coat the pieces of meat lightly, shaking off the excess. Heat the oil in a large frying pan and fry the meat, in several batches, until brown on both sides. Transfer the meat to a plate.

2. Add the onions to the pan and cook for about 5 minutes over low heat to soften but not brown. Add the tomatoes, wine and stock to the pan and bring to the boil.

3. Return the meat to the pan, cover and cook over low heat for about 30-40 minutes or until the meat is tender. Check the level of liquid and add some reserved tomato juice if necessary.

4. Cut the hard-boiled egg in half and remove the yolk. Cut the white into thin shreds. Five minutes before the end of cooking time, add the ham, egg white, olives and parsley to the sauce.

5. To serve, place pork slices on individual plates or on a large serving dish and spoon over the sauce. Push the egg yolks through a metal sieve to garnish the top of the pork. Serve immediately.

Step 2
Cook the onions
until soft, but not
colored.

Step 5
Push egg yolk
through a sieve to
garnish the pork.

Cook's Notes

Time
Preparation takes about 25 minutes and cooking takes about 30-40 minutes.

Serving Ideas
Serve with rice or potatoes and a green vegetable.

Buying Guide
Pitted black olives are available in delicatessens and large supermarkets.

SERVES 4

SHERRIED PORK WITH FIGS

Another popular Spanish fruit and meat combination.
Figs look especially attractive as a garnish and
really complement the sherry sauce.

2lb pork tenderloin
3 tbsps butter or margarine
1 bay leaf
1 sprig fresh thyme
½ cup medium-dry sherry
1 cup brown stock
Juice and zest of 1 large orange
1½ tbsps cornstarch
Pinch cinnamon
Salt and pepper
4 fresh figs

1. Slice the pork diagonally into pieces about ½ inch thick. Melt the butter or margarine in a large sauté pan and, when foaming, place in the slices of pork. Cook quickly on both sides to brown.

2. Pour away most of the fat and add the sherry. Bring to the boil and cook for about 1 minute. Pour on the stock and add the bay leaf and thyme. Bring to the boil and then lower the heat, cover and simmer for about 30 minutes or until the pork is tender.

3. When the pork is cooked, remove it from the pan and boil the liquid to reduce slightly. Add the orange zest to the liquid and mix the juice and cornstarch together. Spoon in a bit of the hot liquid and then return the mixture to the pan. Bring to the boil, whisking constantly until thickened and cleared. Stir in a pinch of cinnamon, salt and pepper. Return the pork to the pan and cook to heat through.

4. If the figs are small, quarter them. If they are large, slice lengthwise. Remove the pork to a serving dish and spoon over the sauce. Garnish with the sliced or quartered figs.

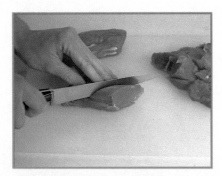

Step 1
Slice the pork tenderloin into diagonal pieces about 1/2 inch thick.

Step 1
Use a large sauté pan or frying pan to brown the slices of pork on both sides.

Step 3
Cook the pork over moderate heat until tender to the point of a knife. Do not allow the pork to boil rapidly.

Cook's Notes

Time
Preparation takes about 25 minutes and cooking takes about 45 minutes.

Preparation
Pork tenderloin can toughen if cooked too rapidly or over heat that is too high. Simmer gently in the liquid.

Serving Ideas
Serve with rice, either saffron or plain.

SERVES 4

PEPPERED FILLET OF LAMB WITH FRUIT

In Catalonia, on the border with France,
meat cooked with fruit is extremely popular.

2¼lbs lamb neck fillets
1 tbsp coarsely crushed black peppercorns
8oz dried fruit salad
4 tbsps butter or margarine
2 tbsps flour
1 cup light stock
½ cup medium dry sherry
3 tbsps heavy cream
Pinch salt
Coriander leaves to garnish

brown slightly. Stir in the stock gradually to blend well and add the sherry. Bring to the boil.

5. Drain the fruit, add to the pan and return the lamb fillets. Cover and cook over gentle heat for about 15-20 minutes or until lamb and fruit are tender.

6. When the lamb is cooked, remove it from the pan and slice into diagonal pieces about ¼ inch thick. Arrange on a serving plate and add the cooked fruit.

7. Add the cream to the sauce and bring to the boil. Allow to boil 1 minute to thicken and cook the cream and spoon the sauce over the fruit and meat to serve.

Step 2
Press the peppercorns firmly into the surface of each lamb fillet using your hand, a meat mallet or rolling pin.

Step 3
Fry the lamb fillets in a sauté pan or frying pan to brown evenly on all sides.

1. Place the fruit salad in a saucepan, cover with water and bring to the boil. Once the water boils, remove from the heat and leave to soak for about 2 hours.

2. Sprinkle the black peppercorns on the lamb fillets and press them in firmly with the palm of your hand, or bat them lightly with a meat mallet or rolling pin.

3. Melt the butter or margarine in a large sauté pan and when foaming, add the lamb fillets. Cook over moderately high heat to seal on both sides. When the lamb fillets are brown, remove them to a plate and set them aside.

4. Add the flour to the pan and cook over moderate heat to

Step 6
When lamb is cooked, slice it thinly on the diagonal.

Cook's Notes

Time
Preparation takes about 25 minutes, with 2 hours soaking time for the fruit. Cooking takes about 30-40 minutes.

Variation
Substitute pork tenderloins or fillet steaks for the lamb neck fillet. Lamb chops may also be used. Any combination of dried fruit may be used in this recipe.

Preparation
When coating the fillets with peppercorns, press firmly so that they stick well in the surface and do not fall off during cooking.

SERVES 4

CHICKEN WITH SAFFRON RICE AND PEAS

Saffron is frequently used in Spanish recipes. While it is expensive, it gives rice and sauces a lovely golden color and delicate taste.

2 tbsps oil
2-3lb chicken, cut into 8 pieces and skinned if desired
Salt and pepper
1 small onion, finely chopped
2 tsps paprika
1 clove garlic, crushed
8 tomatoes, peeled, seeded and chopped
10oz rice
2½ cups boiling water
Large pinch saffron or ¼ tsp ground saffron
6oz frozen peas
2 tbsps chopped parsley

1. Heat the oil in a large frying pan. Season the chicken with salt and pepper and place it in the hot oil, skin side down first. Cook over moderate heat, turning the chicken frequently to brown it lightly. Set the chicken aside.

2. Add the onions to the oil and cook slowly until softened but not colored.

3. Add the paprika and cook about 2 minutes, stirring frequently until the paprika loses some of its red color. Add the garlic and the tomatoes.

4. Cook the mixture over high heat for about 5 minutes to evaporate the liquid from the tomatoes. The mixture should be of dropping consistency when done. Add the rice, water and saffron and stir together.

5. Return the chicken to the casserole and bring to the boil over high heat. Reduce to simmering, cover tightly and cook for about 20 minutes. Remove chicken and add the peas and parsley. Cook a further 5-10 minutes, or until rice is tender. Combine with the chicken to serve.

Step 3
Add the paprika and cook until it loses some of its red color.

Step 4
When the garlic and tomatoes are added, cook over a high heat to evaporate the liquid until the mixture is of a dropping consistency.

Step 5
Stir in the peas and parsley and cook for five minutes.

Cook's Notes

Time
Preparation takes about 20-25 minutes and cooking takes about 25-35 minutes.

Variation
If using fresh peas, allow about 14oz of peas in their pods. Cook fresh peas with the rice and chicken.

Serving Ideas
This is a very casual, peasant-type dish which is traditionally served in the casserole in which it was cooked.

SERVES 4

Spring Chickens with Bitter Chocolate Sauce

A small amount of unsweetened chocolate lends a rich depth of color
and a delightfully mysterious flavor to a savory sauce.

4 tbsps olive oil
4 Rock Cornish hens
Salt and pepper
3 tbsps flour
1 clove garlic, crushed
1 cup chicken stock
4 tbsps dry white wine
2 tsps unsweetened cooking chocolate, grated
Lemon slices to garnish

Step 2
Cook the flour in
the oil until it turns
a pale straw color.

Step 1
Brown the hens in
the hot oil, turning
carefully to avoid
tearing the skin.

Step 5
Stir the grated
chocolate into the
sauce and cook
over low heat to
melt it.

1. Heat the oil in a heavy-based pan or casserole. Season the hens and place them, breast side down first, in the hot oil. Cook until golden brown on all sides, turning frequently.

2. Transfer the hens to a plate and add flour to the casserole. Cook until a pale straw color.

3. Add the garlic and cook to soften. Pour on the stock gradually, mixing well. Add the wine and bring to the boil.

4. Reduce to simmering, replace the hens and cover the casserole. Cook 20-30 minutes, or until the hens are tender.

5. Transfer the cooked hens to a serving dish and skim any fat from the surface of the sauce. Add the grated chocolate and cook, stirring quickly, over low heat for 2-3 minutes. Pour some of the sauce over the hens and garnish with lemon slices. Serve the rest of the sauce separately.

Cook's Notes

Time
Preparation takes about 20 minutes, cooking takes about 25-35 minutes.

Buying Guide
Unsweetened baking chocolate is not the same as semi-sweet chocolate, which must not be used as a substitute. Unsweetened chocolate is available in large supermarkets and specialty shops.

Serving Ideas
Serve with rice and a vegetable such as peas or asparagus, or with a green salad.

SERVES 4

VEAL WITH PEACHES AND PINENUTS

This dish is quite expensive, but very easy
and quick to prepare and cook.

4 ripe peaches
6 tbsps brandy or sherry
8 veal cutlets
Salt and pepper
½ cup dry white wine
Pinch cinnamon
1 small bay leaf
2 tbsps butter or margarine
4 tbsps pinenuts
1 tbsps cornstarch mixed with 2 tbsps water
Pinch sugar

1. Peel the peaches by dropping them into boiling water for about 30 seconds. Remove immediately to a bowl of cold water and leave to cool completely. Use a small, sharp knife to remove the peels.

2. Cut the peaches in half and twist the halves to separate. Remove the stones and place the peaches in a deep bowl with the brandy or sherry. Stir the peach halves to coat them completely.

3. Place the veal cutlets between 2 sheets of wax paper and use a rolling pin or meat mallet to bat out to flatten slightly. This may not be necessary. Heat the oil and fry the cutlets on both sides until golden brown. Pour on the wine and add the cinnamon, bay leaf, salt, pepper and cover the pan. Cook over low heat for about 15 minutes or until the veal is tender and cooked through.

4. While the veal is cooking, melt the butter in a small frying pan and add the pinenuts. Cook over moderate heat, stirring continuously until they are golden brown. Remove from the butter and set them aside to drain.

5. When the veal is cooked, remove it to a serving dish and keep it warm. Add cornstarch and water mixture to the pan and bring to the boil. Cook until thickened and cleared.

6. Remove the peaches from the brandy and slice them. Add the peaches and the brandy to the thickened sauce mixture and bring to the boil. Allow to cook rapidly for about 1 minute. Add the sugar, if using. Spoon the peaches and sauce over the veal cutlets and sprinkle on the browned pinenuts. Serve immediately.

Step 1
Place peaches in boiling water for 30 seconds.

Step 1
Transfer to cold water to cool completely — the peel will be easy to remove with a small knife.

Cook's Notes

Time
Preparation takes about 25-30 minutes, cooking takes about 25-30 minutes in total.

Variation
The recipe may be prepared with pork tenderloin, chicken breasts or duck breasts. Use nectarines or apricots instead of peaches and do not peel them.

SERVES 4

CHOCOLATE ALMOND STUFFED FIGS

A positively luxurious pudding that is deceptively easy to prepare. Try it when an elegant sweet is needed.

---

4 ripe figs
2 tbsps liquid honey
1 square unsweetened cooking chocolate
¾ cup ground almonds

Cinnamon Sauce

1 cup light cream
1 stick cinnamon
2 egg yolks
4 tbsps sugar
Ground cinnamon and blanched almond halves to
    garnish

---

1. Make a cross cut in each fig without cutting right down through the base. Carefully press the 4 sections of the fig out so that it looks like a flower.

2. Melt the honey and chocolate together over a very gentle heat in a small, heavy-based saucepan.

3. Set aside to cool slightly and then mix in the ground almonds.

4. When the mixture has cooled completely, spoon an equal amount into the center of each fig.

5. Meanwhile, prepare the sauce. Pour the cream into a deep saucepan and add the cinnamon stick. Bring just to the boil, draw off the heat and leave to infuse.

6. Beat the egg yolks and the sugar together until light, and gradually strain on the infused cream.

Step 6
Whisk egg yolks and sugar together until light.

Step 7
Combine cream and eggs and cook over gentle heat until mixture coats the back of a spoon.

7. Return the mixture to the saucepan and stir over gentle heat until it just coats the back of a spoon. Leave to cool until just warm.

8. To serve, pour some of the custard onto a serving plate and tilt the plate slowly to coat the base. Place a filled fig on top of the custard and sprinkle around some of the ground cinnamon, topping each fig with a blanched almond.

Cook's Notes

Time
Preparation takes about 20 minutes and cooking takes about 25 minutes.

Cook's Tip
While the custard is cooling, place a sheet of damp wax paper or plastic wrap directly onto the surface of the custard. This will prevent a skin from forming. Alternatively, leave out half of the sugar quantity and sprinkle the remainder over the top of the custard skin.

Preparation
Cook the custard over very gentle heat or in a double boiler to prevent curdling. If the custard should curdle, whisk vigorously or process in a food processor or blender and then strain.

MAKES 4 CUPS

FROZEN MERINGUE CREAM

This is a richer version of a typical
iced milk sweet found all over Spain.

4 cups light cream
⅓ cup sugar
1 whole vanilla bean
4 tbsps brandy
2 egg whites

Step 6
Freeze the cream mixture in shallow containers or ice cube trays until slushy.

Step 5
Whisk the egg whites until stiff but not dry and fold into the cooled cream mixture.

Step 7
Mix with an electric mixer or in a food processor until the mixture is smooth, and then refreeze.

1. Combine the cream, sugar and vanilla bean in a deep, heavy-based saucepan.

2. Cook over very gentle heat for about 10 minutes, stirring frequently to dissolve the sugar. Do not allow the cream to boil.

3. Cover the pan and leave to infuse for about 15 minutes. Strain into a bowl to remove the vanilla bean and set aside to cool completely.

4. Beat the egg whites until stiff but not dry.

5. Fold them into the cooled cream mixture. Add brandy and chill completely.

6. Pour into a shallow pan or ice cube tray and freeze until slushy.

7. Spoon the mixture into a food processor and work until smooth. Alternatively, use an electric mixer. Return the mixture to the freezer and freeze until nearly solid. Repeat the mixing procedure and then freeze in a rigid plastic container until firm. Allow the container to stand at room temperature for about 10 minutes before serving.

Cook's Notes

Time
Preparation takes about 20 minutes. Allow at least 2 hours for the freezing and mixing procedure.

Preparation
The freezing and mixing procedure eliminates large ice crystals from the sorbet. If desired, the sorbet may be processed again just before serving, but this will result in a very soft mixture.

Serving Ideas
Serve with chocolate sauce, fruit sauce or fresh fruit, cookies, or simply sprinkled with ground cinnamon or nutmeg.

SERVES 4-6

BANANA FRITTERS

Fritters, plain or made with fruit, are
a favorite sweet in Spain. Bananas are
especially nice prepared this way.

1 cup all-purpose flour, sifted
Pinch salt
¼ tsp ground cinnamon
1 egg, beaten
1 tbsp oil
⅓ cup milk
1 egg white, stiffly beaten
⅓ cup brandy or rum
2 tbsps sugar
1 tbsp lemon juice
6 ripe bananas, peeled and cut into sharp diagonal slices
    about ½ inch thick
Oil for frying
Powdered sugar

3. While the batter is resting, place the brandy or rum and sugar in a large bowl and stir well to help the sugar dissolve. Add the lemon juice and then slice the bananas. Place the bananas in the bowl, stirring to coat them completely. Set the bananas aside for about 20 minutes, turning them occasionally.

4. Heat the oil in a deep fat fryer or a large, heavy-based frying pan to a temperature of 375°F.

5. Dip the bananas in the batter using tongs or two forks. Drain off excess and fry a few pieces at a time in the hot fat. Drain on paper towels and sprinkle with powdered sugar before serving.

Step 2
When ready to use, fold in stiffly beaten egg white using a large metal spoon or rubber spatula.

Step 1
Mix the liquid ingredients in a well in the center of the flour, gradually drawing in the dry ingredients from the outside.

1. Sift half the flour with the salt and cinnamon into a large bowl and make a well in the center. Pour the beaten egg, oil and milk into the well and stir with a wooden spoon to gradually incorporate the flour from the outside. Stir just until the batter is smooth, but do not overbeat. Set the batter aside at room temperature for at least 30 minutes.

2. Whisk the egg white until stiff but not dry and fold into the batter just before ready to use.

Step 5
Dip the prepared banana slices into the batter using tongs or a fork. Allow the excess to drain away before frying.

Cook's Notes

Time
Preparation takes about 30 minutes and cooking takes about 2-3 minutes per batch of 5 or 6 fritters.

Preparation
When preparing batters for fritters or pancakes, it is best to let them stand for at least 30 minutes before using. This gives the batter a better consistency and makes it easier to use.

Variation
Pineapple, fresh or canned, or peeled apples may be used instead of the bananas.

MAKES 1 CAKE

CINNAMON BUTTERCREAM CAKE

A cake that doesn't need baking is convenient any time, and perfect
for summer. It's very rich, though, so it will go a long way.

1¼ cups sugar
1 cinnamon stick
⅓ cup water
8 egg yolks
1lb unsalted butter, softened
24 ladyfingers
⅓ cup brandy
¾ cup toasted almonds, roughly chopped
3oz semi-sweet chocolate, coarsely grated

1. Combine the sugar, water and cinnamon stick in a small, heavy-based saucepan and bring to the boil, stirring until the sugar dissolves.

2. Allow to boil briskly without stirring until the syrup reaches a temperature of 236°F on a sugar thermometer, or until a small amount dropped into cold water forms a soft ball.

3. While the sugar syrup is boiling, beat the egg yolks in a large bowl with an electric mixer until they are thick and lemon colored. Soften the butter until light and fluffy.

4. When the syrup is ready, quickly pour it in a thin, steady stream into the egg yolks, beating constantly with an electric mixer.

5. Continue beating until the mixture is thick, smooth and creamy. This will take about 10-15 minutes. Allow to cool to room temperature.

6. Beat in the softened butter, a spoonful at a time. Chill the mixture until it is of spreading consistency.

7. Cut the ladyfingers to fit closely together in an 8 inch square pan. Line the pan with lightly greased foil or paper.

8. Spread some of the buttercream lightly on one side of the ladyfingers and place them, powdered side down, in the pan. Cut small pieces of ladyfingers to fill in any corners, if necessary.

9. Sprinkle over half of the brandy, soaking each lady-finger well. Spread over another layer of buttercream and place on the remaining ladyfingers, pushing them down to stick them into the cream. Sprinkle over the remaining brandy and cover the top with buttercream, reserving some for the sides. Place the cake in the refrigerator and chill until firm.

10. When the icing is firm, remove the cake from the refrigerator and lift it out of the pan using the foil or paper. Slide the cake off the paper onto a flat surface and spread the sides with the remaining buttercream. Press the chopped almonds into the sides and decorate the top with grated chocolate. Transfer to a serving dish and serve immediately.

Step 4
Pour the prepared syrup in a thin, steady stream onto the egg yolks while beating with an electric whisk.

Step 6
Beat in the softened butter, a spoonful at a time.

Cook's Notes

Time
Preparation takes about 45 minutes, with about 3 hours in the refrigerator to set the buttercream.

Variation
The icing may be flavored with 2 tsps instant coffee powder. Add when making the syrup. 2oz semi-sweet chocolate may be grated into the syrup once it is made and stirred to dissolve.

Preparation
The syrup must be at exactly the right temperature when it is beaten into the egg yolks or the icing will be soft and runny.

SERVES 8

CARAMEL CUSTARD WITH ORANGE AND CORIANDER

This is one of the best loved puddings in Spain. Fragrant coriander gives it
new appeal and its flavor is marvelous with orange.

6oz sugar
6 tbsps water
3 small oranges
3 cups milk
1 tbsp coriander seeds, crushed
6 eggs
2 egg yolks
6oz sugar

Step 1
Dissolve the sugar in water over gentle heat until it forms a clear syrup.

Step 2
Bring the syrup to the boil over high heat and watch carefully as it begins to turn brown.

1. To prepare the caramel, put the sugar and water in a heavy-based saucepan and bring to the boil over gentle heat to dissolve the sugar.

2. Once the sugar is dissolved, bring to the boil over high heat and cook to a golden brown, watching the color carefully.

3. While the caramel is cooking, heat 8 custard cups to warm them. When the caramel is brown, pour an equal amount into each cup and swirl quickly to coat the base and sides with caramel. Leave the caramel to cool and harden in the cups.

4. Grate the oranges and combine the rind, milk and crushed coriander seeds in a deep saucepan. Set the oranges aside for later use. Bring the milk almost to the boiling point and set it aside for the flavors to infuse.

5. Beat the eggs, yolks and sugar together until light and fluffy. Gradually strain on the milk, stirring well in between each addition. Pour the milk over the caramel in each cup. Place the cups in a bain-marie and place in a preheated 325°F oven for about 40 minutes, or until a knife inserted into the center of the custards comes out clean. Lower the oven temperature slightly if the water begins to boil around the cups.

6. When the custards are cooked, remove the cups from the bain-marie and refrigerate for at least 3 hours or overnight until the custard is completely cold and set.

7. To serve, loosen the custards from the sides of the cup with a small knife and turn them out onto individual plates. Peel the white pith from around the oranges and segment them. Place some of the orange segments around the custards and serve immediately.

Cook's Notes

Time
Preparation takes about 30-40 minutes, cooking time for the custards is about 40 minutes.

Watchpoint
The sugar and water can burn easily once it comes to the boil, so watch it carefully.

Preparation
A bain-marie literally means a water bath. To make one, pour warm water into a roasting pan, the level to come half way up the sides of the dish or dishes being used. This protects delicate egg custard mixtures from the direct heat of the oven. Check from time to time to see that the water is not boiling.

Cook's Tip
It is usual for some of the caramel to stick in the bottom of the dish when the custards are turned out. To make cleaning easier, pour boiling water into the bottom of each dish and leave until it dissolves the residue of caramel.

SERVES 6-8
FRIED MILK SQUARES

An unusual way with custard, this recipe requires
good organization for delicious results.

2 tbsps cornstarch
2½ cups milk
½ cup sugar
Vanilla extract
2 eggs, beaten
Dry breadcrumbs
Cinnamon sugar
Oil for deep frying

1. Place the cornstarch in a heavy-based saucepan and gradually whisk in the milk until completely blended. Add the sugar, stir well and bring the mixture slowly to the boil, stirring constantly until thickened. Stir in the vanilla extract.

2. Pour the mixture into an 8 inch square dish lined with lightly buttered foil.

3. Chill the mixture for at least 4 hours in a refrigerator, or until completely firm.

4. When set, lift out the paper and cut the mixture into squares with a knife dipped in hot water.

5. Coat the squares carefully with egg, using a fish slice.

6. Coat carefully with crumbs, patting them in place with your hands. Place the coated squares on a plate and set them aside.

7. Heat the oil in a deep fat fryer or deep saucepan and place in the squares, one at a time. Brown for about 2 minutes per side, turning over carefully. Drain on paper towels and transfer to a serving dish. Repeat with remaining squares. Sprinkle with sugar and cinnamon and serve immediately.

Step 4
When set, cut through the mixture with a knife dipped in hot water.

Step 5
Coat the squares carefully with beaten egg.

Step 6
Place crumbs on a sheet of paper. Use paper to toss the crumbs over the egg-coated squares.

Cook's Notes

 Time
Preparation takes about 25 minutes, with 4 hours chilling time. Cooking takes about 4 minutes or longer if the squares are cooked in several batches.

Preparation
The milk mixture must be chilled until very firm before slicing. The squares must be completely cold before frying or they will begin to melt and fall apart. Using a knife dipped in hot water makes it easier to slice cleanly through the mixture.

 Serving Ideas
The fried milk squares may be served with cream, either pouring or whipped. Fresh fruit such as strawberries, raspberries or sliced peaches make a nice accompaniment.

SERVES 4-6

SANGRIA

This is the ideal drink with hors d'oeuvres
on warm summer evenings and the perfect complement
to the flavor of Spanish food anytime.

4-6 tbsps sugar
1 lime
1 orange
1 lemon
4 tbsps brandy
1 bottle dry red wine
Soda water or sparkling mineral water
Ice cubes

Step 1
Slice the fruit
thinly and place in
a bowl or jug with
the sugar.

1. Slice the lime and lemon into rounds about ¼ inch thick. Remove any pips.

2. Slice the oranges in half and then cut each half into ¼ inch thick slices, removing any pips. Place all the fruit in a large bowl or jug.

3. Add the sugar, brandy and wine and stir until well mixed. If desired, add a bit more sugar to taste.

4. Refrigerate the mixture for about 1 hour or until thoroughly chilled. Chill the soda or mineral water separately. Just before serving, pour in the soda or mineral water, adding about 2½ cups. Pour over ice into large wine glasses, adding some of the sliced fruit to each glass, and serve immediately.

Step 3
Add the wine and
brandy and mix
all the ingredients
to help dissolve
the sugar.

Step 4
Just before
serving, pour in
soda water or
carbonated
mineral water.

Cook's Notes

Time
Preparation takes about 20 minutes, with 1 hour chilling time.

Cook's Tip
If Sangria is made more than an hour or two in advance, the fruit may discolor slightly because of the wine. This will not affect the taste, but fresh fruit may be substituted for serving.

Variation
May also be made with dry white wine.

SERVES 8

SPANISH LEMONADE

Spanish lemonade has a definite
kick, with the unusual combination
of both red and white wines.

¾ cup sugar
6 lemons
1 quart dry red wine
1 quart dry white wine
Fresh mint

Step 2
Slowly heat the peel, sugar and lemon juice, stirring occasionally to dissolve the sugar.

Step 1
Remove the peel from the lemons in thin strips, using a serrated knife or a vegetable peeler. Do not remove the white pith.

Step 3
Add the lemon slices and the other ingredients and pour into a glass serving jug.

1. Place the sugar in a heavy-based saucepan. Peel the rind carefully from three of the lemons using a sharp serrated knife or a vegetable peeler. Do not take any of the white pith off with the peel. Squeeze the lemons for juice and strain them into the saucepan.

2. Place the saucepan over gentle heat to dissolve the sugar, stirring occasionally. Set aside to cool completely.

3. Slice the remaining lemons about ¼ inch thick. Mix all the

ingredients together and pour into a large glass jug. Refrigerate for at least 4 hours or overnight, stirring occasionally.

4. Add just the leaves or small sprigs of mint to the lemonade, stirring them in well. To serve, pour into tall glasses over ice.

Cook's Notes

Time
Preparation takes about 20 minutes with overnight chilling time.

Variation
Use 7 or 8 limes or 3 oranges in place of the lemons.

Preparation
Taste and add more sugar, it necessary, before chilling the lemonade.

CHINESE COOKING

INTRODUCTION

To say China is vast seems a gross oversimplification. But it is this vastness that is the key to unlocking the mysteries of the country's cuisine. Because of the great land area, China has a great range of climates which influence the crops that grow and hence the dishes of the regions. It is usual, for culinary purposes, to divide the country into four regions: North or Peking, South or Cantonese, East or Shanghai, West or Szechuan.

In the North, noodles are eaten more often than rice, because that is the wheat growing region. Rich sauces and meat dishes are featured, as are pancakes and dumplings. From this region comes the legendary Peking duck.

In the South, the weather is warmer and the meals lighter. Stir-fried dishes with crisp vegetables are popular. The salty tang of fermented black beans or oyster sauce lends interest to meat and poultry stir-fries. Rice is the staple rather than wheat noodles.

In the East, rice and noodles compete for popularity. Noodles, combined with vegetables, poultry or sea-food, make a favorite snack in tea houses. Fish, both freshwater and saltwater, are plentiful.

In the West, hearty dishes with a fiery taste are a specialty. The Szechuan peppercorn grows here, with a taste very different from the pepper we in the Western world are used to. The edible tree fungus – cloud ear – is a highly-prized ingredient.

Cooking Chinese food takes only minutes for most recipes, but preparation often involves much slicing and chopping, so it is best to have everything ready to go. Ingredients are generally cut to approximately the same size so that they cook in almost the same length of time. To slice meat to the necessary thinness, use it partially frozen.

Stir-frying is probably the most important Chinese cooking method used in this book. This involves cooking over high heat in a small amount of oil. A wok is best for this, but, if necessary, a large heavy-based frying pan can be used. Woks usually sit on a stand which keeps the base slightly elevated to give greater control over cooking.

Chinese food is becoming more and more popular, but some ingredients may still prove mystifying and in need of definition:

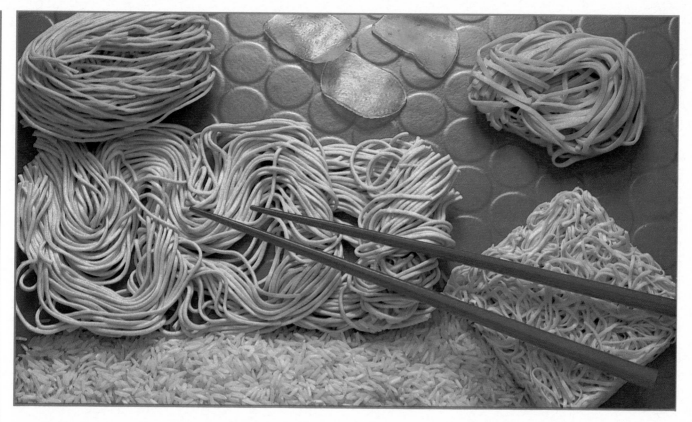

Bamboo shoots – first growth of the bamboo plant, cut just as it emerges from the ground. Crisp, ivory colored and slightly sweet, usually sold canned, sliced or in whole pieces which can be cut to various shapes.

Baby corn – miniature variety of corn. Sold in cans and often available fresh. Needs very brief cooking.

Black beans – used often in Cantonese cooking. Available in pre-prepared sauce or salted to preserve them. Salted beans should be soaked.

Chili peppers – available dried or fresh. Usually red, they are used in Szechuan cooking. Seeds are the hottest part, so remove for less heat.

Chili sauce – available hot or sweet and made from fresh, red chili peppers.

Chinese cabbage – usually refers to Chinese celery cabbage. Some varieties have thicker, whiter spines. Readily available in greengrocers or supermarkets. Smaller, stronger-tasting bok choy is rarely seen outside Chinese markets.

Chinese parsley – also coriander leaves or cilantro. A pungent green herb with a leaf similar to flat parsley.

Five-spice powder – a combination of star anise, anise pepper, fennel, cloves and cinnamon. Use sparingly.

Ginger – knobbly root that must be peeled before use. Use in small amounts, grated or thinly sliced. Also available in powder form or preserved in sugar syrup.

Hoisin sauce – a thick, vegetable-based sauce used often in Chinese barbecue cooking. Useful for stir-fried dishes and as a dipping sauce.

Mushrooms, dried Chinese – brown-black in color, must be soaked for 15-30 minutes before use. Stronger in taste than fresh mushrooms, they also have a chewier texture.

Red bean paste – made from boiled red beans or bean flour mixed with water and flour. Usually sweetened and used in desserts.

Rice wine – available from Chinese groceries, it has a flavor ranging from dry sherry to sweet white wine depending on the variety bought. Substitute either sherry or white wine.

Rice vinegar – made from rice and quite pale in color. Substitute white wine vinegar.

Sesame oil – pressed from sesame seeds it is golden in color with a nutty flavor. Expensive, so use as flavoring at the end of cooking.

Soy sauce – made from fermented soy beans. There are various strength, which will affect the color and flavor of the finished dish.

Star anise – star-shaped seed pod with a liquorice taste. Used in meat, poultry and sweet dishes.

Szechuan peppercorns – also called wild pepper. Not readily available, so substitute black peppercorns.

Water chestnuts – fresh variety is very difficult to obtain. Usually found canned, peeled, sliced or whole. Creamy white in color and crisp in texture.

White radish or mooli – very large, with a delicious, crisp texture and white, translucent appearance. Barely needs cooking.

Wonton skins or wrappers – thin sheets of egg noodle dough in large or small squares. The traditional wrapping for green rolls and dumplings with various stuffings. Can be steamed or cooked in liquid.

Wood or tree ears – grayish-black tree fungus. Sold dried and must be soaked before use.

Yellow beans – whole in brine or in paste or sauce form. Golden brown in color and very salty.

MAKES 12

SPRING ROLLS

One of the most popular Chinese hors
d'oeuvres, these are delicious dipped
in sweet-sour sauce or plum sauce.

Wrappers

1 cup bread flour
1 egg, beaten
Cold water

Filling

8oz pork, trimmed and finely shredded
4oz shrimp, shelled and chopped
4 green onions, finely chopped
2 tsps chopped fresh ginger
4oz Chinese cabbage leaves, shredded
3½oz bean sprouts
1 tbsp light soy sauce
Dash sesame seed oil
1 egg, beaten

1. To prepare the wrappers, sift the flour into a bowl and make a well in the center. Add the beaten egg and about 1 tbsp cold water. Begin beating with a wooden spoon, gradually drawing in the flour from the outside to make a smooth dough. Add more water if necessary.

2. Knead the dough until it is elastic and pliable. Place in a covered bowl and chill for about 4 hours or overnight.

3. When ready to roll out, allow the dough to come back to room temperature. Flour a large work surface well and roll the dough out to about ¼ inch thick.

4. Cut the dough into 12 equal squares and then roll each piece into a larger square about 6x6 inches. The dough should be very thin. Cover while preparing the filling.

5. Cook the pork in a little of the frying oil for about 2-3 minutes. Add the remaining filling ingredients, except the beaten egg, cook for a further 2-3 minutes and allow to cool.

6. Lay out the wrappers on a clean work surface with the point of each wrapper facing you. Brush the edges lightly with the beaten egg.

7. Divide the filling among all 12 wrappers, placing it just above the front point. Fold over the sides like an envelope.

8. Then fold over the point until the filling is completely covered, Roll up as for a jelly roll. Press all the edges to seal well.

9. Heat the oil in a deep fat fryer or in a deep pan to 375°F. Depending upon the size of the fryer, place in 2-4 spring rolls and fry until golden brown on both sides. The rolls will float to the surface when one side has browned and should be turned over. Drain thoroughly on paper towels and serve hot.

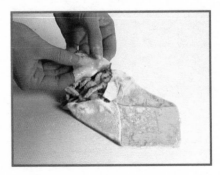

Step 7 Fill the dough and fold up sides like an envelope before rolling up.

Cook's Notes

Time
Preparation takes about 50 minutes for the wrapper dough, the filling and for rolling up. Dough must be allowed to rest for at least 4 hours before use. Cooking takes about 20 minutes.

Serving Ideas
Serve with a sauce dip. Sweet and sour sauce or hot mustard sauce are available bottled from specialty shops and Chinese supermarkets.

Freezing
Rolls may be frozen uncooked. Line a baking sheet with plastic wrap, place on the rolls and freeze until nearly solid. Wrap each roll individually, place in a large plastic bag, seal, label and freeze for up to 2 months. Defrost completely before frying.

SERVES 4-6

HOT & SOUR SOUP

A very warming soup, this is a favorite
in winter in Peking. Add chili sauce and
vinegar to suit your taste.

2oz pork
3 dried Chinese mushrooms, soaked in boiling water for
     5 minutes and chopped
2oz peeled, uncooked shrimp
5 cups chicken stock
1oz bamboo shoots, sliced
3 green onions, shredded
Salt and pepper
1 tbsp sugar
1 tsp dark soy sauce
½ tsp light soy sauce
1-2 tsps chili sauce
1½ tbsps vinegar
Dash sesame seed oil and rice wine or sherry
1 egg, well beaten
2 tbsps water mixed with 1 tbsp cornstarch

Step 1 Cut the pork into thin shreds, long enough to fit comfortably into a soup spoon.

1. Trim any fat from the pork and slice it into shreds about 2 inches long and less than ¼ inch thick.

2. Soak the mushrooms in boiling water until softened. Place the pork in a large pot with the shrimp and stock. Bring to the boil and then reduce the heat to allow to simmer gently for 4-5 minutes. Add all the remaining ingredients except for the egg and cornstarch and water mixture. Cook a further 1-2 minutes over low heat.

3. Remove the pan from the heat and add the egg gradually, stirring gently until it forms threads in the soup.

4. Mix a spoonful of the hot soup with the cornstarch and water mixture and add to the soup, stirring constantly.

5. Bring the soup back to simmering point for 1 minute to thicken the cornstarch. Serve immediately.

Step 2 Soak the dry mushrooms in boiling water for 5 minutes until they soften and swell. Remove the stalks before chopping.

Step 3 Pour the egg into the hot soup and stir gently to form threads.

Cook's Notes

Time
Preparation takes about 25 minutes, cooking takes 7-8 minutes.

Preparation
Vary the amount of chili sauce to suit your own taste.

Variation
Hot and Sour Soup is very versatile. Substitute other ingredients such as chicken, crabmeat, bean sprouts, spinach or green cabbage.

Watchpoint
The soup must be hot enough to cook the egg when it is added, but not so hot that the egg sets immediately.

POT STICKER DUMPLINGS

So called because they are fried in very little
oil, they will stick unless they are brown and
crisp on the bottom before they are steamed.

Dumpling Pastry

1½ cups all-purpose flour
½ tsp salt
3 tbsps oil
Boiling water

Filling

4oz finely ground pork or chicken
4 water chestnuts, finely chopped
3 green onions, finely chopped
½ tsp five spice powder
1 tbsp light soy sauce
1 tsp sugar
1 tsp sesame oil

Step 3 Place a mound of filling on half of each dough circle.

1. Sift the flour and salt into a large bowl and make a well in the center. Pour in the oil and add enough boiling water to make a pliable dough. Add about 4 tbsps water at first and begin stirring with a wooden spoon to gradually incorporate the flour. Add more water as necessary. Knead the dough for about 5 minutes and allow to rest for 30 minutes.

2. Divide the dough into 12 pieces and roll each piece out to a circle about 6 inches in diameter.

3. Mix all the filling ingredients together and place a mound of filling on half of each circle. Fold over the top and press the edges together firmly. Roll over the joined edges using a twisting motion and press down to seal.

4. Pour about ⅛ inch of oil in a large frying pan, preferably cast iron. When the oil is hot, add the dumplings flat side down and cook until nicely browned.

5. When the underside is brown, add about ⅓ cup water to the pan and cover it tightly. Continue cooking gently for about 5 minutes, or until the top surface of dumplings is steamed and appears cooked. Serve immediately.

Step 3 Fold over the dough and press edges to seal in filling.

Step 3 Twist the edges together to seal firmly.

 Cook's Notes

 Time
Preparation takes about 50 minutes including the standing time for the dough. Cooking takes about 10-20 minutes.

Preparation
The pan used for cooking must have a flat base. Do not use a wok.

 Watchpoint
Make sure the dumplings are brown and crisp on the bottom before adding the water otherwise they really will be pot stickers!

SERVES 4-6

CRAB & SWEETCORN SOUP

Creamy sweetcorn and succulent crabmeat
combine to make a velvety rich soup. Whisked
egg whites add an interesting texture.

3½ cups chicken or fish stock
12oz cream style corn
4oz crabmeat
Salt and pepper
1 tsp light soy sauce
2 tbsps cornstarch
3 tbsps water or stock
4 green onions for garnish
2 egg whites, whisked
4 green onions for garnish

Step 3 Whisk the egg whites until soft peaks form and stir into the hot soup.

Step 2 Mix the cornstarch and water together with some of the hot soup and return the mixture to the pan.

1. Bring the stock to the boil in a large pan. Add the corn, crabmeat, seasoning and soy sauce. Allow to simmer for 4-5 minutes.

2. Mix the cornstarch and water or stock and add a spoonful of the hot soup. Return the mixture to the soup and bring back to the boil. Cook until the soup thickens.

3. Whisk the egg whites until soft peaks form. Stir into the hot soup just before serving.

4. Slice the onions thinly on the diagonal and scatter over the top to serve.

Cook's Notes

 Time
Preparation takes about 10 minutes, cooking takes about 8-10 minutes.

 Preparation
Adding the egg whites is optional.

 Watchpoint
Do not allow the corn and the crab to boil rapidly; they will both toughen.

 Economy
Use crab sticks instead of crabmeat.

 Variation
Chicken may be used instead of the crabmeat and the cooking time increased to 10-12 minutes.

SERVES 6-8

WONTON SOUP

Probably the best-known Chinese soup,
this recipe uses pre-made wonton
wrappers for ease of preparation.

20-24 wonton wrappers
2 tbsps chopped Chinese parsley
3oz finely ground chicken or pork
3 green onions, finely chopped
1 inch piece fresh ginger, peeled and grated
1 egg, lightly beaten
5 cups chicken stock
1 tbsps dark soy sauce
Dash sesame oil
Salt and pepper
Chinese parsley or watercress for garnish

Step 2 Place a spoonful of filling on half of each wrapper

Step 3 Fold over the tops and press firmly with the fingers to seal.

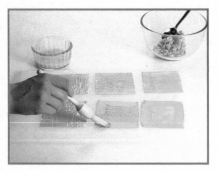

Step 1 Place the wonton wrappers out on a clean surface. Brush edges with beaten egg.

1. Place all the wonton wrappers on a large, flat surface. Mix together the chicken or pork, chopped parsley, green onions and ginger. Brush the edges of the wrappers lightly with beaten egg.

2. Place a small mound of mixture on one half of the wrappers and fold the other half over the top to form a triangle.

3. Press with the fingers to seal the edges well.

4. Bring the stock to the boil in a large saucepan. Add the filled wontons and simmer 5-10 minutes or until they float to the surface. Add remaining ingredients to the soup, using only the leaves of the parsley or watercress for garnish.

Cook's Notes

 Time
Preparation takes 25-30 minutes and cooking takes about 5-10 minutes.

 Variation
Use equal quantities of crabmeat or shrimp to fill the wontons instead of chicken or pork.

 Buying Guide
Wonton wrappers are sometimes called wonton skins. They are available in speciality shops, delicatessens and Chinese supermarkets. Chinese parsley is also known as coriander or cilantro and is available from greengrocers and supermarkets.

SERVES 4-6

BARBECUED SPARE RIBS

Although Chinese barbecue sauce is nothing like
the tomato-based American-style sauce, these
ribs are still tasty cooked on an outdoor grill.

4lbs fresh spare-ribs
3 tbsps dark soy sauce
6 tbsps hoisin sauce (Chinese barbecue sauce)
2 tbsps dry sherry
¼ tsp five spice powder
1 tbsp brown sugar
4-6 green onions for garnish

Step 2 Cut both ends of the onions into thin strips, leaving the middle whole.

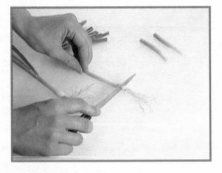

Step 1 Trim the root ends and the green tops from the onions.

Step 3 Place in ice water and leave to stand 4 hour or overnight until the ends curl.

1. First prepare the garnish. Trim the root ends and the dark green tops from the onions.

2. Cut both ends into thin strips, leaving about ½ inch in the middle uncut.

3. Place the onions in ice water for several hours or overnight for the ends to curl up.

4. Cut the spare-ribs into one-rib pieces. Mix all the remaining ingredients together, pour over the ribs and stir to coat evenly. Allow to stand for 1 hour.

5. Put the spare-rib pieces on a rack in a roasting pan containing 2 cups water and cook in a preheated 350°F oven for 30 minutes. Add more hot water to the pan while cooking, if necessary.

6. Turn the ribs over and brush with the remaining sauce. Cook 30 minutes longer, or until tender. Serve garnished with the onion brushes.

Cook's Notes

Time
Preparation takes about 45 minutes. The onion brushes must soak for at least 4 hours and the ribs must marinate for 1 hour. Cooking takes about 1 hour.

Preparation
If the ribs are small and not very meaty, cut into two-rib pieces before cooking, then into one-rib pieces just before serving.

Cook's Tip
The ribs may be prepared in advance and reheated at the same temperature for about 10 minutes.

SERVES 8

SESAME CHICKEN WINGS

This is an economical appetizer that is
also good as a cocktail snack or as a
light meal with stir-fried vegetables.

12 chicken wings
1 tbsp salted black beans
1 tbsp water
1 tbsp oil
2 cloves garlic, crushed
2 slices fresh ginger, cut into fine shreds
3 tbsps soy sauce
1½ tbsps dry sherry or rice wine
Large pinch black pepper
1 tbsp sesame seeds

1. Cut off and discard the wing tips. Cut between the joint to separate into two pieces.

2. Crush the beans and add the water. Leave to stand.

3. Heat the oil in a wok and add the garlic and ginger. Stir briefly and add the chicken wings. Cook, stirring, until lightly browned, about 3 minutes. Add the soy sauce and wine and cook, stirring, about 30 seconds longer. Add the soaked black beans and pepper.

4. Cover the wok tightly and allow to simmer for about 8-10 minutes. Uncover and turn the heat to high. Continue cooking, stirring until the liquid is almost evaporated and the chicken wings are glazed with sauce. Remove from the

Step 1 Use a knife or scissors to cut through thick joint and separate the wing into two pieces.

Step 3 Fry garlic and ginger briefly, add the chicken wings and cook, stirring, until lightly browned.

heat and sprinkle on sesame seeds. Stir to coat completely and serve. Garnish with green onions or Chinese parsley, if desired.

Cook's Notes

Time
Preparation takes about 25 minutes, cooking takes about 13-14 minutes.

Watchpoint
Sesame seeds pop slightly as they cook.

Cook's Tip
You can prepare the chicken wings ahead of time and reheat them. They are best reheated in the oven for about 5 minutes at 350°F.

Serving Ideas
To garnish with scallion brushes, trim the roots and green tops of green onions and cut both ends into thin strips, leaving the middle intact. Place in ice water for several hours or overnight for the cut ends to curl up. Drain and use to garnish.

SERVES 4-6

QUICK FRIED SHRIMP

Prepared with either raw or cooked
shrimp, this is an incredibly delicious
appetizer that is extremely easy to cook.

2lbs cooked shrimp in their shells
2 cloves garlic, crushed
1 inch piece fresh ginger, finely chopped
1 tbsp chopped fresh Chinese parsley (coriander)
3 tbsps oil
1 tbsp rice wine or dry sherry
1½ tbsps light soy sauce
Chopped green onions to garnish

Step 2 Peel the shells from the shrimp, leaving only the tail ends on.

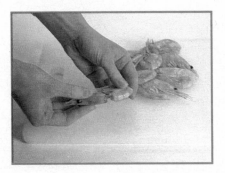

Step 1 Carefully pull the head of the shrimp away from the body.

1. Shell the shrimp except for the very tail ends. Place the shrimp in a bowl with the remaining ingredients. except for the garnish, and leave to marinate for 30 minutes.

2. Heat the wok and add the shrimp and their marinade. Stir-fry briefly to heat the shrimp.

3. Chop the onions roughly or cut into neat rounds. Sprinkle over the shrimp to serve.

Cook's Notes

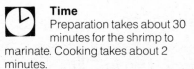 **Time**
Preparation takes about 30 minutes for the shrimp to marinate. Cooking takes about 2 minutes.

 Watchpoint
Do not overcook the shrimp as they will toughen.

 **Variation**
If uncooked shrimp are available, stir-fry with their marinade until they turn pink.

SERVES 4

EGGPLANT & PEPPER SZECHUAN STYLE

Authentic Szechuan food is fiery hot.
Outside China, restaurants often tone down the taste for Western palates.

1 large eggplant
2 cloves garlic, crushed
1 inch piece fresh ginger, shredded
1 onion, cut into 1 inch pieces
1 small green pepper, seeded, cored and cut into 1 inch pieces
1 small red pepper, seeded, cored and cut into 1 inch pieces
1 red or green chili, seeded, cored and cut into thin strips
½ cup chicken or vegetable stock
1 tsp sugar
1 tsp vinegar
Pinch salt and pepper
1 tsp cornstarch
1 tbsp soy sauce
Dash sesame oil
Oil for cooking

Step 1 Cut eggplant in half and lightly score the surface.

Step 2 Sprinkle lightly with salt and leave on paper towels or in a colander to drain.

1. Cut the eggplants in half and score the surface.

2. Sprinkle lightly with salt and leave to drain in a colander or on paper towels for 30 minutes.

3. After 30 minutes, squeeze the eggplant gently to extract any bitter juices and rinse thoroughly under cold water. Pat dry and cut the eggplant into 1 inch cubes.

4. Heat about 3 tbsps oil in a wok. Add the eggplant and stir-fry for about 4-5 minutes. It may be necessary to add more oil as the eggplant cooks. Remove from the wok and set aside.

5. Reheat the wok and add 2 tbsps oil. Add the garlic and ginger and stir-fry for 1 minute. Add the onions and stir-fry for 2 minutes. Add the green pepper, red pepper and chili pepper and stir-fry for 1 minute. Return the eggplant to the wok along with the remaining ingredients.

6. Bring to the boil, stirring constantly, and cook until the sauce thickens and clears. Serve immediately.

Cook's Notes

Time
Preparation takes about 30 minutes, cooking takes about 7-8 minutes.

Cook's Tip
Lightly salting the aubergine will help draw out any bitterness.

Serving Suggestions
Serve as a vegetarian stir-fry dish with plain or fried rice, or serve as a side dish.

SERVES 4

SPECIAL MIXED VEGETABLES

This dish illustrates the basic stir-frying
technique for vegetables. Use other varieties
for an equally colorful side dish.

1 tbsp oil
1 clove garlic, crushed
1 inch piece fresh ginger, sliced
4 Chinese cabbage leaves, shredded
2oz flat mushrooms, thinly sliced
2oz bamboo shoots, sliced
3 sticks celery, diagonally sliced
2oz baby corn, cut in half if large
1 small red pepper, cored, seeded and thinly sliced
2oz bean sprouts
2 tbsps light soy sauce
Dash sesame oil
Salt and pepper
3 tomatoes, peeled, seeded and quartered

1. Heat the oil in a wok and add the ingredients in the order given, reserving the tomatoes until last.

2. To make it easier to peel the tomatoes, remove the stems and place in boiling water for 5 seconds.

3. Remove from the boiling water with a draining spoon and place in a bowl of cold water. This will make the peels easier to remove. Cut out the core end using a small sharp knife.

4. Cut the tomatoes in half and then in quarters. Use a teaspoon or a serrated edged knife to remove the seeds and the cores.

5. Cook the vegetables for about 2 minutes. Stir in the soy sauce and sesame oil and add the tomatoes. Heat through for 30 seconds and serve immediately.

Step 2 To peel the tomatoes, place them first in a pan of boiling water for 5 seconds. Tomatoes that are very ripe need less time.

Step 3 Place in cold water to stop the cooking. The skin will then peel away easily.

Step 4 Cut into quarters and remove the seeds, core and juice with a teaspoon, or use a serrated edged knife.

Cook's Notes

Time
Preparation takes about 25 minutes, cooking takes about 2½-3 minutes.

Variation
Other vegetables such as broccoli flowerets, cauliflower flowerets, pea pods, zucchini or green beans may be used.

Serving Ideas
Serve as a side dish or as a vegetarian main dish with plain or fried rice.

SERVES 4-6

PORK & SHRIMP CHOW MEIN

Chinese chow mein dishes are usually based on
noodles, using more expensive ingredients in small
amounts. This makes economical everyday fare.

8oz medium dried Chinese noodles
8oz pork fillet, thinly sliced
1 carrot, peeled and shredded
1 small red pepper, cored, seeded and thinly sliced
3oz bean sprouts
2oz pea pods
1 tbsp rice wine or dry sherry
2 tbsps soy sauce
4oz peeled, cooked shrimp

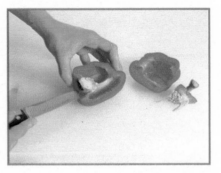

Step 3 Cut peppers in half and remove the cores and seeds. Make sure all the white pith is also removed before slicing thinly.

Step 1 Place whole sheets of noodles into rapidly boiling salted water. Stir as the noodles start to soften.

Step 4 Add the cooked noodles to the other ingredients in the wok and use chopsticks or a spatula to toss over high heat.

1. Cook the noodles in plenty of boiling salted water for about 4-5 minutes. Rinse under hot water and drain thoroughly.

2. Heat the wok and add oil. Stir-fry the pork 4-5 minutes or until almost cooked. Add the carrots to the wok and cook for 1-2 minutes.

3. Core, seed and slice the red pepper and add the remaining vegetables, wine and soy sauce. Cook for about 2 minutes.

4. Add the cooked, drained noodles and shrimp and toss over heat for 1-2 minutes. Serve immediately.

Cook's Notes

Time
Preparation takes about 20 minutes. The noodles take 4-5 minutes to cook and the stir-fried ingredients need to cook for about 5-6 minutes for the pork and about 3 minutes for the vegetables.

Variation
Use green pepper instead of red, or add other vegetables such as baby corn ears, mushrooms or peas.

Buying Guide
Dried Chinese noodles are available in three thicknesses. Thin noodles are usually reserved for soup, while medium and thick noodles are used for fried dishes.

SERVES 2-3

CANTONESE EGG FU YUNG

As the name suggests, this dish is from
Canton. However, fu yung dishes are popular
in many other regions of China, too.

5 eggs
2oz shredded cooked meat, poultry or fish
1 stick celery, finely shredded
4 Chinese dried mushrooms, soaked in boiling water for
    5 minutes
2oz bean sprouts
1 small onion, thinly sliced
Pinch salt and pepper
1 tsp dry sherry
Oil for frying

Sauce

1 tbsp cornstarch dissolved in 3 tbsps cold water
1 cup chicken stock
1 tsp tomato ketchup
1 tbsp soy sauce
Pinch salt and pepper
Dash sesame oil

1. Beat the eggs lightly and add the shredded meat and celery.

2. Squeeze all the liquid from the dried mushrooms. Remove the stems and cut the caps into thin slices. Add to the egg mixture along with the bean sprouts and onion. Add a pinch of salt and pepper and the sherry and stir well.

3. Heat a wok or frying pan and pour in about 4 tbsps oil. When hot, carefully spoon in about ⅓ cup of the egg mixture.

4. Brown on one side, turn gently over and brown the other side. Remove the cooked patties to a plate and continue until all the mixture is cooked.

5. Combine all the sauce ingredients in a small, heavy-based pan and bring slowly to the boil, stirring continuously until thickened and cleared. Pour the sauce over the Egg Fu Yung to serve.

Step 3 Heat the oil in a wok and spoon in the egg mixture to form patties.

Step 5 Bring sauce ingredients to the boil and cook until thick and clear.

Cook's Notes

Time
Preparation takes 25 minutes, cooking takes about 5 minutes for the patties and 8 minutes for the sauce.

Variation
Use cooked shellfish such as crab, shrimp or lobster, if desired. Fresh mushrooms may be used instead of the dried ones. Divide mixture in half or in thirds and cook one large patty per person.

Economy
Left-over cooked meat such as beef, pork or chicken can be used as an ingredient.

SERVES 6-8

FRIED RICE

A basic recipe for a traditional Chinese accompaniment
to stir-fried dishes, this can be more substantial
with the addition of meat, poultry or seafood.

1lb cooked rice, well drained and dried
3 tbsps oil
1 egg, beaten
1 tbsp soy sauce
2oz cooked peas
2 green onions, thinly sliced
Dash sesame oil
Salt and pepper

1. Heat a wok and add the oil. Pour in the egg and soy sauce and cook until just beginning to set.

2. Add the rice and peas and stir to coat with the egg mixture. Allow to cook for about 3 minutes, stirring continuously. Add seasoning and sesame oil.

3. Spoon into a serving dish and sprinkle over the green onions.

Step 2 Add rice and peas on top of egg mixture.

Step 2 Stir to coat the rice with egg, and toss mixture over heat to separate grains of rice.

Cook's Notes

 Time
The rice will take about 10 minutes to cook. Allow at least 20 minutes for it to drain as dry as possible. The fried rice dish will take about 4 minutes to cook.

Variation
Cooked meat, poultry or seafood may be added to the rice along with the peas.

 Cook's Tip
The 1lb rice measurement is the cooked weight.

SERVES 4

SHANGHAI NOODLES

In general, noodles are more popular in northern and eastern China, where wheat is grown, than in other parts of the country. Noodles make a popular snack in Chinese tea houses.

3 tbsps oil
4oz chicken breasts
4oz Chinese cabbage
4 green onions, thinly sliced
2 tbsps soy sauce
Freshly ground black pepper
Dash sesame oil
1lb thick Shanghai noodles, cooked

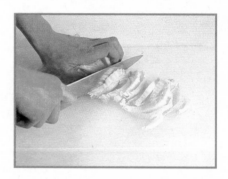

Step 3 Stack up the Chinese leaves and, using a large, sharp knife, cut across into thin strips.

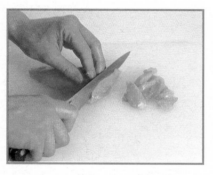

Step 1 Cut the chicken into thin strips across the grain.

Step 3 Toss in the cooked noodles, stir well and heat through.

1. Heat the oil in the wok and add the chicken cut into thin shreds. Stir-fry for 2-3 minutes.

2. Meanwhile, cook the noodles in boiling salted water until just tender, about 6-8 minutes. Drain in a colander and rinse under hot water. Toss in the colander to drain and leave to dry.

3. Add the shredded Chinese cabbage and green onions to the chicken in the wok along with the soy sauce, pepper and sesame oil. Cook about 1 minute and toss in the cooked noodles. Stir well and heat through. Serve immediately.

Cook's Notes

Time
Preparation takes about 10 minutes, cooking takes 6-8 minutes.

Variation
Pork may be used instead of the chicken. Add fresh spinach, shredded, if desired and cook with the Chinese cabbage.

Buying Guide
Shanghai noodles are available in Chinese supermarkets and also some delicatessens. If unavailable, substitute tagliatelle or dried Chinese noodles.

SERVES 2

SWEET-SOUR FISH

In China this dish is almost always
prepared with freshwater fish, but
sea bass is also an excellent choice.

1 sea bass, gray mullet or carp, weighing about 2lbs,
  cleaned
1 tbsp dry sherry
Few slices fresh ginger
½ cup sugar
6 tbsps cider vinegar
1 tbsp soy sauce
2 tbsps cornstarch
1 clove garlic, crushed
2 green onions, shredded
1 small carrot, peeled and finely shredded
1oz bamboo shoots, shredded

1. Rinse the fish well inside and out. Make three diagonal
cuts on each side of the fish with a sharp knife.

2. Trim off the fins, leaving the dorsal fin on top.

3. Trim the tail to two neat points.

4. Bring enough water to cover the fish to the boil in a wok.
Gently lower the fish into the boiling water and add the
sherry and ginger. Cover the wok tightly and remove at
once from the heat. Allow to stand 15-20 minutes to let the
fish cook in the residual heat.

5. To test if the fish is cooked, pull the dorsal fin – if it comes
off easily the fish is done. If not, return the wok to the heat
and bring to the boil. Remove from the heat and leave the
fish to stand a further 5 minutes. Transfer the fish to a heated
serving dish and keep it warm. Take all but 4 tbsps of the fish
cooking liquid from the wok. Add the remaining ingredients
including the vegetables and cook, stirring constantly, until
the sauce thickens. Spoon some of the sauce over the fish
to serve and serve the rest separately.

Step 1 Rinse the fish well and make three diagonal cuts on each side.

Step 2 Using kitchen scissors, trim all of the fins except the dorsal fin at the top.

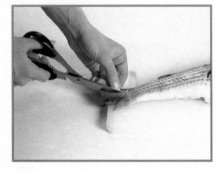

Step 3 Using kitchen scissors again, trim the ends of the tail to two sharp points.

Cook's Notes

Time
Preparation takes about 25
minutes, cooking takes about
15-25 minutes.

Cook's Tip
The diagonal cuts in the side
of the fish ensure even
cooking.

Variation
If desired, use smaller fish
such as trout or red mullet and
shorten the cooking time to 10-15
minutes.

Preparation
The fish may also be cooked
in the oven in a large roasting
pan or in greased foil sprinkled with
sherry. Cook at 375°F for 10 minutes
per ½ inch thickness, measured
around the middle of the fish.

SERVES 6

SINGAPORE FISH

The cuisine of Singapore was much influenced by
that of China. In turn, the Chinese brought
ingredients like curry powder into their own cuisine.

1lb whitefish fillets
1 egg white
1 tbsp cornstarch
2 tsps white wine
Salt and pepper
Oil for frying
1 large onion, cut into ½ inch-thick wedges
1 tbsp mild curry powder
1 small can pineapple pieces, drained and juice
    reserved, or ½ fresh pineapple, peeled and cubed
1 small can mandarin orange segments, drained and
    juice reserved
1 small can sliced water chestnuts, drained
1 tbsp cornstarch mixed with juice of 1 lime
2 tsps sugar (optional)
Pinch salt and pepper

1. Starting at the tail end of the fillets, skin them using a
sharp knife.

2. Slide the knife back and forth along the length of each
fillet, pushing the fish flesh along as you go.

3. Cut the fish into even-sized pieces, about 2 inches.

4. Mix together the egg white, cornstarch, wine, salt and
pepper. Place the fish in the mixture and leave to stand
while heating the oil.

5. When the oil is hot, fry a few pieces of fish at a time until
light golden brown and crisp. Remove the fish to paper
towels to drain, and continue until all the fish is cooked.

6. Remove all but 1 tbsp of the oil from the wok and add the
onion. Stir-fry the onion for 1-2 minutes and add the curry

powder. Cook the onion and curry powder for a further 1-2
minutes. Add the juice from the pineapple and mandarin
oranges and bring to the boil.

7. Combine the cornstarch and lime juice and add a
spoonful of the boiling fruit juice. Return the mixture to the
wok and cook until thickened, about 2 minutes. Taste and
add sugar if desired. Add the fruit, water chestnuts and
fried fish to the wok and stir to coat. Heat through 1 minute
and serve immediately.

Step 2 Hold
filleting knife at a
slight angle and
slide knife along
length of fillet in a
sawing motion.

Step 3 Cut fish
into even-sized
pieces, about 2
inches.

Cook's Notes

Time
Preparation takes about 25
minutes, cooking takes about
10 minutes.

Variation
Chicken may be used in place
of the fish and cooked in the
same way. Garnish with Chinese
parsley leaves if desired.

Serving Ideas
Serve with plain rice, fried rice
or cooked Chinese noodles.

SERVES 2-4

SNOW PEAS WITH SHRIMP

Snow peas, pea pods and mangetout are
all names for the same vegetable – bright
green, crisp and edible, pods and all.

3 tbsps oil
½ cup split blanched almonds, halved
4oz pea pods
2oz bamboo shoots, sliced
2 tsps cornstarch
2 tsps light soy sauce
¾ cup chicken stock
2 tbsps dry sherry
Salt and pepper
1lb cooked, peeled shrimp

Step 2 Tear stems
downward to
remove strings
from pea pods.

1. Heat the oil in a wok. Add the almonds and cook over moderate heat until golden brown. Remove from the oil and drain on paper towels.

2. To prepare the pea pods, tear off the stems and pull them downwards to remove any strings. If the pea pods are small, just remove the stalks. Add the pea pods to the hot oil and cook for about 1 minute. Remove and set aside with the almonds.

3. Drain all the oil from the wok and mix together the cornstarch and the remaining ingredients, except the shrimp and bamboo shoots. Pour the mixture into the wok and stir constantly while bringing to the boil. Allow to simmer for 1-2 minutes until thickened and cleared. Stir in the shrimp and all the other ingredients and heat through for about 1 minute. Serve immediately.

Step 2 If pea
pods are very
large, cut in half
on the diagonal.

Step 3 Add all
the ingredients to
the wok and stir-
fry, tossing with
chopsticks or a
spatula.

Cook's Notes

Time
Preparation takes about 10
minutes, cooking takes
6-8 minutes.

Variation
If using green onions, celery
or water chestnuts, cook with
the pea pods.

Watchpoint
Do not cook the shrimp too
long or on heat that is too high
– they toughen quite easily.

SERVES 6

SZECHUAN FISH

The piquant spiciness of Szechuan pepper is quite different from that of black or white pepper. Beware, though, too much can numb the mouth temporarily!

1lb whitefish fillets
Pinch salt and pepper
1 egg
5 tbsps flour
6 tbsps white wine
Oil for frying
2oz cooked ham, cut in small dice
1 inch piece fresh ginger, finely diced
½-1 red or green chili pepper, cored, seeded and finely diced
6 water chestnuts, finely diced
4 green onions, finely chopped
3 tbsps light soy sauce
1 tsp cider vinegar or rice wine vinegar
½ tsp ground Szechuan pepper (optional)
1 cup light stock
1 tbsp cornstarch dissolved with 2 tbsps water
2 tsps sugar

1. To prepare the garnish, choose unblemished chili peppers with the stems on. Using a small, sharp knife, cut the peppers in strips, starting from the pointed end.

2. Cut down to within ½ inch of the stem end. Rinse out the seeds under cold running water and place the peppers in iced water.

3. Leave the peppers to soak for at least 4 hours or overnight until they open up like flowers.

4. Cut the fish fillets into 2 inch pieces and season with salt and pepper. Beat the egg well and add flour and wine to make a batter. Dredge the fish lightly with flour and then dip into the batter. Mix the fish well.

5. Heat a wok and when hot, add enough oil to deep-fry the fish. When the oil is hot, fry a few pieces of fish at a time, until golden brown. Drain and proceed until all the fish is cooked.

6. Remove all but 1 tbsp of oil from the wok and add the ham, ginger, diced chili pepper, water chestnuts and green onions. Cook for about 1 minute and add the soy sauce and vinegar. If using Szechuan pepper, add at this point. Stir well and cook for a further 1 minute. Remove the vegetables from the pan and set them aside.

7. Add the stock to the wok and bring to the boil. When boiling, add 1 spoonful of the hot stock to the cornstarch mixture. Add the mixture back to the stock and reboil, stirring constantly until thickened.

8. Stir in the sugar and return the fish and vegetables to the sauce. Heat through for 30 seconds and serve at once.

Step 1 Cut the tip of each chili pepper into strips.

Step 3 Allow to soak 4 hours or overnight to open up.

Cook's Notes

Time
Preparation takes about 30 minutes. Chili pepper garnish takes at least 4 hours to soak. Cooking takes about 10 minutes.

Serving Ideas
Serve with plain or fried rice. Do not eat the chili pepper garnish.

Buying Guide
Szechuan peppercorns are available in Chinese supermarkets or delicatessens. If not available, substitute extra chili pepper.

SERVES 6

KUNG PAO SHRIMP WITH CASHEW NUTS

It is said that Kung Pao invented this dish,
but to this day no one knows who he was!

½ tsp chopped fresh ginger
1 tsp chopped garlic
1½ tbsps cornstarch
¼ tsp bicarbonate of soda
Salt and pepper
¼ tsp sugar
1lb uncooked shrimp
4 tbsps oil
1 small onion, cut into dice
1 large or 2 small zucchini, cut into ½ inch cubes
1 small red pepper, cut into ½ inch cubes
½ cup cashew nuts

Sauce

¾ cup chicken stock
1 tbsp cornstarch
2 tsps chili sauce
2 tsps bean paste (optional)
2 tsps sesame oil
1 tbsp dry sherry or rice wine

1. Mix together the ginger, garlic, 1½ tbsps cornstarch, bicarbonate of soda, salt, pepper and sugar.

2. If the shrimp are unpeeled, remove the peels and the dark vein running along the rounded side. If large, cut in half, Place in the dry ingredients and leave to stand for 20 minutes.

3. Heat the oil in a wok and when hot add the shrimp. Cook, stirring over high heat for about 20 seconds, or just until the shrimp change color. Transfer to a plate.

4. Add the onion to the same oil in the wok and cook for about 1 minute. Add the zucchini and red pepper and cook about 30 seconds.

5. Mix the sauce ingredients together and add to the wok. Cook, stirring constantly, until the sauce is slightly thickened. Add the shrimp and the cashew nuts and heat through completely.

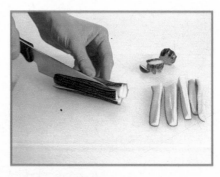

Step 4 To dice the zucchini quickly, top and tail and cut into ½ inch strips.

Step 4 Cut the strips across with a large sharp knife into ½ inch pieces.

Cook's Notes

 Time
Preparation takes about 20 minutes, cooking takes about 3 minutes.

 Variation
If using cooked shrimp, add with the vegetables. Vary amount of chili sauce to suit your taste.

 Serving Ideas
Serve with plain or fried rice.

SERVES 8

PEKING BEEF

In China, meat is often simmered in large earthenware casseroles placed on asbestos mats. A wok is a convenient substitute and the stand does the work of the traditional mat.

2lb sirloin tip or rump roast
1½ cups white wine
2 cups water
2 whole green onions, roots trimmed
1 inch piece fresh ginger
3 star anise
2 tsps sugar
½ cup soy sauce
1 carrot, peeled
2 sticks celery
½ mooli (daikon) radish, peeled

Step 3 Cut the celery into three strips and then into thin strips.

Step 3 Cut the vegetables into 3 inch lengths. To shred carrots, cut each length into thin slices, stack the slices 3-4 at a time and cut through into thin strips with a sharp knife.

1. Place the beef in a wok and add the white wine, water, green onions, ginger and anise. Cover and simmer for about 1 hour.

2. Add the soy sauce and sugar, stir and simmer for 30 minutes longer, or until the beef is tender. Allow to cool in the liquid.

3. Shred all the vegetables finely. Blanch them all, except the green onion, in boiling water for about 1 minute. Rinse under cold water, drain and leave to dry.

4. When the meat is cold, remove it from the liquid and cut into thin slices. Arrange on a serving plate and strain the liquid over it. Scatter over the shredded vegetables and serve cold.

Cook's Notes

Time
Preparation takes about 25 minutes if shredding the vegetables by hand. This can also be done with the fine shredding blade of a food processor. Cooking takes about 1½ hours.

Economy
Because of the long cooking time, less expensive cuts of meat may be used for this dish.

Cook's Tip
If using a rolled roast, remove as much of the fat from the outside as possible. Skim off any fat that rises to the surface of the liquid as it cools, before pouring over the meat to serve.

SERVES 6

BEEF WITH TOMATO & PEPPER IN BLACK BEAN SAUCE

Black beans are a specialty of Cantonese cooking
and give a pungent, salty taste to stir-fried dishes.

2 tbsps salted black beans
2 tbsps water
2 large tomatoes
4 tbsps dark soy sauce
1 tbsp cornstarch
1 tbsp dry sherry
1 tsp sugar
1lb rump steak, cut into thin strips
4 tbsps oil
1 small green pepper, seeded and cored
¾ cup beef stock
Pinch pepper

1. Core tomatoes and cut them into 16 wedges. Crush the black beans, add the water and set aside.

2. Combine soy sauce, cornstarch, sherry, sugar and meat in a bowl and set aside.

3. Cut pepper into ½ inch diagonal pieces. Heat the wok and add the oil. When hot, stir-fry the green pepper pieces for about 1 minute and remove.

4. Add the meat and the soy sauce mixture to the wok and stir-fry for about 2 minutes. Add the soaked black beans and the stock. Bring to the boil and allow to thicken slightly. Return the peppers to the wok and add the tomatoes and pepper. Heat through for 1 minute and serve immediately.

Step 1 Remove cores from the tomatoes with a sharp knife. Cut into even-sized wedges.

Step 4 Add the beef mixture to the hot wok and stir-fry until liquid ingredients glaze the meat.

Cook's Notes

 Time
Preparation takes about 25 minutes, cooking takes about 5 minutes.

 Serving Ideas
Serve with plain boiled rice.

 Watchpoint
Do not add the tomatoes too early or stir the mixture too vigorously once they are added or they will fall apart easily.

 Variation
Substitute pea pods for the green peppers in the recipe. Mushrooms may also be added and cooked with the peppers or pea pods.

SERVES 2-3

BEEF WITH BROCCOLI

The traditional Chinese method of cutting meat
for stir-frying used in this recipe ensures that
the meat will be tender and will cook quickly.

1lb rump steak, partially frozen
4 tbsps dark soy sauce
1 tbsp cornstarch
1 tbsp dry sherry
1 tsp sugar
8oz fresh broccoli
6 tbsps oil
1 inch piece ginger, peeled and shredded
Salt and pepper

1. Trim any fat from the meat and cut into very thin strips across the grain. Strips should be about 3 inches long.

2. Combine the meat with the soy sauce, cornstarch, sherry and sugar. Stir well and leave long enough for the meat to completely defrost.

3. Trim the flowerets from the stalks of the broccoli and cut them into even-sized pieces. Peel the stalks of the broccoli and cut into thin, diagonal slices.

4. Slice the ginger into shreds. Heat a wok and add 2 tbsps of the oil to it. Add the broccoli and sprinkle with salt. Stir-fry, turning constantly, until the broccoli is dark green. Do not cook for longer than 2 minutes. Remove from the wok and set aside.

5. Place the remaining oil in the wok and add the ginger and beef. Stir-fry, turning constantly, for about 2 minutes. Return the broccoli to the pan and mix well. Heat through for 30 seconds and serve immediately.

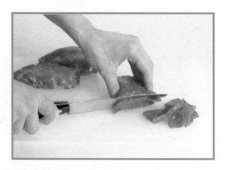

Step 1 Use partially frozen meat and slice it thinly across the grain.

Step 3 Cut the broccoli stalks in thin diagonal slices.

Step 4 To shred ginger quickly, cut into thin slices, stack up the slices and cut into thin strips.

Cook's Notes

Time
Preparation takes about 25 minutes and cooking takes about 4 minutes.

Preparation
Using meat that is partially frozen makes it easier to get very thin slices.

Cook's Tip
If more sauce is desired, double the quantities of soy sauce, cornstarch, dry sherry and sugar.

SERVES 2-4

SWEET & SOUR PORK

This really needs no introduction because of its popularity. The dish originated in Canton, but is reproduced in most of the world's Chinese restaurants.

1 cup all-purpose flour
4 tbsps cornstarch
1½ tsps baking powder
Pinch salt
1 tbsp oil
Water
8oz pork tenderloin, cut into ½ inch cubes

Sweet and Sour Sauce

2 tbsps cornstarch
½ cup light brown sugar
Pinch salt
½ cup cider vinegar or rice vinegar
1 clove garlic, crushed
1 tsp fresh ginger, grated
6 tbsps tomato ketchup
6 tbsps reserved pineapple juice

1 onion, sliced
1 green pepper, seeded, cored and sliced
1 small can pineapple chunks, juice reserved
Oil for frying

1. To prepare the batter, sift the flour, cornstarch, baking powder and salt into a bowl. Make a well in the center and add the oil and enough water to make a thick, smooth batter. Using a wooden spoon, stir the ingredients in the well, gradually incorporating flour from the outside, and beat until smooth.

2. Heat enough oil in a wok to deep-fry the pork. Dip the pork cubes one at a time into the batter and drop into the hot oil. Fry 4-5 pieces of pork at a time and remove them with a draining spoon to paper towels. Continue until all the pork is fried.

3. Pour off most of the oil from the wok and add the sliced onion, pepper and pineapple. Cook over high heat for 1-2 minutes. Remove and set aside.

4. Mix all the sauce ingredients together and pour into the wok. Bring slowly to the boil, stirring continuously until thickened. Allow to simmer for about 1-2 minutes or until completely clear.

5. Add the vegetables, pineapple and pork cubes to the sauce and stir to coat completely. Reheat for 1-2 minutes and serve immediately.

Step 2 Dip the pork cubes into the batter and then drop into the hot oil. Chopsticks are ideal to use for this.

Step 3 Place the onion half flat on a chopping board and use a large, sharp knife to cut across to thick or thin slices as desired. Separate these into individual strips.

Cook's Notes

 Time
Preparation takes about 15 minutes, cooking takes about 15 minutes.

Variation
Use beef or chicken instead of the pork. Uncooked, peeled shrimp may be used as can whitefish, cut into 1 inch pieces.

 Cook's Tip
If pork is prepared ahead of time, this will have to be refried before serving to crisp up.

SERVES 4

CHICKEN LIVERS WITH CHINESE CABBAGE & ALMONDS

Chicken livers need quick cooking, so they are
a perfect choice for the Chinese stir-frying method.

8oz chicken livers
3 tbsps oil
½ cup split blanched almonds
1 clove garlic, peeled
2oz pea pods
8-10 Chinese cabbage leaves
2 tsps cornstarch mixed with 1 tbsp cold water
2 tbsps soy sauce
½ cup chicken stock

Step 2 Cook the almonds slowly in the oil to brown evenly, stirring often.

Step 1 Cut off any yellowish or greenish portions from the livers and divide them into even-sized pieces.

Step 3 Quickly stir-fry the livers until lightly browned on the outside. May be served slightly pink in the middle.

1. Pick over the chicken livers and remove any discolored areas or bits of fat. Cut the chicken livers into even-sized pieces.
2. Heat a wok and pour in the oil. When the oil is hot, turn the heat down and add the almonds. Cook, stirring continuously, over gentle heat until the almonds are a nice golden brown. Remove and drain on paper towels.
3. Add the garlic, cook for 1-2 minutes to flavor the oil and remove. Add the chicken livers and cook for about 2-3 minutes, stirring frequently. Remove the chicken livers and

set them aside. Add the pea pods to the wok and stir-fry for 1 minute. Shred the Chinese cabbage leaves finely, add to the wok and cook for 1 minute. Remove the vegetables and set them aside.

4. Mix together the cornstarch and water with the soy sauce and stock. Pour into the wok and bring to the boil. Cook until thickened and clear. Return all the other ingredients to the sauce and reheat for 30 seconds. Serve immediately.

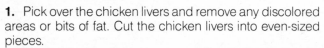

Cook's Notes

 Time
Preparation takes about 25 minutes, cooking takes about 4-5 minutes.

Preparation
Remove any discolored portions from the livers as these can cause a bitter taste. Livers may be served slightly pink in the middle.

 Serving Ideas
Serve with plain or fried rice. Chinese noodles also make a good accompaniment.

SERVES 4

CHICKEN WITH WALNUTS & CELERY

Oyster sauce lends a subtle, slightly salty taste to this Cantonese dish.

8oz boned chicken, cut into 1 inch pieces
2 tsps soy sauce
2 tsps brandy
1 tsp cornstarch
Salt and pepper
2 tbsps oil
1 clove garlic
1 cup walnut halves
3 sticks celery, cut in diagonal slices
½ cup water or chicken stock
2 tsps oyster sauce

Step 3 Add the walnuts to the wok and cook until they are crisp.

Step 3 Cook the chicken until done but not brown.

Step 4 Use a large, sharp knife to cut the celery on the diagonal into thin slices.

1. Combine the chicken with the soy sauce, brandy, cornstarch, salt and pepper.

2. Heat a wok and add the oil and garlic. Cook for about 1 minute to flavor the oil.

3. Remove the garlic and add the chicken in two batches.

Stir-fry quickly without allowing the chicken to brown. Remove the chicken and add the walnuts to the wok. Cook for about 2 minutes until the walnuts are slightly brown and crisp.

4. Slice the celery, add to the wok and cook for about 1 minute. Add the oyster sauce and water and bring to the boil. When boiling, return the chicken to the pan and stir to coat all the ingredients well. Serve immediately.

Cook's Notes

Time
Preparation takes about 20 minutes, cooking takes about 8 minutes.

Watchpoint
Nuts can burn very easily. Stir them constantly for even browning.

Variation
Almonds or cashew nuts may be used instead of the walnuts. If the cashew nuts are already toasted, add them along with the celery.

Serving Ideas
Serve with boiled or fried rice.

Buying Guide
Oyster sauce, made from oysters and soy sauce, is available from Chinese supermarkets.

SERVES 6

CHICKEN WITH CLOUD EARS

Cloud ears is the delightful name
for an edible tree fungus which is
mushroom-like in taste and texture

12 cloud ears, wood ears or other dried Chinese
　　mushrooms, soaked in boiling water for 5 minutes
1lb chicken breasts, boned and thinly sliced
1 egg white
2 tsps cornstarch
2 tsps white wine
2 tsps sesame oil
1 inch piece fresh ginger, left whole
1 clove garlic
1 cup oil
1 cup chicken stock
1 tbsp cornstarch
3 tbsps light soy sauce
Pinch salt and pepper

1. Soak the mushrooms until they soften and swell.
Remove all the skin and bone from the chicken and cut it
into thin slices. Mix the chicken with the egg white,
cornstarch, wine and sesame oil.

2. Heat the wok for a few minutes and pour in the oil. Add
the whole piece of ginger and whole garlic clove to the oil
and cook for about 1 minute. Take them out and reduce the
heat.

3. Add about a quarter of the chicken at a time and stir-fry
for about 1 minute. Remove and continue cooking until all
the chicken is fried. Remove all but about 2 tbsps of the oil
from the wok.

4. Drain the mushrooms and squeeze them to extract all
the liquid. If using mushrooms with stems, remove the
stems before slicing thinly. Cut cloud ears or wood ears into

smaller pieces. Add to the wok and cook for about 1 minute.
Add the stock and allow it to come almost to the boil. Mix
together the cornstarch and soy sauce and add a spoonful
of the hot stock. Add the mixture to the wok, stirring
constantly, and bring to the boil. Allow to boil 1-2 minutes or
until thickened. The sauce will clear when the cornstarch
has cooked sufficiently.

5. Return the chicken to the wok and add salt and pepper.
Stir thoroughly for about 1 minute and serve immediately.

Step 1 Soak the cloud ears or mushrooms in boiling water for five minutes, they will swell in size.

Step 3 Stir-fry the chicken in small batches, placing in the oil with chopsticks.

Cook's Notes

Time
Preparation takes about 25 minutes, cooking takes about 5 minutes.

Preparation
If desired, the chicken may be cut into 1 inch cubes. If slicing, cut across the grain as this helps the chicken to cook more evenly.

Variation
Flat, cup or button mushrooms may be used instead of the dried mushrooms. Eliminate the soaking and slice them thickly. Cook as for the dried variety. 2 tsps bottled oyster sauce may be added with the stock.

Buying Guide
Cloud ears or wood ears are a type of edible Chinese tree fungus. They are both available from Chinese supermarkets and some delicatessens. Chinese mushrooms are more readily available. Both keep a long time in their dried state. Chinese ingredients are becoming more readily available. Check supermarket shelves for bottled sauces like Oyster Sauce.

SERVES 4

SPUN FRUITS

Often called toffee fruits, this sweet
consists of fruit fried in batter and
coated with a thin, crisp caramel glaze.

Batter

1 cup all-purpose flour, sifted
Pinch salt
1 egg
½ cup water and milk mixed half and half
Oil for deep frying

Caramel Syrup

1 cup sugar
3 tbsps water
1 tbsp oil
1 large apple, peeled, cored and cut into 2 inch chunks
1 banana, peeled and cut into 1 inch pieces
Ice water

1. To prepare the batter, combine all the ingredients, except the oil for deep frying, in a liquidizer or food processor and process to blend. Pour into a bowl and dip in the prepared fruit.

2. In a heavy-based saucepan, combine the sugar with the water and oil and cook over very low heat until the sugar dissolves. Bring to the boil and allow to cook rapidly until a pale caramel color.

3. While the sugar is dissolving, heat the oil in a wok and fry the batter-dipped fruit, a few pieces at a time.

4. While the fruit is still hot and crisp, use chopsticks or a pair of tongs to dip the fruit into the hot caramel syrup. Stir each piece around to coat evenly.

5. Dip immediately into ice water to harden the syrup and place each piece on a greased dish. Continue cooking all the fruit in the same way.

6. Once the caramel has hardened and the fruit has cooled, transfer to a clean serving plate.

Step 2 Cook the syrup until the sugar dissolves and is a pale golden brown.

Step 4 Using tongs or chopsticks, immediately dip the fried fruit into the hot syrup, swirling to coat evenly.

Step 5 Dip the caramel coated fruit into ice water to harden. Place on a greased dish to cool.

Cook's Notes

Time
Preparation takes about 25 minutes, cooking takes from 10-15 minutes.

Variation
Lychees may be used either fresh or canned. Organization is very important for the success of this dish. Have the batter ready, syrup prepared, fruit sliced and ice water on hand before beginning.

Watchpoint
Watch the syrup carefully and do not allow it to become too brown. This will give a bitter taste to the dish.

ALMOND COOKIES

In China these are often eaten as a
between-meal snack. In Western style cuisine, they
make a good accompaniment to fruit or sorbet.

1 stick butter or margarine
4 tbsps granulated sugar
2 tbsps light brown sugar
1 egg, beaten
Almond extract
1 cup all-purpose flour
1 tsp baking powder
Pinch salt
¼ cup ground almonds, blanched or unblanched
2 tbsps water
30 whole blanched almonds

Step 2 Add egg and flavoring and beat until smooth.

Step 3 Shape into small balls with floured hands on a floured surface. Place well apart on baking sheets.

Step 1 Cream the butter and sugars until light and fluffy.

1. Cream the butter or margarine together with the two sugars until light and fluffy.

2. Divide the beaten egg in half and add half to the sugar mixture with a few drops of the almond extract and beat until smooth. Reserve the remaining egg for later use. Sift the flour, baking powder and salt into the egg mixture and add the ground almonds. Stir well by hand.

3. Shape the mixture into small balls and place well apart on a lightly greased baking sheet. Flatten slightly and press an almond on to the top of each one.

4. Mix the reserved egg with the water and brush each cookie before baking.

5. Place in a preheated 350°F oven and bake for 12-15 minutes. Cookies will be a pale golden color when done.

Cook's Notes

 Time
Preparation takes about 10 minutes. If the dough becomes too soft, refrigerate for 10 minutes before shaping. Cooking takes about 12-15 minutes per batch.

 Cook's Tip
Roll the mixture on a floured surface with floured hands to prevent sticking.

 Watchpoint
Do not over beat once the almonds are added. They will begin to oil and the mixture will become too soft and sticky to shape.

 Serving Ideas
Serve with fruit, ice cream or sorbet. Do not reserve just for Chinese meals.

 Freezing
Cookies may be frozen baked or unbaked. Defrost un-cooked dough completely at room temperature before baking. Baked cookies may be re-crisped by heating in the oven for about 2 minutes and then allowed to cool before serving.

SERVES 6

SWEET BEAN WONTONS

Wonton snacks, either sweet or savory, are another popular
tea house treat. Made from prepared wonton wrappers and
ready-made bean paste, these couldn't be more simple.

15 wonton wrappers
8oz sweet red bean paste
1 tbsp cornstarch
4 tbsps cold water
Oil for deep frying
Honey

1. Take a wonton wrapper in the palm of your hand and
place a little of the red bean paste slightly above the center.

2. Mix together the cornstarch and water and moisten the
edge around the filling.

3. Fold over, slightly off center.

4. Pull the sides together, using the cornstarch and water
paste to stick the two together.

5. Turn inside out by gently pushing the filled center.

6. Heat enough oil in a wok for deep-fat frying and when
hot, put in 4 of the filled wontons at a time. Cook until crisp
and golden and remove to paper towels to drain. Repeat
with the remaining filled wontons. Serve drizzled with honey.

Step 4 Bring the
two sides together
and stick with
cornstarch and
water paste.

Step 5 Push the
filled portion
gently through the
middle to turn
inside out.

Cook's Notes

Variation
Add a small amount of grated
ginger to the red bean paste
for a slight change in flavor. Wontons
may also be sprinkled with sugar
instead of honey.

Buying Guide
Wontons, wonton wrappers
and red bean paste are
available in Chinese supermarkets.

SERVES 6-8

ALMOND FLOAT WITH FRUIT

Sweet dishes are not often served in the course
of a Chinese meal. Banquets are the exception, and
this elegant fruit salad is certainly special enough.

1 envelope unflavored gelatine
6 tbsps cold water
⅓ cup sugar
1 cup milk
1 tsp almond extract
Few drops red or yellow food coloring (optional)

Almond Sugar Syrup

⅓ cup sugar
2 cups water
½ tsp almond extract

Fresh fruit such as kiwi, mango, pineapple, bananas,
    lychees, oranges or satsumas, peaches, berries,
    cherries, grapes or starfruit
Fresh mint for garnish

1. Allow the gelatine to soften in the cold water for about 10 minutes or until spongy. Put in a large mixing bowl.

2. Bring ⅓ cup water to the boil and stir in the sugar. Pour into the gelatine and water mixture and stir until gelatine and sugar dissolves.

3. Add milk, flavoring and food coloring if using. Mix well and pour into an 8 inch square pan. Chill in the refrigerator until set.

4. Mix the sugar and water for the syrup together in a heavy-based pan. Cook over gentle heat until the sugar dissolves. Bring to the boil and allow to boil for about 2 minutes, or until the syrup thickens slightly. Add the almond extract and allow to cool at room temperature. Chill in the refrigerator until ready to use.

5. Prepare the fruit and place in attractive serving dish. Pour over the chilled syrup and mix well.

6. Cut the set almond float into 1 inch diamond shapes or cubes. Use a spatula to remove them from the pan and stir them gently into the fruit mixture. Decorate with sprigs of fresh mint to serve.

Step 2 Add boiling water and sugar, and stir until the mixture is clear and not grainy.

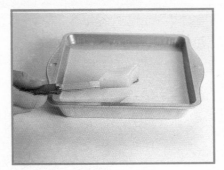

Step 6 Cut the set almond float mixture into cubes and remove from the pan with a palette knife.

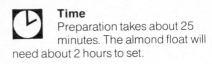

Cook's Notes

Time
Preparation takes about 25 minutes. The almond float will need about 2 hours to set.

Preparation
To prepare kiwi fruit, peel with a swivel vegetable peeler and cut into thin rounds. To prepare lychees, peel off the rough outer skin. Cut around the stone or leave it in. To prepare mangoes, peel and cut into thin slices around the large stone. To prepare starfruit, wash and cut crosswise into thin slices. The shape of the slices will resemble a star.

Buying Guide
Use whatever fruits are in season at the moment, or use good quality canned fruit. Exotic fruits are available in most large supermarkets and some greengrocers. Allow about 2lbs of fruit for 6-8 people.

MEXICAN COOKING

INTRODUCTION

In Mexico, as in most countries of the world that enjoy warm climates, the food is spicy. The addition of spices to food cooked in these climates has a two-fold purpose: they act as a preservative while also stimulating appetites flagging in the heat. But just because food is spicy, it need not be very hot. Cumin, coriander and cinnamon are favorite choices in Mexico and lend their fragrance and flavor without bringing tears to the eyes! For those who like things hot, fresh or dried chili peppers or cayenne pepper will add fire to any dish. Green chilies and Jalapeno peppers, another variety, are also available canned.

If any one ingredient really symbolizes Mexican cooking, it is the tortilla. In Mexico, tortillas in one form or another appear at every meal. Even if they are not an integral part of a recipe they are served warm as an accompaniment, even with eggs at breakfast. There are two types of tortilla, each made with different flours. Corn tortillas are made with Masa Harina, a fine corn flour that is not always easy to find. These corn tortillas are also slightly more difficult to make and to work with even though they are the more popular choice in Mexico. However, in the northern part of the country more wheat is grown, so tortillas are more often made with wheat flour. These are easy to make and more pliable, so they are easier to use in recipes and many people prefer them to the corn variety. Our recipe for flour tortillas can be used interchangeably with corn tortillas and you can even cut the tortillas into triangles or rounds and deep-fry them to make your own tortilla chips.

The use of cocoa powder in savory dishes may seem a startling idea, but don't be put off. It gives a depth of color and flavor to meat dishes without making them taste of chocolate. Spanish settlers in Mexico first used the plentiful cocoa bean in their cooking, adapting it to both sweet and savory dishes. While the Spanish also introduced sugar and milk into the cuisine, sweets have not become overly popular in Mexico.

Over the past few years more and more prepared ingredients for Mexican cooking have appeared on the market. Corn tortillas come ready made and even shaped exactly right for tacos, making the cook's job easy. But, there is fun to be had in cooking this colorful and exciting cuisine in the traditional way, too.

MAKES ½ PINT

TACO SAUCE

This basic recipe has many uses in Mexican
cooking – sauce, topping, dip or as an
ingredient to give a dish extra flavor.

1 tbsp oil
1 onion, diced
1 green pepper, diced
½-1 red or green chili pepper
½ tsp ground cumin
½ tsp ground coriander
½ clove garlic, crushed
Pinch salt, pepper and sugar
14oz canned tomatoes
Tomato paste (optional)

Step 3 Add remaining ingredients and use a potato masher or fork to break up tomatoes.

Step 2 Cut the chili in half, remove the seeds and chop flesh finely.

Step 4 Cook the sauce over moderate heat to reduce and thicken.

1. Heat the oil in a heavy-based saucepan and when hot, add the onion and pepper. Cook slowly to soften slightly.

2. Chop the chili and add with the cumin, coriander, garlic and cook a further 2-3 minutes.

3. Add sugar, seasonings and tomatoes with their juice.

Break up the tomatoes with a fork or a potato masher.

4. Cook a further 5-6 minutes over moderate heat to reduce and thicken slighly. Add tomato paste for color, if necessary. Adjust seasoning and use hot or cold according to your recipe.

Cook's Notes

Time
Preparation takes about 15-20 minutes, cooking takes about 8-10 minutes.

Serving Ideas
Use as a sauce or topping for fish, meat or poultry main dishes. Use in tacos, tostadas, nachos and as a dip for tortilla chips or vegetable crudités.

Freezing
Fill rigid containers with sauce at room temperature. Label and freeze for up to 3 months. Defrost at room temperature, breaking the sauce up as it thaws.

MAKES 12

FLOUR TORTILLAS

Tortillas made with wheat instead of corn are traditional in northern Mexico. Flour tortillas are easier to make and use than the corn variety.

1lb all-purpose or whole-wheat flour
1 tbsp salt
6 tbsps lard
1 cup hot water

Step 2 Knead a ball of prepared dough until smooth and pliable.

1. Sift flour and salt into a mixing bowl and rub in the lard until the mixture resembles fine breadcrumbs. Mix in the water gradually to form a soft, pliable dough. Whole-wheat flour may need more water.

2. Knead on a well-floured surface until smooth and no longer sticky. Cover with a damp tea towel.

3. Cut off about 3 tbsps of dough at a time, keeping the rest covered. Knead into a ball.

4. Roll the ball of dough out into a very thin circle with a floured rolling pin. Cut into a neat round using a 10 inch plate as a guide. Continue until all the dough is used.

5. Stack the tortillas as you make them, flouring each well to prevent sticking. Cover with a clean tea towel.

6. Heat a heavy-based frying pan and carefully place in a tortilla. Cook for about 10 seconds per side. Stack and keep covered until all are cooked. Use according to chosen recipe.

Step 4 Roll out the ball of dough thinly and cut into a 10 inch circle.

Step 6 Cook for 10 seconds per side in a hot frying pan.

Cook's Notes

Time
Preparation takes about 60 minutes to make the dough and roll out all the tortillas, cooking takes about 5 minutes.

Serving Ideas
Use with any recipe that calls for tortillas. Also, serve hot as an accompaniment to any Mexican dish.

Freezing
Tortillas can be prepared and cooked in advance and frozen. Stack the tortillas between sheets of non-stick or wax paper. Place in plastic bags, seal, label and freeze for up to 2 months. Defrost at room temperature before using.

SERVES 8

GUACAMOLE

This is one of Mexico's most famous dishes.
It is delicious as a first course on its
own or as an ingredient in other recipes.

1 medium onion, finely chopped
1 clove garlic, crushed
Grated rind and juice of ½ lime
½ quantity Taco Sauce recipe
3 large avocados
1 tbsp chopped fresh coriander
Pinch salt
Coriander leaves to garnish
1 package tortilla chips

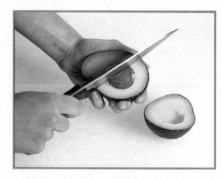

Step 3 Hit the stone with a large knife and twist to remove the stone.

Step 2 Cut avocados in half and twist the halves to separate.

Step 6 Use a potato masher to mash the avocado until nearly smooth.

1. Mix the onion, garlic, rind and juice of lime and the taco sauce together in a large mixing bowl.

2. Cut the avocados in half lengthwise. Twist the halves gently in opposite directions to separate.

3. Hit the stone with a large, sharp knife and twist the knife to remove the stone.

4. Place the avocado halves cut side down on a chopping board. Lightly score the skin lengthwise and gently pull

back to peel. Alternatively, scoop out avocado flesh with a spoon, scraping the skin well.

5. Chop the avocado roughly and immediately place in the bowl with the onion and lime.

6. Use a potato masher to break up the avocado until almost smooth. Do not over-mash. Season with salt and stir in the chopped coriander. Spoon into a serving bowl and garnish with coriander leaves.

7. Surround the bowl with tortilla chips for dipping.

Cook's Notes

Time
Preparation takes about 25 minutes.

Preparation
Do not prepare too long in advance. The avocado will darken even with the addition of lime juice if left too long.

Cook's Tip
Try leaving the avocado stone in the mixture. This is said to retard discoloration.

SERVES 4

MOYETTES

While these sandwiches seem like lunch fare, they
are very popular for breakfast in Mexico.

4 crusty rolls
2 tbsps butter or margarine
8oz canned refried beans
2 green onions, chopped
4 tbsps grated Tilsit cheese

1. Cut the rolls in half and remove some of the inside.

Step 1 Remove
some of the
insides of each
roll. Use a
teaspoon to
scrape out
crumbs or cut out
with a small knife.

Step 2 Spread
both sides of
each roll with
softened butter or
margarine, then fill
the rolls with the
refried beans.

2. Soften the butter and spread on both sides of the rolls.

3. Fill the rolls with the refried beans.

4. Sprinkle with the green onion and top with the grated cheese.

5. Place the rolls on a baking sheet and cook in a pre-heated 325°F oven for 15-20 minutes, or until the cheese has melted and the beans are hot. Serve immediately.

Cook's Notes

Time
Preparation takes about 15
minutes and cooking takes
about 15-20 minutes.

Cook's Tip
Sandwiches may be prepared
in advance and heated
through just before serving. Once
heated, they do not reheat
successfully.

Variation
Use red onion and Cheddar
or Monterey Jack cheese, if
available.

MAKES 12

TACOS

Packaged taco shells make this famous
Mexican snack easy to prepare, so spend
the extra time on imaginative fillings.

12 taco shells

Beef Filling

1 tbsp oil
1lb ground beef
1 medium onion, chopped
2 tsps ground cumin
1 clove garlic, crushed
2 tsps chili powder
Pinch paprika
Salt and pepper

Chicken Filling

3 tbsps butter or margarine
1 medium onion, chopped
1 small red pepper, seeded and chopped
2 tbsps sliced almonds
12oz chicken breasts, skinned and finely chopped
Salt and pepper
1 piece fresh ginger, peeled and chopped
6 tbsps milk
2 tsps cornstarch
½ cup sour cream

Toppings

Shredded lettuce
Grated cheese
Tomatoes, seeded and chopped
Chopped green onions
Avocado slices
Sour cream
Jalapeno peppers
Taco sauce

1. Heat oil for beef filling in a large frying pan and brown the beef and onions, breaking the meat up with a fork as it cooks. Add spices, garlic and seasoning and cook about 20 minutes. Set aside.

2. Melt the 2 tbsps butter or margarine in a medium saucepan and add the onion. Cook slowly until softened.

3. Add the red pepper and almonds and cook slowly until the almonds are lightly browned. Stir often during cooking. Remove to a plate and set aside.

4. Melt the remaining butter in the same saucepan and cook the chicken for about 5 minutes, turning frequently. Season and return the onion mixture to the pan along with the chopped ginger.

5. Blend milk and cornstarch and stir into the chicken mixture. Bring to the boil and stir until very thick. Mix in the sour cream and cook gently to heat through. Do not boil.

6. Heat the taco shells on a baking sheet in a preheated 350°F oven for 2-3 minutes. Place on the sheet with the open ends down.

7. To fill, hold the shell in one hand and spoon in about 1 tbsp of either beef or chicken filling.

8. Next, add a layer of shredded lettuce, followed by a layer of grated cheese.

9. Add choice of other toppings and finally spoon on some taco sauce.

Step 7 Hold taco shell in the palm of the hand and fill with about 1 tbsp filling.

Cook's Notes

Time
Preparation takes about 40 minutes. Cooking takes about 20 minutes for the beef filling, 15 minutes for the chicken filling and 2-3 minutes to heat the taco shells.

Cook's Tip
Placing the taco shells on their open ends when reheating keeps them from closing up and makes filling easier.

Serving Ideas
For a buffet, place all the ingredients out separately for guests to help themselves and create their own combinations.

SERVES 8-10

NACHOS

These make excellent cocktail savories
and the variety of toppings and flavor
combinations is almost endless.

1 package round tortilla chips
1 can refried beans
1 can Jalapeno bean dip
Full quantity Taco Sauce recipe
8-10 cherry tomatoes, sliced
½ cup sour cream or natural yogurt
Sliced black and stuffed green olives
Grated Cheddar cheese

Taco Filling

2 tsps oil
8oz ground beef
2 tsps chili powder
Pinch ground coriander
Pinch cayenne pepper
Salt and pepper

1. Prepare taco filling as for Tacos recipe. Top half of the tortilla chips with refried beans and half with beef taco filling.

2. Place a spoonful of taco sauce on the bean-topped chips and Jalapeno bean dip in the beef-topped chips.

3. Top the tortilla chips with tomatoes, sour cream or yogurt, olives or cheese in any desired combination, and serve.

Step 2 Spoon on taco sauce and Jalapeno bean dip on top of beans or beef.

Step 1 Use a teaspoon to top chips with beans and beef mixture. Spread out carefully with the bowl of the spoon.

Step 3 Top with chosen ingredients and serve. Heat through to melt cheese if desired.

Cook's Notes

Time
Preparation takes about 25 minutes.

Variation
If desired, heat through for 5 minutes in a moderate oven before topping with tomatoes, sour cream or olives. Cheese may be sprinkled on to melt before serving.

Cook's Tip
Tortilla chips will become slightly soggy if topped too soon before serving.

MAKES 12

TOSTADAS

These are popular all over Mexico and the toppings reflect the food available in each area. They are delicious, but difficult to eat!

2 tsps oil
1lb ground beef or pork
2 tsps chili powder
1 tsp ground cumin
1 tsp ground coriander
1 can refried beans
1 package tostada shells

Toppings

Shredded lettuce
Grated Cheddar cheese
Tomatoes, seeded and chopped
Sour Cream
Olives
Shrimp
Green onions, chopped
Taco sauce

Step 4 Spoon some of the meat mixture over the beans, pushing it down gently so that it sticks to the beans.

Step 5 Top with your choice of topping ingredients.

Step 3 Spread refried beans carefully over each tostada shell.

1. Cook the meat in the oil in a medium frying pan. Sprinkle on the spices and cook quickly to brown.

2. Reheat the beans and place the tostada shells on a baking sheet. Heat 2-3 minutes in a moderate oven.

3. Spread 1-2 tbsps of the beans on each tostada shell.

4. Top each shell with some of the beef mixture.

5. Add the topping ingredients in different combinations and serve immediately.

Cook's Notes

Time
Preparation takes about 40 minutes, cooking takes about 10-15 minutes.

Preparation
All the ingredients can be prepared ahead of time. The tostadas cannot be reheated once assembled.

Variation
Add chopped green or red peppers to the list of toppings along with chopped green chilies or Jalapeno peppers and guacamole.

SERVES 6

FLAUTAS

Traditionally, these are long, thin
rolls of tortillas with savory
fillings, topped with sour cream.

8oz chicken, skinned, boned and ground or finely
   chopped
1 tbsp oil
1 small onion, finely chopped
½ green pepper, finely chopped
½-1 chili pepper, seeded and finely chopped
3oz frozen sweetcorn
6 black olives, pitted and chopped
½ cup heavy cream
Salt
12 prepared tortillas (see recipe for Flour Tortillas)
Taco sauce, guacamole and sour cream for toppings.

1. Use a food processor or meat grinder to prepare the
chicken, or chop by hand.

2. Heat the oil in a medium frying pan and add the
chicken, onion and green pepper. Cook over moderate
heat, stirring frequently to break up the pieces of chicken.

3. When the chicken is cooked and the vegetables are
softened, add the chili, sweetcorn, olives, cream and salt.
Bring to the boil over heat and boil rapidly, stirring
continuously, to reduce and thicken the cream.

4. Place 2 tortillas on a clean work surface, overlapping
them by about 2 inches. Spoon some of the chicken
mixture onto the tortillas, roll up and secure with wooden
picks.

5. Fry the flautas in about ½ inch oil in a large frying pan.
Do not allow the tortillas to get very brown. Drain on paper
towels.

6. Arrange flautas on serving plates and top with sour
cream, guacamole and taco sauce.

Step 4 Place
tortillas slightly
overlapping on
work surface and
fill with chicken.

Step 4 Use
wooden picks to
secure tortillas.

Step 5 Fry slowly
and turn carefully
so the filling does
not leak.

Cook's Notes

Time
Preparation takes about 1
hour for the tortillas and about
30 minutes to finish the dish.

Variation
Use pork or beef in place of
the chicken. Green olives,
may be substituted for black, and red
peppers for green.

Serving Ideas
Flautas are often served with
rice, refried beans and a
salad.

SERVES 6

BURRITOS

The name means 'little donkeys' and the dish is
a very popular one. Beans are the traditional
filling, but meat may be used as well.

6 flour tortillas
1 onion, chopped
1 tbsp oil
1lb canned refried beans
6 lettuce leaves, shredded
2 tbsps snipped chives
2 tomatoes, sliced
4oz Cheddar cheese, grated
Full quantity Taco Sauce recipe
½ cup sour cream
Chopped coriander leaves

Step 3 Use
kitchen scissors to
make snipping
chives easy.

Step 3 Spoon
some of the bean
mixture down the
center of each
tortilla.

Step 3 Fold the
ends and sides of
each tortilla
around the filling
to make
rectangular
parcels.

sides to form long rectangular parcel. Make sure the filling
is completely enclosed.

1. Wrap tortillas in foil and heat in a warm oven to soften.

2. Cook the onion in the oil until soft but not colored. Add
the beans and heat through.

3. Spoon the mixture down the center of each tortilla. Top
with lettuce, cheese, tomatoes and chives. Fold over the

4. Place burritos in an ovenproof dish, cover and cook in a
preheated 350°F oven for about 20 minutes.

5. Spoon over the taco sauce. Top with sour cream and
sprinkle with chopped coriander to serve.

Cook's Notes

Time
Preparation takes about 25
minutes, not including making
the tortillas. Cooking takes about 20
minutes.

Preparation
Heat just before serving.
Burritos do not reheat well.
Add extra chili pepper to the taco
sauce recipe if desired.

Serving Ideas
Serve with rice and
guacamole.

SERVES 6

CHIMICHANGAS

A strange sounding name for a delicious snack
which is something like a deep-fried taco.

6 flour tortillas
Half quantity Chili Con Carne recipe
6 lettuce leaves, shredded
6 green onions, chopped
3oz Cheddar cheese, grated
Oil for frying
Half quantity Guacamole recipe
½ cup sour cream
1 tomato, seeded and chopped

Step 4 Lower the chimichangas carefully into hot oil in a large frying pan, folded side first.

Step 3 Fold the tortillas over the filling to enclose it completely and form a parcel.

Step 5 After about 3 minutes, turn chimichangas over with a draining spoon or spatula to cook the other side.

1. Wrap the tortillas in foil and place in a warm oven for 5 minutes to make them pliable.

2. Heat the chili briefly and spoon about 2 tbsps onto the center of each tortilla. Top with lettuce, onions and cheese.

3. Fold in the sides to make a parcel, making sure all the filling is enclosed.

4. Heat about 1 inch of oil in a large frying pan and when

hot lower in the chimichangas, folded side down first. Cook 2-4 at a time depending on the size of the pan.

5. Cook for 3 minutes and carefully turn over. Cook a further 3 minutes and remove to paper towels and drain. Repeat with remaining chimichangas.

6. Spoon the guacamole over the top of each and drizzle over the sour cream. Sprinkle over the chopped tomato and serve immediately.

Cook's Notes

Time
Preparation takes about 30 minutes. This does not include time to prepare the tortillas or the chilli. Cooking time for the chimichangas is about 12-18 minutes.

Preparation
Tortillas and chili can be made in advance and the chimichangas cooked just before serving. They do not reheat successfully.

Serving Idea
Serve with rice and refried beans.

SERVES 6

ENCHILADAS

Although fillings and sauces vary, enchiladas
are one of the tastiest Mexican dishes.

10 ripe tomatoes, peeled, seeded and chopped
1 small onion, chopped
1-2 green or red chilies, seeded and chopped
1 clove garlic, crushed
Salt
Pinch sugar
1-2 tbsps tomato paste
2 tbsps butter or margarine
2 eggs
1 cup heavy cream
4 tbsps grated cheese
12oz ground pork
1 small red pepper, seeded and chopped
4 tbsps raisins
4 tbsps pine nuts
Salt and pepper
12 prepared tortillas (see recipe for Flour Tortillas)
Sliced green onions to garnish

1. Place tomatoes, onion, chilies, garlic, salt and sugar in a
blender or food processor and purée until smooth.

2. Melt butter or margarine in a large saucepan. Add the
paste and simmer for 5 minutes.

3. Beat together the eggs and cream, mixing well. Add a
spoonful of the hot tomato paste to the cream and eggs and
mix quickly. Return mixture to the saucepan with the rest of
the tomato paste. Reserve cheese for topping.

4. Heat slowly, stirring constantly, until the mixture thickens. Do not boil.

5. While preparing the sauce, cook the pork and pepper
slowly in a large frying pan. Use a fork to break up the meat
as it cooks. Turn up the heat when the pork is nearly cooked
and fry briskly for a few minutes. Add the raisins, pine nuts

and seasoning.

6. Combine about ¼ of the sauce with the meat and divide
mixture evenly among all the tortillas. Spoon on the filling to
one side of the center and roll up the tortilla around it,
leaving the ends open and some of the filling showing.

7. Place enchiladas seam side down in a baking dish and
pour over the remaining sauce, leaving the ends uncovered. Sprinkle over the cheese and bake in a preheated
350°F oven for 15-20 minutes, or until the sauce begins
to bubble. Sprinkle with the sliced onions and serve
immediately.

Step 3 Mix the
eggs and cream
with some of the
hot sauce and
then return it to
the pan, stirring
constantly.

Step 6 Spoon
meat filling to one
side of the tortillas
and roll them up,
leaving ends
open.

Cook's Notes

Time
Preparation takes about 60
minutes to make the tortillas
and about 30 minutes more to finish the
dish.

Watchpoint
When preparing the sauce, do
not allow it to boil or it
will curdle.

Economy
Left-over meat or chicken can
be ground in a food processor
or finely chopped and used in place of
the freshly cooked meat.

SERVES 4

SHRIMP ACAPULCO

These make a stylish appetizer or a quickly
prepared snack. Make the bread slices
smaller to serve with cocktails.

4 slices bread, crusts removed
6 tbsps softened butter
6oz cooked and peeled shrimp
½ tsp chili powder
¼ tsp paprika
¼ tsp cumin
Salt and pepper
Watercress to garnish

1. Cut the bread slices in half and spread with 2 tbsps butter. Butter both sides sparingly.

2. Place the bread on a baking sheet and cook in a preheated 350°F oven for 10-15 minutes until golden brown. Keep warm.

3. Melt the remaining butter in a small pan and add the shrimp, spices and seasoning and stir well.

4. Heat through completely and spoon on top of the bread slices. Garnish with watercress and serve hot.

Step 2 Cook the bread on a baking sheet until golden brown and crisp.

Step 3 Cook the shrimp and chili mixture over gentle heat, stirring continuously.

Cook's Notes

Time
Preparation takes about 15 minutes. The bread will take 15-20 minutes to cook until golden, and the shrimp take about 5 minutes to heat through.

Watchpoint
Do not heat the shrimp too long or at too high a temperature; they toughen easily.

Cook's Tip
The bread may be prepared in advance and reheated 5 minutes in the oven. Do not reheat the shrimp.

SERVES 4

CHILI VEGETABLE SOUP

A simple-to-make and delicious soup
that makes a light first course.

1 tbsp oil
1 onion, chopped
4oz canned whole green chilies, quartered
4 cups chicken stock
1 large potato, peeled and cut into short strips
Full quantity Taco Sauce recipe
1 tbsp lime juice
Tortilla chips and lime slices to garnish
Salt

Step 1 Cook the onion slowly in the oil until translucent. Do not brown.

1. Heat the oil in a large saucepan and sauté the onion until translucent. Add the green chilies, stock, potato and taco sauce.

2. Cover the pan and simmer soup for 20 minutes. Stir in the lime juice and add salt.

3. Serve in individual bowls with tortilla chips.

4. Cut a thin slice of lime to float in each bowl of soup.

Step 1 Add the remaining ingredients and simmer for 20 minutes.

Cook's Notes

 Time
Preparation takes about 20 minutes and cooking takes 20 minutes.

 Variation
Use only half a can green chilies if desired, or cook green peppers with the onions instead.

 Serving Ideas
For a more filling soup, add cooked rice.

SERVES 4

BEEF & BEAN SOUP

In Mexico, the day's main meal is
eaten at around 2.00 pm and this
soup is a popular appetizer.

1 large onion, peeled and finely chopped
2 sticks celery, chopped
1 red pepper, deseeded and finely chopped
2 tbsps oil
8oz ground beef
6 tomatoes, peeled, seeded and chopped
15oz canned refried beans
1 tsp ground cumin
1 tsp chili powder
1 tsp garlic powder or paste
Pinch cinnamon and cayenne pepper
2 cups beef stock
Salt and pepper

spices, garlic and seasoning and mix well.

3. Stir in the stock and bring to the boil. Cover and simmer gently for 30 minutes, stirring occasionally.

4. Pour the soup into a blender or food processor and purée. The soup will be quite thick and not completely smooth.

5. Adjust the seasoning and serve with tortilla chips. Top with sour cream if desired.

Step 2 Cook the beef over medium heat until well browned.

Step 1 Cook the onion, celery and pepper in oil to soften. Stir frequently.

Step 4 Purée the soup in several batches until nearly smooth.

1. Fry the onion, pepper and celery in the oil in a large saucepan until softened.

2. Add the beef and fry over medium heat until well browned. Add the tomatoes and refried beans with the

Cook's Notes

Time
Preparation takes about 20 minutes and cooking takes about 50 minutes to soften vegetables, brown meat and simmer soup.

Watchpoint
Make sure the blender or food processor lid is closed securely before puréeing the hot soup. Purée in 2 or 3 small batches for safety.

Freezing
Allow the pasted soup to cool completely and skim any fat from the surface. Pour into freezer containers, label and freeze for up to 3 months.

SERVES 6

Mexican Chicken & Pepper Salad

This is the perfect lunch or light supper dish
during the summer, and it can be prepared in advance.

1lb cooked chicken, cut in strips
½ cup mayonnaise
½ cup natural yogurt
1 tsp chili powder
1 tsp paprika
Pinch cayenne pepper
½ tsp tomato paste
1 tsp onion paste
1 green pepper, seeded and finely sliced
1 red pepper, seeded and finely sliced
6oz frozen sweetcorn, defrosted
6oz long grain rice, cooked

1. Place the chicken strips in a large salad bowl.

2. Mix the mayonnaise, yogurt, spices, tomato and onion pastes together and leave to stand briefly for flavors to blend. Fold dressing into the chicken.

3. Add the peppers and sweetcorn and mix gently until all the ingredients are coated with dressing.

4. Place the rice on a serving dish and pile the salad into the center. Serve immediately.

Step 3 Fold all ingredients together gently so that they do not break up Use a large spoon or rubber spatula.

Step 4 Arrange rice on a serving plate and spoon salad into the center.

Cook's Notes

Time
Preparation takes about 30 minutes.

Buying Guide
Onion paste is available in tubes like tomato paste.

Preparation
Chicken salad may be prepared several hours in advance and kept covered in the refrigerator. Spoon onto rice just before serving.

Variation
Add sliced or diced green chilies or Jalapeno peppers for hotter flavor. Try chili sauce or taco sauce as an alternative seasoning.

SERVES 6

CHILI SHRIMP QUICHE

Fresh chili peppers give a Mexican flavor
to this quiche with its shrimp filling.

Pastry

1 cup all-purpose flour
Pinch salt
2 tbsps butter or margarine
2 tbsps white cooking fat
2-4 tbsps cold water

Filling

4 eggs
½ cup milk
½ cup light cream
½ clove garlic, crushed
1 cup Cheddar cheese, grated
3 green onions, chopped
2 green chilies, seeded and chopped
8oz cooked and peeled shrimp
Salt
Cooked, unpeeled shrimp and parsley sprigs for garnish

1. Sift the flour with a pinch of salt into a mixing bowl, or place in a food processor and mix once or twice.

2. Rub in the butter and fat until the mixture resembles fine breadcrumbs, or work in the food processor, being careful not to over-mix.

3. Mix in the liquid gradually, adding enough to bring the pastry together into a ball. In a food processor, add the liquid through the funnel while the machine is running.

4. Wrap the pastry well and chill for 20-30 minutes.

5. Roll out the pastry on a well-floured surface with a floured rolling pin.

6. Wrap the circle of pastry around the rolling pin to lift it into a 10 inch flan dish. Unroll the pastry over the dish.

7. Carefully press the pastry onto the bottom and up the sides of the dish, taking care not to stretch it.

8. Roll the rolling pin over the top of the dish to remove excess pastry, or cut off with a sharp knife.

9. Mix the eggs, milk, cream and garlic together. Sprinkle the cheese, onion, chilies and shrimp onto the base of the pastry and pour over the egg mixture.

10. Bake in a preheated 400°F oven for 30-40 minutes until firm and golden brown. Peel the tail shells off the shrimp and remove the legs and roe if present. Use to garnish the quiche along with the sprigs of parsley.

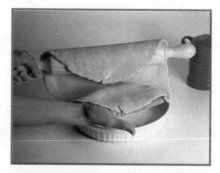

Step 6 Use the rolling pin to help lift the pastry into the flan dish.

Step 7 Carefully press the pastry into the dish to line the base and sides.

Cook's Notes

Time
Preparation takes about 40 minutes, which includes time for the pastry to chill. Cooking takes 30-40 minutes.

Variation
Add diced red or green peppers and chopped coriander leaves to the filling before baking.

Serving Ideas
Serve as a starter, cut in thin wedges or baked in individual dishes. Serve hot or cold with a salad for a snack or light meal.

SERVES 6

SHRIMP VERACRUZ

Veracruz is a port on the Gulf of Mexico
which lends its name to a variety
of colorful seafood dishes.

1 tbsp oil
1 onion, chopped
1 large green pepper, cut into 1½ inch strips.
2-3 green chilies, seeded and chopped
Double quantity Taco Sauce recipe
2 tomatoes, skinned and roughly chopped
12 pimento-stuffed olives, halved
2 tsps capers
¼ tsp ground cumin
Salt
1lb shrimp, uncooked
Juice of 1 lime

Refresh in cold water. The skins will now peel away easily.

Step 2 Combine all the sauce ingredients in a heavy-based pan.

Place the tomatoes in a pan of boiling water for a few seconds.

1. Heat the oil in a large frying pan and add the onion and green pepper. Cook until soft but not colored.

2. Add chilies, taco sauce, tomatoes, olives, capers, cumin

and salt. Bring to the boil and then lower the heat to simmer for 5 minutes.

3. Remove black veins, if present, from the rounded side of the shrimp with a wooden pick.

4. Add the shrimp to the sauce and cook until they curl up and turn pink and opaque. Add the lime juice to taste and serve.

Cook's Notes

 Time
Preparation takes about 25 minutes and cooking takes about 15 minutes.

 Preparation
Sauce may be prepared in advance and reheated while cooking the shrimp.

Variation
If using cooked shrimp, reheat for about 5 minutes. Do not overcook.

SERVES 4

PLAICE WITH SPICY TOMATO SAUCE

This piquant fish dish is popular along
Mexico's Gulf coast.

3oz cream cheese
1 tsp dried oregano
Pinch cayenne pepper
4 whole fillets of plaice
Lime slices and dill to garnish

Tomato Sauce

1 tbsp oil
1 small onion, chopped
1 stick celery, chopped
1 chili pepper, seeded and chopped
¼ tsp each ground cumin, coriander and ginger
½ red and ½ green pepper, seeded and chopped
14oz canned tomatoes
1 tbsp tomato paste
Salt, pepper and a pinch sugar

1. Heat the oil in a heavy-based pan and cook the onion, celery, chili pepper and spices for about 5 minutes over very low heat.

2. Add red and green peppers and the remaining ingredients and bring to the boil. Reduce heat and simmer 15-20 minutes, stirring occasionally. Set aside while preparing the fish.

3. Mix the cream cheese, oregano and cayenne pepper together and set aside.

4. Skin the fillets using a filleting knife. Start at the tail end and hold the knife at a slight angle to the skin.

5. Push the knife along using a sawing motion, with the blade against the skin. Dip fingers in salt to make it easier to hold onto the fish skin. Gradually separate the fish from the skin.

6. Spread the cheese filling on all 4 fillets and roll each up. Secure with wooden picks.

7. Place the fillets in a lightly greased baking dish, cover and cook for 10 minutes in a preheated 350°F oven.

8. Pour over the tomato sauce and cook a further 10-15 minutes. Fish is cooked when it feels firm and looks opaque. Garnish with lime slices and dill.

Step 5 Using a filleting knife held at an angle, push the knife along, cutting against the fish skin. Use a sawing motion to separate flesh from skin.

Step 6 Spread cheese filling on the fish and roll up each fillet.

Cook's Notes

Time
Preparation takes about 30 minutes and cooking takes 20-25 minutes.

Serving Ideas
Add rice and an avocado salad.

Special Occasions
Add shrimp or crabmeat to the filling for a dinner party dish.

MAKES 6

EMPANADAS
(SAVORY TURNOVERS)

Fillings for these turnovers can also be sweet.
They are Spanish in origin and widely popular.

Triple quantity pastry recipe from Chili Shrimp Quiche
1 egg

Filling

1 onion, chopped
1 clove garlic, finely chopped
1 small green pepper, seeded and chopped
1 tbsp oil
8oz ground beef
1 tsp cocoa powder
1 tbsp flour
½ tsp ground cumin
½ tsp paprika
½ tsp dried oregano, crushed
Salt and pepper
1-2 chilies, seeded and chopped
2 tbsps tomato paste
3 tbsps water
2 tbsps sliced almonds
2 tbsps raisins

1. Prepare the pastry according to the recipe for Chili Shrimp Quiche, or use packaged shortcrust pastry.

2. Cook the onion, garlic and green pepper in the oil until soft but not colored. Add the meat and fry quickly until well browned. Add the cocoa, flour, spices, oregano, and seasonings, stir well and cook briefly before adding the chilies, tomato paste and water. Cook slowly for 10-15 minutes. Add nuts and raisins and allow to cool.

3. Roll out the pastry on a floured surface and cut out 6 rounds using a 6 inch plate or saucepan lid as a guide.

4. Place the cooled filling on one side of the rounds of pastry and dampen the edges with water.

5. Fold over and press to seal the edges. Crimp the edges if desired.

6. Place on baking sheets and brush with a mixture of beaten egg and salt. Make sure the egg glaze is brushed on evenly. Prick once or twice with a fork and bake at 425°F for about 15 minutes, or until golden brown.

Step 5 Fold over and press the edges to seal firmly. Crimp if desired.

Step 6 Brush the surface of each turnover with beaten egg and prick the tops with a fork to let out steam.

Cook's Notes

Time
Preparation takes about 30 minutes. Dough should chill for about 30 minutes before rolling out. Filling takes about 20 minutes to cook and turnovers take about 15 minutes to bake.

Preparation
Turnovers may be baked in advance and reheated for about 5 minutes in a hot oven before serving. They may also be served cold.

Serving Ideas
Serve hot or cold as a snack or light meal accompanied with a salad. Perfect for picnics.

SERVES 4

CHILI CON CARNE

Although this dish is Mexican in
origin, the version everyone knows
best is really more American.

1 tbsp oil
1lb ground beef
2 tsps ground cumin
2 tsps mild or hot chili powder
Pinch oregano
Salt, pepper and pinch sugar
¼ tsp garlic powder
2 tbsps flour
1lb canned tomatoes
1lb canned red kidney beans

1. Heat the oil in a large saucepan and brown the meat, breaking it up with a fork as it cooks. Sprinkle on the cumin, chili powder, oregano, salt, pepper, sugar, garlic and flour. Cook, stirring frequently, over medium heat for about 3 minutes.

2. Add the tomatoes and their liquid and simmer 25-30 minutes.

3. Drain the kidney beans and add just before serving. Heat through about 5 minutes.

Step 1 Sprinkle on the spice mixture and stir it into the meat. Skim off any fat that forms on the surface.

Step 2 Add the tomatoes and their liquid. Use a large spoon or potato masher to break up the tomatoes.

Cook's Notes

Time
Preparation takes about 15 minutes. Cooking takes about 10 minutes to brown the meat and 15-30 minutes to cook after the tomatoes are added.

Serving Ideas
Spoon the chili on top of boiled rice to serve. Top with sour cream, chopped onion, grated cheese, diced avocado or a combination of the four ingredients.

Freezing
Allow the chili to cool completely and place in rigid containers, seal, label and freeze for up to 3 months. Thaw before reheating.

SERVES 4

MEXICAN BEEF PATTIES

Refried beans added to the meat mixture
make moist and flavorsome beefburgers
that are slightly out of the ordinary.

1 onion, finely chopped
1 tbsp oil
12oz ground beef
8oz canned refried beans
4 tbsps breadcrumbs
½ tsp cumin
1 tsp chili powder
1 clove garlic, crushed
Salt and pepper
1 egg, beaten
Flour to coat
Oil for frying
Watercress to garnish

1. Cook the onion in the oil until soft but not browned. Mix in the beef, beans, breadcrumbs, spices, garlic and seasoning and gradually add the egg until the mixture holds together well.

2. Turn the mixture out onto a well-floured surface and divide into 8 pieces.

3. Shape into even-sized patties with well-floured hands. Knead the pieces before shaping, if necessary, to make sure mixture holds together with no cracks.

4. Coat lightly with flour and refrigerate until firm.

5. Pour enough oil into a large frying pan to completely cover the patties. Fry 2 at a time until golden brown on all sides and completely cooked through.

6. Remove from the oil and drain on paper towels. Arrange on a serving plate and garnish with watercress.

Step 3 Shape meat mixture into firm, even-sized patties with well-floured hands.

Step 4 Coat lightly with flour on all sides and place on a plate or baking sheet to refrigerate until firm.

Step 5 Fry 2 patties at a time in hot oil. Make sure they are completely submerged.

Cook's Notes

Time
Preparation takes about 20 minutes. The patties will take at least 1 hour to firm up sufficiently in the refrigerator.

Preparation
If mixture is too soft to shape, add 2 tbsps flour.

Serving Ideas
Serve with sour cream or taco sauce and an avocado and tomato salad. Accompany with warm flour tortillas.

Freezing
Meat patties can be made up ahead of time and frozen on baking sheets until firm. Place in rigid containers with wax paper between each patty. Defrost in the refrigerator before cooking. Do not use ground beef that has been previously frozen or defrosted.

SERVES 4

ALBONDIGAS
(MEATBALLS)

A simple-to-make taco sauce makes plain meatballs
a lot less ordinary and a lot more fun to eat.

8oz ground veal
8oz ground beef
1 clove garlic, crushed
2 tbsps dry breadcrumbs
½ chili pepper, seeded and finely chopped
½ tsp ground cumin
Salt and pepper
1 egg, beaten
Oil for frying
Full quantity Taco Sauce recipe
2 green onions, chopped

Step 2 Divide the meat mixture into 16 equal pieces. Work on a floured surface.

1. Mix together the veal, beef, garlic, breadcrumbs, chili pepper, cumin, salt and egg until well blended. Add the egg gradually.

2. Turn the mixture out onto a floured surface and divide into 16 equal pieces.

3. With floured hands, shape the mixture into balls.

4. Pour about 3 tbsps of oil into a large frying pan and place over high heat.

5. When the oil is hot, place in the meatballs and fry for 5-10 minutes until brown on all sides. Turn frequently during cooking.

6. Remove the browned meatballs and drain well on paper towels. Place in an ovenproof dish and pour over the taco sauce.

7. Heat through in a preheated 350°F oven for 10 minutes. Sprinkle with chopped green onions to serve.

Step 3 Flour hands well and roll each piece into a ball.

Step 5 Brown the meatballs on all sides in hot oil until a good color.

Cook's Notes

Time
Preparation takes about 25 minutes and cooking time about 20 minutes.

Serving Ideas
Serve with rice, refried beans or guacamole. Drizzle with sour cream if desired.

Freezing
Prepare and cook the meatballs and allow to cool completely. Place meatballs on baking sheets and place in the freezer until firm. Transfer to freezer containers, label and store for up to 3 months. Defrost in the refrigerator and reheat according to the recipe.

SERVES 4

MEXICAN KEBABS

Kebabs are a favorite barbecue food
almost everywhere. The spice mixture and
sauce give these their Mexican flavor.

1lb pork or lamb, cut into 2 inch pieces
4oz large button mushrooms, left whole
2 medium onions, quartered
8 bay leaves
1 tsp cocoa powder
2 tsps chili powder
¼ tsp garlic powder
½ tsp dried marjoram
Salt and pepper
6 tbsps oil
6oz cooked rice
½ quantity Taco Sauce recipe

Step 3 Thread the meat and mushrooms onto skewers, alternating with onions and bay leaves.

Step 1 Place meat and mushrooms in a deep bowl with the marinade ingredients and stir to coat thoroughly.

Step 4 Place the kebabs on a lightly oiled rack and grill until meat is tender and onions are cooked. Baste frequently, using a small brush.

1. Place meat and mushrooms in a bowl. Add the bay leaves, cocoa, chili powder, garlic powder, marjoram and seasoning to the oil and stir to coat all the ingredients with the marinade.

2. Cover the bowl and leave to marinate at least 6 hours, preferably overnight.

3. Remove meat, mushrooms and bay leaves from the marinade and reserve it. Thread onto skewers, alternating meat, onions, mushrooms and bay leaves.

4. Place under a preheated broiler for 15-20 minutes, turning frequently until cooked to desired doneness. If using pork, the meat must be thoroughly cooked and not served pink. Baste with reserved marinade.

5. Mix hot rice with taco sauce and spoon onto a warm serving dish. Place the kebabs on top of the rice to serve.

Cook's Notes

Time
Preparation takes about 15 minutes, with at least 6 hours to marinate meat and mushrooms. Cooking time for the rice is about 12 minutes and 15-20 minutes for the meat.

Preparation
The kebabs may be cooked on an outdoor barbecue grill, if desired.

Variation
Add pieces of red or green pepper, cherry tomatoes or sliced zucchini to the kebabs and cut meat into slightly smaller pieces so everything cooks in the same length of time.

SERVES 4

SPARE RIBS IN CHILI & CREAM SAUCE

Unsweetened cocoa lends color and depth to a sauce for ribs that's slightly more sophisticated than the usual barbecue sauce.

2¼lbs spare ribs
1 tsp cocoa powder
1 tbsp flour
½ tsp cumin
½ tsp paprika
½ tsp dried oregano, crushed
Salt and pepper
1 cup warm water
2 tbsps thin honey
2 tbsps heavy cream
Lime wedges and watercress for garnish

Step 2 Cook the ribs until the meat is tender to the point of a knife and the sauce is reduced.

Step 3 Place ribs on a chopping board and cut into pieces.

Step 1 Cook the ribs until well browned. Remove from the roasting pan and pour off the fat.

further 30 minutes, until the sauce has reduced and the ribs are tender.

3. Cut the ribs into pieces and arrange on a serving dish.

4. Pour the cream into the sauce in the roasting pan and place over moderate heat. Bring to the boil and pour over the ribs.

5. Garnish with lime wedges and serve.

1. Leave the ribs in whole slabs and roast at 400°F for 20-25 minutes, or until well browned. Drain off all the excess fat.

2. Blend together the cocoa, flour, cumin, paprika, oregano, seasoning, water and honey and pour over the ribs. Lower the temperature to 350°F and cook ribs for a

Cook's Notes

Time
Preparation takes about 20 minutes, cooking takes 50-55 minutes.

Preparation
Ribs may be cooked for the last 30 minutes on an outdoor barbecue grill.

Serving Ideas
Serve with rice and an avocado or tomato salad.

SERVES 6

MINUTE STEAKS WITH TACO SAUCE

A quick meal needn't be ordinary. Prepare taco sauce ahead
and keep it on hand to add last-minute spice to a meal.

Full quantity Taco Sauce recipe
2 tbsps butter or margarine
2 tbsps oil
6 minute steaks
Salt and pepper
4oz button mushrooms, left whole
Chopped parsley or coriander leaves

Step 1 Cook steaks over high heat until done to desired degree. To check, make a small cut in the center.

1. Prepare taco sauce according to the recipe directions. Heat the butter or margarine and oil together in a large frying or sauté pan. Season the steaks with salt and pepper and fry 2 or 3 at a time for 2-3 minutes on each side, or to desired doneness.

2. Remove the steaks to a warm serving dish and add the mushrooms to the pan. Sauté over high heat to brown lightly, remove and keep warm.

3. Drain most of the fat from the pan and pour in the taco sauce. Place over low heat until just bubbling. Spoon over the steaks.

4. Top the steaks with the sautéed mushrooms and sprinkle over parsley or coriander before serving.

Step 2 Add mushrooms to the pan and cook briskly until lightly browned.

Cook's Notes

Time
Preparation takes about 15 minutes. Cooking time takes 6-9 minutes per batch of steaks and about 10 minutes more to finish off the dish.

Variation
Substitute turkey escalopes for the steaks, if desired, and cook until juices run clear.

Serving Ideas
Serve with rice or flour tortillas.

SERVES 4

LEG OF LAMB WITH CHILI SAUCE

Give Sunday roast lamb a completely
different taste with a spicy orange sauce.

2¼lb leg of lamb

Marinade

1 tsp cocoa powder
¼ tsp cayenne pepper
½ tsp ground cumin
½ tsp paprika
½ tsp ground oregano
½ cup water
½ cup orange juice
½ cup red wine
1 clove of garlic, crushed
2 tbsps brown sugar
1 tbsp cornstarch
Pinch salt
Orange slices and coriander to garnish

1. If the lamb has a lot of surface fat, trim slightly with a sharp knife. If possible, remove the paper-thin skin on the outside of the lamb. Place lamb in a shallow dish.

2. Mix together the marinade ingredients, except cornstarch, and pour over the lamb, turning it well to coat completely. Cover and refrigerate for 12-24 hours, turning occasionally.

3. Drain the lamb, reserving the marinade, and place in a roasting pan. Cook in a preheated 350°F oven for about 2 hours until meat is cooked according to taste.

4. Baste occasionally with the marinade and pan juices.

5. Remove lamb to a serving dish and keep warm. Skim the fat from the top of the roasting pan with a large spoon and discard.

6. Pour remaining marinade into the pan juices in the roasting pan and bring to the boil, stirring to loosen the sediment. Mix cornstarch with a small amount of water and add some of the liquid from the roasting pan. Gradually stir cornstarch mixture into the pan and bring back to the boil.

7. Cook, stirring constantly, until thickened and clear. Add more orange juice, wine or water as necessary.

8. Garnish the lamb with orange slices and sprigs of coriander. Pour over some of the sauce and serve the rest separately.

Step 6 Pour the marinade into the roasting pan and bring to the boil. Scrape to remove browned juices.

Step 7 Cook, stirring constantly, until thickened and clear. Add more orange juice, wine or water as necessary.

Cook's Notes

 Time
Preparation takes about 15 minutes, with 12-24 hours for the lamb to marinate. Cooking takes about 2 hours for the lamb and 20 minutes to finish the sauce.

 Cook's Tip
The marinade ingredients can also be used with beef or poultry.

Serving Ideas
Serve with rice or boiled potatoes and vegetables.

SERVES 6

MANGO FOOL

To cool the palate after a spicy
Mexican meal, the taste of mango,
lime, ginger and cream is perfect.

2 ripe mangoes
1 small piece fresh ginger, peeled and shredded
1 cup powdered sugar, sifted
Juice of ½ a lime
½ cup heavy cream

Step 3 Whisk the cream to soft peaks.

Step 1 Cut the mango in half, slicing around the stone. Scoop out pulp.

Step 3 Fold the cream into the mango purée using a large spoon or rubber spatula.

1. Cut the mangoes in half, cutting around the stone. Scoop out the pulp into a bowl, blender or food processor. Reserve two slices.

2. Add the ginger, powdered sugar and lime juice and purée in the blender or food processor until smooth. Use a hand blender or electric mixer in the bowl, pushing mixture through a sieve afterwards, if necessary.

3. Whip the cream until soft peaks form and fold into the mango purée.

4. Divide the mixture between 6 glass serving dishes and leave in the refrigerator for 1 hour before serving.

5. Cut the reserved mango slices into 6 smaller slices or pieces and garnish the fool.

Cook's Notes

🕐 **Time**
Preparation takes about 20 minutes. Fool should be refrigerated 1 hour before serving.

 Serving Ideas
Accompany with cookies.

❗ **Watchpoint**
When whipping cream, refrigerate it for at least 2 hours before use. Overwhisked cream turns to butter, so whisk slowly and watch carefully.

SERVES 6

TROPICAL FRUIT SALAD

A refreshing mixture of exotic fruits is the
most popular sweet in Mexico. Add tequila or
triple sec to the syrup for a special occasion.

½ cantaloup or honeydew melon, cubed or made into
  balls
½ small fresh pineapple, peeled, cored and cubed or
  sliced
4oz fresh strawberries, hulled and halved (leave whole, if
  small)
1 mango, peeled and sliced or cubed
8oz watermelon, seeded and cubed
4oz guava or papaya, peeled and cubed
2 oranges, peeled and segmented
1 prickly pear, peeled and sliced (optional)
½ cup sugar
½ cup water
Grated rind and juice of 1 lemon
2 tbsps chopped pecans to garnish (optional)

1. To make melon balls, cut melons in half and scoop out
seeds and discard them. To use a melon baller, press
cutting edge firmly into the melon flesh and twist around to
scoop out round pieces.

2. It is easy to core the pineapple if it is first cut into quarters.
Use a serrated fruit knife to cut the point off the quarter,
removing the core. Slice off the peel. Cut into slices or cubes
and mix with the other fruit.

3. Dissolve the sugar in the water over gentle heat and
when the mixture is no longer grainy, leave it to cool
completely.

4. Add lemon rind and juice to the sugar syrup and pour
over the prepared fruit. Refrigerate well before serving.
Sprinkle with chopped nuts, if desired.

Step 1 Cut melon
in half and scoop
out seeds.

Step 1 Twist
melon baller
around to scoop
out round shaped
pieces.

Step 2 Cut out
pineapple core
with a serrated
fruit knife.

Cook's Notes

Time
Preparation takes about 45
minutes. The syrup will take
about 5-7 minutes to make.

Preparation
Allow the syrup to cool
completely before adding any
fruit. Hot syrup will cook the fruit and
draw out the juices.

Variation
Use other varieties of fruit,
choosing whatever is in
season.

SERVES 4

MEXICAN CHOCOLATE FLAN

Flan in Mexico is a molded custard with
a caramel sauce. Chocolate and cinnamon
is a favorite flavor combination.

½ cup sugar
2 tbsps water
Juice of ½ a lemon
1 cup milk
2oz semi-sweet chocolate
1 cinnamon stick
2 whole eggs
2 egg yolks
4 tbsps sugar

1. Combine the first amount of sugar with the water and lemon juice in a small, heavy-based saucepan.

2. Cook over gentle heat until the sugar starts to dissolve. Swirl the pan from time to time, but don't stir.

3. Once the sugar liquifies, bring the syrup to the boil and cook until golden brown.

4. While preparing the syrup, heat 4 custard cups in a 350°F oven. When the syrup is ready, pour into the cups and swirl to coat the sides and base evenly. Leave to cool at room temperature.

5. Chop the chocolate into small pieces and heat with the milk and cinnamon, stirring occasionally to help chocolate dissolve.

6. Whisk the whole eggs and the yolks together with the remaining sugar until slightly frothy. Gradually whisk in the chocolate milk. Remove cinnamon.

7. Pour the chocolate custard carefully into the custard cups and place them in a roasting pan of hand-hot water.

8. Place the roasting pan in the oven and bake the custards until just slightly wobbly in the center, about 20-30 minutes. Cool at room temperature and refrigerate for several hours or overnight before serving. Loosen custards carefully from the sides of the dishes and invert into serving plates. Shake to allow custard to drop out.

Step 3 Boil sugar syrup rapidly until golden brown.

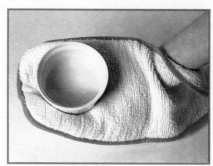

Step 4 Pour caramel into warmed dishes and swirl to coat base and sides.

Cook's Notes

 Time
Preparation takes about 30 minutes, cooking takes about 35-40 minutes.

 Variation
Leave out chocolate, if desired, for cinnamon flan.

 Watchpoint
Do not allow custard to over-cook or it will form a tough skin on top. If the oven temperature is too high, it will cause the custard to boil and spoil the texture.

Serving Ideas
Garnish with pecans or chocolate curls. Also good with fruit such as raspberries or bananas with chocolate; peaches or strawberries with cinnamon.

SERVES 4

TEQUILA SUNRISE

½ cup tequila
1½ cups orange juice
4 tbsp Cointreau or Grand Marnier
Ice
4 tbsps Grenadine syrup

1. Crush ice and place in a blender with the tequila, orange juice and orange liqueur and mix thoroughly.

2. Chill 4 tall glasses in the refrigerator and when cold, pour in the cocktail mixture.

3. Hold each glass at a tilt and carefully pour 1 tbsp

Hold glass at a tilt and carefully pour grenadine down the side for the tequila sunrise.

Grenadine syrup down one side. Syrup will sink to the bottom giving the drink its sunrise effect.

SERVES 2

MARGARITA

1 lime
Coarse salt
½ cup tequila
2 tbsps triple sec
4 ice cubes

1. Squeeze the lime and moisten the rim of two cocktail

glasses with a small amount of juice.

2. Pour salt onto a plate and dip in the moistened rims of the glasses, turning to coat evenly. Refrigerate to chill thoroughly.

3. Crush 4 ice cubes and place in a blender with the tequila and triple sec. Process until well blended and slushy. Pour into the chilled glasses and serve immediately.

Rub rims of cocktail glasses with half a lime to moisten for the margarita.

Pour salt onto a plate and dip in the moistened rims of the glasses.